The Neuroscience of Sleep and Dreams

This book provides a complete introduction to the neuroscience of sleep and dreams in plain language. Patrick McNamara outlines new discoveries in the science of sleep and dreams, places them within an evolutionary context, and brings them together with existing scientific findings and implications for sleep medicine. Unlike other introductory texts, the important evolutionary background and social nature of sleep and dreams is emphasized. Major advances in sleep medicine, sleep and memory, dream content analyses, brain correlates of sleep stages, and lifespan development of sleep are covered in depth. While the text is geared toward students, the general reader and scientists studying other disciplines will find it accessible and informative.

Patrick McNamara is Associate Professor in the Department of Neurology at Boston University and Professor of Psychology, Northcentral University. He has received a VA Merit Review Award as well as two NIH research grant awards for his work on sleep and dreams. Magazines, newspapers, and TV shows have featured his work, including *New Scientist, The Boston Globe, NOVA,* and *PBS Closer to Truth.*

D0583767

Cambridge Fundamentals of Neuroscience in Psychology

Developed in response to a growing need to make neuroscience accessible to students and other non-specialist readers, the *Cambridge Fundamentals of Neuroscience in Psychology* series provides brief introductions to key areas of neuroscience research across major domains of psychology. Written by experts in cognitive, social, affective, developmental, clinical, and applied neuroscience, these books will serve as ideal primers for students and other readers seeking an entry point to the challenging world of neuroscience.

Books in the Series

The Neuroscience of Expertise by Merim Bilalić
The Neuroscience of Intelligence by Richard J. Haier
Cognitive Neuroscience of Memory by Scott D. Slotnick
The Neuroscience of Adolescence by Adriana Galván
The Neuroscience of Suicidal Behavior by Kees van Heeringen
The Neuroscience of Creativity by Anna Abraham
Cognitive and Social Neuroscience of Aging by Angela Gutchess
The Neuroscience of Sleep and Dreams by Patrick McNamara

The Neuroscience of Sleep and Dreams

Patrick McNamara

Boston University

CAMBRIDGE
UNIVERSITY PRESS

CAMBRIDGE
UNIVERSITY PRESS

University Printing House, Cambridge CB2 8BS, United Kingdom

One Liberty Plaza, 20th Floor, New York, NY 10006, USA

477 Williamstown Road, Port Melbourne, VIC 3207, Australia

314–321, 3rd Floor, Plot 3, Splendor Forum, Jasola District Centre,
New Delhi – 110025, India

79 Anson Road, #06–04/06, Singapore 079906

Cambridge University Press is part of the University of Cambridge.

It furthers the University's mission by disseminating knowledge in the pursuit of
education, learning, and research at the highest international levels of excellence.

www.cambridge.org
Information on this title: www.cambridge.org/9781107171107
DOI: 10.1017/9781316817094

First published 2019
Reprinted 2019

Printed in the United Kingdom by TJ International Ltd. Padstow Cornwall

A catalogue record for this publication is available from the British Library.

Library of Congress Cataloging-in-Publication Data
Names: McNamara, Patrick, 1956- author.
Title: The neuroscience of sleep and dreams / Patrick McNamara.
Description: Cambridge, United Kingdom ; New York, NY : Cambridge University Press,
   2019. | Series: Cambridge fundamentals of neuroscience in psychology | Includes
   bibliographical references and index.
Identifiers: LCCN 2018040380| ISBN 9781107171107 (hardback : alk. paper) | ISBN
   9781316629741 (pbk. : alk. paper)
Subjects: LCSH: Sleep–Physiological aspects. | Dreams–Physiological aspects.
Classification: LCC QP425 .M374 2019 | DDC 612.8/21–dc23
LC record available at https://lccn.loc.gov/2018040380

ISBN 978-1-107-17110-7 Hardback
ISBN 978-1-316-62974-1 Paperback

To Ina Livia McNamara,
on her tenth birthday

Contents

List of Figures	*page* viii
List of Tables	ix
Preface	xi
Acknowledgments	xiii
PART I SLEEP	1
1 What Is Sleep?	3
2 From Biological Rhythms to the Sleep Cycle	28
3 Expression of Sleep across the Human Lifespan	40
4 Characteristics of REM and NREM Sleep	60
5 Sleep Disorders	78
6 Theories of REM and NREM Sleep	99
PART II DREAMS	121
7 What Are Dreams?	123
8 Dreams across the Human Lifespan	138
9 Characteristics of REM and NREM Dreams	155
10 Dream Varieties	171
11 Theories of Dreaming	194
Appendix: Methods	208
References	228
Index	253

Figures

1.1 Information processing with the social brain *page* 13
2.1 Human sleep architecture (Hypnogram) 32
3.1 Age-related trends for stage 1 sleep, stage 2 sleep, slow
wave sleep (SWS), rapid eye movement (REM) sleep, wake
after sleep onset (WASO) and sleep latency (in minutes) 58
4.1 Functional neuroanatomy of normal human non-REM
sleep 65
4.2 Functional neuroanatomy of normal human REM sleep 71
9.1 Dreamer-initiated aggression/befriending percentages
out of total number of social interactions in REM, NREM,
and waking reports 159
9.2 Frequency of dreamer's role in social interactions for
REM and NREM dreams 165

Tables

1.1	Sleep hygiene	*page* 6
1.2	Definition of sleep	6
1.3	Sleep traits	8
1.4	Social isolation and sleep	16
2.1	Disorders of biological rhythms	37
3.1	Attachment orientations as a function of Internal Working models of self vs. other	45
3.2	Sleep changes from neonateal to adult period	48
3.3	Sleep in pregnancy	56
4.1	Two spindle types	63
5.1	Sleep disorders and the law	94
6.1	Targeted memory reactivation in sleep	111
6.2	REM-NREM characteristics suggesting opposing functional states	114
7.1	Dreams are sleep-dependent cognitions	124
7.2	Hall/Van de Castle social interaction content ratios	132
8.1	Stage characteristics of the human life cycle	139
8.2	Overlap of social brain with default mode network	142
8.3	Establishing the credibility of children's dreams	144
8.4	Hall/Van de Castle norms on male and female dreams	147
9.1	Frequency of social interactions by state	158
9.2	Hall/Van de Castle social interaction percentages	159
A.1	Drugs that influence sleep	213
A.2	What drug studies have taught us about the neurobiology of sleep and wakefulness	215
A.3	Sources for study of sleep and dreams	217
A.4	Functional neuroimaging methods to study the sleeping brain	220
A.5	Common sleep and dream measures	223
A.6	Hall/Van de Castle content ratios	225

Preface

This introduction to the neuroscience of sleep and dreams is part of the *Cambridge Fundamentals of Neuroscience in Psychology* series published by Cambridge University Press. The goal of this series is to introduce readers to the use of neuroscience methods and research to inform psychological questions. A key theme of this book, therefore, will be to inform readers both about the basic science of sleep and dreams and to illuminate psychological questions that arise around sleep and dreams. This book can serve as a supplemental textbook in college/university courses such as Brain and Behavior, Psychopharmacology, Neuropsychology, Behavioral Neuroscience, Psychology of Dreams, Physiological Psychology and as a trade book for educated lay people, and/or as a main textbook in a college/university course or seminar at the advanced undergraduate level or the graduate level (along with supplemental scientific articles).

Some of the questions I will be addressing include: What is sleep and why are there two basic forms of sleep (REM and NREM; at least among terrestrial mammals)? Why is the amygdala activated and the dorsal-prefrontal cortex downregulated during REM? What is the evidence for immune system repair during slow wave sleep? What is sleep debt and how is it related to brain function? What are the psychological consequences of chronic sleep debt? What do the major parasomnias teach us about conscious states? The many intriguing and bizarre clinical symptoms of various sleep disorders (sleepwalking, REM Behavior Disorder, narcolepsy, parasomnias, etc.) will be discussed, as well as the latest findings on the role of sleep and dreams in memory and learning. With respect to dreams, some of the questions to be addressed are: Why do some people recall very few dreams while others are flooded with dream memories on a daily basis? Why are social interactions so ubiquitous in dreams? Can certain dream experiences signal illness or even death? Why are some dreams extraordinarily moving and others quite banal and forgetful? Why do some people find it easy to realize they are dreaming when they are in fact dreaming ("lucid dreams") while others never achieve "lucidity"? Do we need to dream in order to remember things? Do we need dreams in order to be creative? How is the new rage for using smartphones and apps to track sleep patterns and dreams altering our understanding of sleep and dreams? What about nightmares? Why do they occur and is there anything we can do about them? These are only a few of the fascinating puzzles concerning sleep and dreams that will be addressed in this book.

Unlike other introductory texts on sleep and dreams, I adopt a consistently evolutionary and social neuroscience approach to understanding the neuropsychology of sleep and dreams. I adopt this orientation as functional aspects of physiological systems are more easily understood within the framework of Darwinian evolutionary biology. To study sleep within an evolutionary context inevitably leads us to consider sleep as a social behavior, given that for most animals fitness trade-offs occur within social interactions. I will therefore argue that sleep can be profitably studied and understood, at least in part, as a social phenomenon. For example, fetal and infant sleep cannot be understood in the absence of its social context; that is, the infant's interactions with its mother. Similarly, sleep states from toddlerhood up to adulthood also occur within social contexts (e.g., attachment relationships with parents in childhood and then attachment relationships with sexual partners in adulthood, etc.) that shape all aspects of sleep expression. Sleep expression differs in the solitary sleeper as compared to co-sleepers. Co-sleeping is very likely the evolutionary default for human beings. Our ancestors were all co-sleepers and that fact can help to explain some of sleep's peculiar biologic features. While these elementary facts concerning sleep and social context have been assumed and occasionally acknowledged by sleep scientists, they have never received the sustained or explicit attention they deserve, it seems to me. Placing sleep within its social context will illuminate the everyday functional aspects of sleep and its disorders for readers of this introductory text on the neuropsychology of sleep and dreams.

Acknowledgments

I thank all of the scientists and scholars whose work I have cited and built upon in this book. Parts of this book appeared first in posts at my *Psychology Today* online blog at www.psychologytoday.com/us/blog/dream-catcher/. Other ideas and some text first appeared in the following papers:

McNamara, P., Minsky, A., Pae, V., Harris, E., Pace-Schott, E., & Auerbach, S. (2015). Aggression in nightmares and unpleasant dreams and in people reporting recurrent nightmares. *Dreaming*, 25(3), 190–205. http://dx.doi.org/10.1037/a0039273.

McNamara, P., Ayala, R., & Minsky, A. (2014). REM sleep, dreams, and attachment themes across a single night of sleep: A pilot study. *Dreaming*, 24(4), 290.

McNamara, P., Pace-Schott, E. F., Johnson, P., Harris, E., & Auerbach, S. (2011). Sleep architecture and sleep-related mentation in securely and insecurely attached young people. *Attachment and Human Development*, 13(2), 141–154.

McNamara, P., Johnson, P., McLaren, D., Harris, E., Beauharnais, C., & Auerbach, S. (2010). REM and NREM sleep mentation. *International Review of Neurobiology, 92*, 69–86.

McNamara, P., Auerbach, S., Johnson, P., Harris, E., & Doros, G. (2010). Impact of REM sleep on distortions of self concept, mood and memory in depressed/anxious participants. *Journal of Affective Disorders, 122*(3), 198–207. PMID: 19631989.

Capellini, I., McNamara, P., Preston, B. T., Nunn, C. L., & Barton, R. A. (2009). Does sleep play a role in memory consolidation? A comparative test. *PLoS ONE*, 4(2), e4609. PMID: 19240803.

Preston, B. T., Capellini, I., McNamara, P., Barton, R. A., & Nunn, C. L. (2009). Parasite resistance and the adaptive significance of sleep. *BMC Evolutionary Biology, 9*, 7. PMID: 19134175.

Capellini, I., Nunn, C. L., McNamara, P., Preston, B. T., & Barton, R. A. (2008). Energetic constraints, not predation, influence the evolution of sleep patterning in mammals. *Functional Ecology*, 22(5), 847–853.

Stavitsky, K., McNamara, P., Durso, R., Harris, E., Auerbach, S., & Cronin-Golomb, A. (2008). Hallucinations, dreaming and frequent dozing in Parkinson's disease: Impact of right-hemisphere neural networks. *Cognitive and Behavioral Neurology*, 21(3), 143–149. PMID: 18797256.

McNamara, P., Belsky, J., & Fearon, P. (2003). Infant sleep disorders and attachment: Sleep problems in infants with insecure-resistant versus insecure-avoidant attachments to mother. *Sleep and Hypnosis*, 5(1), 7–16.

McNamara, P., Durso, R., & Auerbach, S. (2002). Dopaminergic syndromes of sleep, mood and mentation: Evidence from Parkinson's disease and related disorders. *Sleep and Hypnosis*, 4(3), 119–131.

McNamara, P., Dowdall, J., & Auerbach, S. (2002). REM sleep, early experience and the development of reproductive strategies. *Human Nature*, 13(4), 404–435.

McNamara, P., Andresen, J., Arrowood, J., & Messer, G. (2002). Counterfactual cognitive operations in dreams. *Dreaming*, 12(3), 121–133.

McNamara, P., Andresen, J., Clark, J., Zborowski, M., & Duffy, C. (2001). Impact of attachment styles on sleep and dreams: A test of the attachment hypothesis of REM sleep. *Journal of Sleep Research*, 10, 117–127.

McNamara, P. (2000). Counterfactual thought in dreams. *Dreaming*, 10(4), 232–245.

Zborowski, M., & McNamara, P. (1998). The evolutionary psychology of REM sleep. *Psychoanalytic Psychology*, 15(1), 115–140.

PART I

Sleep

CHAPTER 1

What Is Sleep?

Learning Objectives

- Identify the homeostatic nature of sleep
- Evaluate the key elements in the scientific definition of sleep
- Evaluate the evidence for the social nature of sleep
- Distinguish biologic characteristics of reptilian, avian, mammalian, nonhuman primate sleep, and human sleep

1.1 Introduction

What happens if you do not get enough sleep? You become easily distractible, your tolerance for other's foibles declines, you are less able to think clearly, and you act as if you are drunk during social interactions. If you go without sleep for more than just a single night you find that social interactions become difficult; you find it harder to control your emotions, you get irritable with others very easily, your self-control declines; your primary drives for food, aggression and sex increase; you become more susceptible to viral infection, especially for things like cold and flu; minor aches and pains get amplified into major pains, and you just want to get some sleep.

But if you go without sleep for more than a couple of nights, things go from bad to worse: You find it harder to regulate your internal body temperature, you feel weak, you walk through the day like a zombie, you may even start to hallucinate all kinds of weird visions, and you may begin to develop paranoid delusions that people are out to get you. Admittedly, the paranoid delusions are rare after prolonged sleep loss, but thinking problems are not; nor is it rare to experience subtle visual hallucinations after sleep loss. These visual effects may be due to intrusion of dreams into waking consciousness. In any case, the thing that happens invariably, without fail and most insistently and prominently when you do not get enough sleep is that you become extremely sleepy. You will get more and more sleepy until one of two things happen: Either you die or you eventually succumb to sleep. Sleep, therefore, is a biological need for human beings. We need it and we therefore need to understand it. Increasing evidence also suggests that dreams are vital for normal human cognitive and social functioning. Thus, the purpose of this book is to help all of us to better understand sleep and dreams.

More than sixty million Americans, or approximately one in three adults, experience inadequate sleep that can interfere with daily activities. Sleep loss has been linked with several leading causes of death in the United States, including cardiovascular disease, cancer, stroke, diabetes, and hypertension (Kochanek et al., 2014). Sleep loss not only adversely affects our health, it also costs us and the economy. Lack of sleep can lead to traffic accidents, industrial accidents (e.g., Exxon Valdez oil spill, etc.), medical errors, and loss of work time (Pack et al., 1995).

Employers should be worried about sleep-deprived employees. Workers who sleep less than six hours per day call in sick more often than workers who get a regular night's sleep. A worker sleeping less than six hours a night loses around six working days per year, *more* than a worker sleeping seven to nine hours. On an annual basis, the United States loses an equivalent of about 1.23 million working days due to insufficient sleep (Hafner et al., 2016).

Chronic sleep loss is not limited to the fast paced, highly industrialized economies of the North. People in the global South, especially those in poor countries, are also complaining that they do not get enough sleep. Stranges et al. (2017) surveyed large numbers of people from eight countries across Africa and Asia participating in the INDEPTH WHO-SAGE multicenter study during 2006–2007. The participating sites included rural populations in Ghana, Tanzania, South Africa, India, Bangladesh, Vietnam, and Indonesia, and an urban area in Kenya. There were 24,434 women and 19,501 men age fifty years and older. Two measures of sleep quality, over the past thirty days, were assessed alongside a number of sociodemographic variables, measures of quality of life, and health disorders. Overall, 16.6 percent of participants reported severe/extreme sleep problems. When the authors attempted to identify causes of sleep loss in this group of people, several social factors emerged as leading culprits: Being a solitary sleeper (not living in partnership), poorer self-rated overall quality of life, and feelings of depression and anxiety were consistently strong, independent predictors of sleep problems.

Why are so many people, both in rich and poor countries, so sleep-deprived? Social conditions seem to be a major contributing factor to sleep loss. When we worry, we lose sleep and we worry most often due to social problems: A fight with a friend, inability to pay the rent or to adequately feed your kids, pressing job deadlines or no luck in finding a job, neighborhood crime, or even neighborhood noise can all lead to sleep loss. People who live in poor neighborhoods are more vulnerable than others to many of these sorts of worries and sleep-loss-inducing stressors. Recent community surveys have found that upwards of 53 percent of non-Hispanic African Americans living in poor neighborhoods sleep less than six hours a night (Durrence and Lichstein, 2006).

While insufficient sleep can have detrimental impacts on all age cohorts, regardless of socioeconomic status, sleep deprivation among children and adolescents across economic classes may trigger irreversible long-term consequences. For instance, there is strong evidence for the association of quality and quantity of sleep with school performance and cognitive ability among school-aged children and adolescents (DeWald et al., 2010). In addition, according to a National Sleep Foundation (2014) survey, over half (58 percent) of fifteen- to seventeen-year-olds sleep seven hours or less per night and only 10 percent sleep nine hours or more. Among six to eleven year olds, 8 percent sleep seven hours or less per night and 23 percent sleep only eight hours per night. Smartphones and TVs are disrupting sleep of children. Eighty-nine percent of adults and 75 percent of children have at least one electronic device in their bedrooms; 68 percent of parents and 51 percent of children had two or more devices in their bedroom at night. Use of smartphone apps, such as addicting game apps, at bedtime by children as young as four- or five-years-old is not uncommon and is severely disruptive to sleep. More than 10 percent of children awaken during the night to send or read a text message; again this is very disruptive for sleep. At the other end of the age spectrum, over half of the thirty-three million adults over sixty-five years of age in the USA have some chronic sleep complaint which contributes to personal discomfort and illness, to caregiver burden, and to overall health care costs.

In short, there appears to be a global epidemic of sleep loss. This is despite the fact that some simple behavioral habits can often restore adequate sleep times and sleep quality (see Table 1.1). For all these reasons we need a better understanding of sleep.

The first step one needs to take to study sleep effectively is to define sleep.

1.2 What Is Sleep?

Here is a definition I propose for human sleep (Table 1.2): Sleep is a restorative process that is brain state–regulated, reversible, homeostatic,

Table 1.1 Sleep hygiene

1. Establish a regular and consistent bedtime routine. Set a consistent wake-up time.
2. Get adequate exposure to natural light during daytime and reduce exposure to light from all sources including electronic devices before bedtime.
3. Limit the consumption of stimulants like caffeine, soda, alcohol and nicotine which may impair sleep quality.
4. Exercise. As little as 10 minutes of aerobic exercise during the daytime can improve sleep.
5. Limit daytime napping.
6. Practice some form of mental and physical relaxation routine before bedtime in order to quiet socially related anxieties and ruminations at bedtime.

Table 1.2 Definition of sleep

Sleep is a restorative process that is brain state-regulated, reversible, homeostatic, embedded in a circadian and social–physiologic organization and involving a species-specific quiescent posture, some amount of perceptual disengagement, and elevated arousal thresholds.

- Restorative process indicates that one feels refreshed after high quality sleep.
- Reversible means that once we fall asleep we can easily return to wake if aroused sufficiently via noise, shaking, etc. There is no quick reversibility in other quiescent states like coma.
- Homeostatic means that if we go without sleep we need to at least partially make up for that lost sleep.
- Brain state–regulated indicates that the brain is what triggers and maintains sleep and that different forms of sleep are associated with distinctive patterns of brain activation and deactivation; we will see in later chapters that the "social brain" is particularly important for sleep and vice versa.
- Circadian and social-physiologic organization refers to the fact that sleep occurs every 24 hours and is entrained to social cues in the environment such that interactions with conspecifics are optimized.
- Quiescent posture indicates that for most animals sleep is associated with a relatively motionless posture – most often recumbency (lying down).
- Perceptual disengagement indicates that the sleeper exhibits reduced responsiveness to normal environmental stimuli.
- Elevated threshold means that it takes a sufficiently loud noise or hard shake to wake us up.

embedded in both a circadian and social–physiologic organization and involving a species-specific quiescent posture, some amount of perceptual disengagement, and elevated arousal thresholds. Admittedly, that is a mouthful. But I assure you there is a good reason for including every single element in that long definition. We will define and discuss each of these terms shortly. This definition best captures human sleep but it can encompass sleep of other organisms if we allow relaxation of some of the components of the definition. For example, even organisms as genetically and neurally simple as the worm *Caenorhabditis elegans*, exhibits a regularly occurring period of inactivity or quiescence. Other simple organisms like the fruit fly and some insects also display regularly occurring periods of quiescence and some evidence of compensatory "sleep" rebound or homeostatically regulated periods of quiescence. The role of brain state–regulated transitions between different phases of activity and inactivity becomes more prominent in organisms with more complex nervous systems like animals and humans. Thus, the definition is broad enough to capture the essentials of sleep expression from the simplest to the most complex of organisms. To fill out this definition in more detail we need to quickly identify some common traits or characteristics normally associated with sleep in animals and in humans.

Sleep can be thought of as composed of behavioral, functional, physiologic, and electrophysiological traits (see Table 1.3). For most animals, sleep can only be identified via measurement of its behavioral and functional sleep traits, as their nervous systems do not support what has become known as full polygraphic sleep or sleep that can be measured with an electroencephalograph or EEG machine that records brain waves through the skull.

Full polygraphic sleep refers to electrophysiologic measures of both REM (rapid eye movement) and NREM (non-rapid eye movement) sleep stages N1, N2, and N3, identified via the electroencephalogram or EEG. It has become common however to use the term "full polygraphic sleep" to refer to an animal who exhibits most or all of the other three major components of sleep in addition to the electrophysiologic measures. When an animal exhibits all four major components of sleep including the behavioral, electrophysiologic, physiologic, and functional components of sleep, then it is said that the animal exhibits full polygraphic sleep. Full polygraphic sleep, in this sense, has so far only been documented in primates (including humans). In humans and other mammals (and perhaps some reptiles) sleep comes in two forms or phases: REM (rapid eye movement) and NREM (non-REM) sleep. While REM and NREM phases of sleep have been identified in a large

Table 1.3 Sleep traits

1. Behavioral
   - Typical usually quiescent body posture.
   - Specific sleeping site.
   - Behavioral rituals before sleep (e.g., circling, yawning).
   - Physical quiescence.
   - Elevated threshold for arousal and reactivity.
   - Rapid state reversibility.
   - Circadian organization of rest–activity cycles.
   - Entrained to and sensitive to social cues and to activities of conspecifics.
   - Different from hibernation/torpor.
2. Electrophysiological
   EEG
       NREM: high voltage slow waves, Delta power (quiet sleep).
   - Spindles in some animals.
   - K-complexes in some primates.
       REM: low voltage fast waves (REM, Paradoxical sleep or AS [active sleep]).
   - Hippocampal theta; PGO waves.
       Electro-oculogram (EOG)
       NREM: absence of eye movements or presence of slow rolling eye movements.
       REM: rapid eye movements.
       EMG
   - Progressive loss of muscle tone from Wake → NREM → REM.
3. Physiological
   - REM: instabilities in heart-rate, breathing, body temperature, etc. Other: penile tumescence.
   - NREM: reduction in physiologic/metabolic processes; reduction of about 2C in core body temperature.
4. Functional
   Compensation of sleep deficit: (homeostatic regulation)
   - Enhancement of sleep time after sleep deprivation.
   - Intensification of the sleep process (e.g., enhanced EEG power in the Delta range).

number of mammalian species, NREM in most of these species cannot be differentiated into distinct substages as it is in several primate species.

Behavioral traits of sleep include a species-specific body posture that typically involves a recumbent non-moving animal (quiescence), though some animals can engage in some limited sleep while standing (e.g., cows). There is also typically a species-specific sleeping site that is constructed to conserve warmth and to protect the sleeping animal from predators. Before relaxing into the sleep site an animal usually engages in behavioral rituals such as circling the nest and yawning before laying down to sleep. It is unclear why these behavioral rituals are needed before sleep. Other behavioral indicators of sleep include reduced muscle tone, reduction in neck/nuchal muscle tone, paralysis of the antigravity muscles in some species, increased arousal threshold, and rapid reversibility to wakefulness. Physiologic indices of sleep include significant reductions in core body temperature and metabolism during NREM and significant lability in the autonomic nervous system activity (ANS), as well as cardio-vascular and respiratory measures during REM. Electrophysiologic meas-ures of REM include low voltage fast waves, rapid eye movements, theta rhythms in the hippocampus, and pontine-geniculo-occipital or PGO waves. PGO waves are electrical discharges in all the visual centers (from the pons to the occipital cortex) of the brain. Electrophysiologic measures of NREM include high voltage slow waves, spindles, and k-complexes. Functional indices of sleep include increased amounts of sleep after sleep deprivation and increased sleep intensity after sleep deprivation.

We say that *sleep is a restorative process that is brain state–regulated, reversible, homeostatic, embedded in a circadian and social-physiologic organization and involving a species-specific quiescent posture, some amount of perceptual disengagement, and elevated arousal thresholds.*

1.3 What Do Each of These Terms Mean?

1.3.1 Restorative Process

When you have a night of high quality sleep you wake up feeling refreshed and no longer tired. Sleep, therefore, reverses some process that makes you feel worn, ragged, socially inept, and tired. That process is the waking state. Since both the waking state and sleep are mediated by the brain, we need neuroscience to understand sleep. Genetic and neurochemical analyses of the sleep state reveal that housekeeping, metabolic, and energy-related genes are differentially expressed during sleep and there is cumulative evidence that sleep restores glycogen (the fuel for the brain) levels in the brain.

1.3.2 Reversible State

By reversible state we mean that when you go to sleep, you are not stuck there as may be the case with an irreversible coma; with appropriate forms of stimulation such as a loud noise and a vigorous shaking you can return to wakefulness. Typically the brain spontaneously shifts itself out of sleep and back into waking after about five to eight hours in adult human beings.

1.3.3 Homeostatic

By homeostatically regulated we mean that the *amount* and *intensity* of sleep you experience is controlled by a kind of internal thermostat. If you get too little sleep you cumulate a sleep debt that needs to eventually be paid back or made up. To make up for lost sleep time you sleep a bit longer and a bit more intensely on subsequent nights. In short, you sleep in proportion to wake time. The longer the wake time (or the greater the amount of sleep deprivation), the greater the subsequent sleep time and intensity. Lots of people sleep little during the work week and then sleep in (or sleep longer) during the weekend. In other words, we make up for lost sleep time during the work week by sleeping more on the weekends.

If we use an electroencephalograph or EEG (to be discussed more fully later and in the Appendix) to record brain waves during catch-up sleep, we see that the brain exhibits a lot of so-called *delta power*. The longer the wake time before sleep, the stronger or higher the delta power during sleep. Once you go to sleep, however, delta power begins to decline across the night, indicating that delta signal's "need for sleep," or the intensity with which you sleep during catch-up sleep. The greater the delta power the more intense the catch-up sleep. When delta power is high at the beginning of the night and declines across the night, people report high-quality sleep. So it is not so much the amount of sleep but the intensity of sleep that counts in catch-up sleep. The more intense the sleep as measured by delta power, the more refreshing the sleep. Thus, we can pay back a sleep deficit by sleeping more intensely as well as by sleeping longer.

The phenomenon of catch-up sleep suggests that something, some chemical process within the body or the brain perhaps, builds up during wake and is discharged during sleep. Delta activity (during slow wave sleep; N3) indexes the efficiency with which this wake-related chemical process, call it Process S, is discharged. Delta power is doing something that reverses whatever Process S induces during wake. For example, if Process S is some sort of fuel for body and brain that gets depleted during waking, then delta power would presumably index some sort of manufacturing process that produces some chemical that would refuel the body and brain. If we could identify the physical factor responsible for Process S, we could possibly gain insight about the actual function of sleep. The relationships between sleep deprivation and the nature of catch-up or recovery sleep are important because they gives us clues as to what it is that sleep actually does for us, i.e., the function of sleep.

In addition to the exponential decline of delta power across a single night of sleep, local transient increases in various regions of the brain in delta power can also occur, in relation to the amount of use of that area of the brain. These local increases in sleep or delta power indicate use-dependent functions of recovery sleep. That is, if you use a part of the brain intensely during some waking activity, that area of the brain will evidence local increases in delta wave activity, thus indicating some sort of recuperative process for that particular brain region. The regular, more global changes in delta wave activity that occur each night appears to be more strongly related to use or engagement of particular regions of the frontal lobes and its interconnected regions than it is to other areas of the brain (Halasz et al., 2014). Sleep deprivation, in general, has been shown to enhance the frontal predominance of delta-indexed slow wave activity or SWA during recovery sleep (Horne, 1993; Cajochen et al., 1999; Finelli et al., 2001), especially in the left hemisphere (Achermann et al., 2001).

While it is clear that the deprivation of NREM sleep leads to a dramatic increase of EEG delta slow waves, particularly within the frontal lobes, there is also evidence of sleep rebound phenomena associated with deprivation of REM sleep. REM sleep is also homeostatically regulated, but it is unclear whether an intensity dimension (as measured by delta waves in NREM) exists for REM sleep. With REM rebound we see an increase in the density of rapid eye movements but it is unclear if that indexes increased sleep intensity. In any case, for both REM and NREM rebound phenomena this homeostatic component of sleep regulation is regulated separately from the circadian regulatory sites/processes. While both are linked to hypothalamic networks, the circadian system depends on the suprachiasmatic nucleus within the hypothalamus while the homeostatic system does not.

1.3.4 Brain State–Regulated

The brain initiates sleep, maintains sleep, promotes transitions between one form of sleep and another, and triggers wakefulness – it is therefore a brain-dependent and regulated process through and through. In addition, dreaming is integral to human sleep. Dreaming phenomenology also depends crucially on brain activation and deactivation patterns, thus underlining the fact once again that sleep and dreams are essentially linked to brain state changes.

It is a theme of this book that one brain network in particular may be crucial for sleep and vice versa (i.e., sleep is crucial for that brain region) – namely the "social brain" network (e.g., Dunbar, 1998; Kennedy and Adolphs, 2012; Mars et al., 2012; Lieberman, 2014). The brain network that is typically called "the social brain network" is that set of interconnected brain regions that handles or mediates all of the thinking and emotional work we have to do to keep track of and regulate our social interactions with others. Since we are an intensely social species, most of what our brains preferentially process is composed of socially relevant information; things like: Who did what to whom and why?; What social alliances/groups am I in, and am I in good standing with those alliances?; Who can I trust and how do I remain on cooperative terms with various groups of people I have to interact with on a daily basis?; and so on. The network of structures that make up the social brain include the amygdala, which is known to be involved in emotional memory, threat appraisal and fear; the fusiform gyrus supports rapid recognition and processing of faces; the ventromedial and dorsomedial prefrontal regions are known to support processing of self-related information as well as understanding the mental states of others (i.e., Theory of Mind or ToM tasks). The frontopolar region (BA 10) is involved in multitasking, working memory, and cognitive branching and likely supports processing of 3rd and 4th, etc. orders of social intentionality. The superior temporal sulcus contains mirror neurons that support social imitation behaviors and possibly emotional empathy while the temporal–parietal junction supports ToM tasks and language processing. The insula supports empathetic responses as well as moral emotions and the precuneus is involved in a range of activities from mental simulation to self-awareness. The core of the social brain is the mentalizing and the amygdala networks, the amygdala, the ventromedial prefrontal cortex, the cingulate cortex, and the temporal–parietal junction.

These interconnected brain structures allow us to fluently and more or less expertly, process huge amounts of strategic social information daily that is vital to our well-being and the well-being of those closest to us. Incoming information (see Figure 1.1) important for social interactions is typically associated with face perception of others, which is handled by fusiform gyrus; information on trustworthiness of that person is then evaluated via amygdala and other limbic and paralimbic regions. Then intentional states of that individual are evaluated by ventromedial prefrontal cortex and related regions and all of this processing is done in

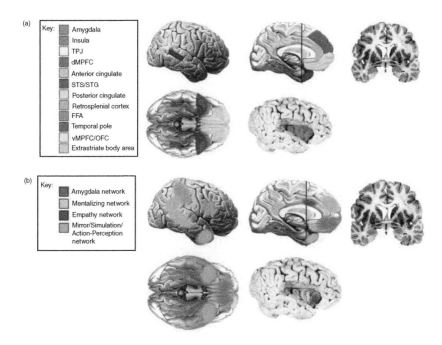

(a)

Key:
- Amygdala
- Insula
- TPJ
- dMPFC
- Anterior cingulate
- STS/STG
- Posterior cingulate
- Retrosplenial cortex
- FFA
- Temporal pole
- vMPFC/OFC
- Extrastriate body area

(b)

Key:
- Amygdala network
- Mentalizing network
- Empathy network
- Mirror/Simulation/Action-Perception network

Figure 1.1 Information processing with the social brain.
(with permission Elsevier Press; Cell; TINS from Kennedy and Adolphs, 2012)

relation to the self, which is mediated via midline structures in limbic and medial prefrontal cortex as well as subcortically in the insula and precuneus. It is no wonder that a network of interconnected structures specialize in handling all of this social information. Interestingly, the sleeping brain appears to be vitally important for this brain network. *The set of structures comprising the social brain (particularly the mentalizing and amygdala networks) are gradually taken off-line after sleep onset and throughout NREM sleep (basically the first half of the night) and then are gradually put back together or reconnected and reactivated during each subsequent episode of REM until the brain fully comes back online after waking* (Maquet, 2000; Muzur et al., 2002; Dang Vu et al., 2005; Maquet et al., 2005;). There is no perfect correspondence between the social brain and brain regions implicated in sleep. Nevertheless, there is certainly a striking overlap between brain regions implicated in sleep and the social brain network. It will be worth keeping this overlap in mind as it may be more than coincidental.

Brain structures such as the dorsolateral prefrontal cortex that help to regulate structures within the social brain are the first that are taken off-line during sleep onset. Then the structures of the social brain itself are shut down in piecemeal fashion with each progressive episode of NREM (N1, N2, and N3 slow wave sleep). For example, in the first NREM episode of the night, there is relatively greater delta indexed slow wave activity (SWA) in frontal than in parietal and occipital regions (Werth et al., 1996, 1997; Finelli et al., 2001). Synchronization of slow wave activity then spreads progressively to posterior and subcortical regions (De Gennaro et al., 2004).

Both PET (Dang-Vu et al., 2005; Hofle et al., 1997; Maquet, 1995) and fMRI (Czisch et al., 2004; Kaufmann et al., 2005) studies have shown that global cerebral activity, including that of frontal areas, continues to diminish with deepening NREM sleep. While the transition from waking to NREM involves a prominent thalamic deactivation in addition to widespread cortical and subcortical deactivations (Dang-Vu, 2005; Hofle et al., 1997), once sleep is achieved further thalamic deactivation does not appear to characterize deepening NREM (Dang-Vu et al., 2005). Instead, a PET study showed that progressive deactivation within NREM sleep is centered on regions in the social brain network including the medial prefrontal cortex anterior medial areas in BA 9 and 10, orbitofrontal cortices (BA 11) including caudal orbital basal forebrain, anterior cingulate (BA24), bilateral anterior insula, basal forebrain/ anterior hypothalamus, bilateral putamen, and left precuneus (Dang Vu et al., 2005; Kaufmann et al., 2006). Thus sleep is both regulated by brain structures and in turn shapes these brain structures with the social brain network playing an important role in sleep.

1.3.5 Circadian and Social-Physiologic Organization

Sleep occurs within a circadian or twenty-four-hour cycle and within a social context. In humans and other primates, sleep is usually monopha-sic or consolidated into one large sleep period at night, although some studies of sleep among hunter gatherers suggest that human sleep may be naturally biphasic with one long bout at night and then another short bout in late afternoon. In most mammals, however, sleep is polyphasic, with bouts of sleep occurring during the day and night. In species such as the cat and the guinea pig, sleep occurs in short bouts at virtually any time of the day or night. The factors responsible for the different patterns of sleep cycle phasing remain unclear but keeping open the ability to pursue social interactions is likely one such factor. Prolonged quiescence makes an animal vulnerable to predation and it also increases the chances that it will miss out on opportunities for social alliances or reproductive opportunities. Therefore, if an animal can obtain the benefits of sleep in a few short bouts rather than in one long prolonged bout, that option will be common.

In nonhuman primates and in humans sleep is exquisitely sensitive to social cues. Although biological rhythms are entrained to light-dark phases, social cues can dramatically influence expression of sleep. We cannot fall asleep when crossing time zones not simply because the light cycle is off but also because the people around us are not sleeping. In nonhuman primates and possibly also in humans, contagious yawning signals to conspecifics that a sleep phase is approaching and sleep partnerships need to be initiated. Once sleep commences individual physiologic systems appear to assume that individuals are not sleeping alone. For example, in REM thermoregulatory reflexes are relaxed probably because warmth can be conserved by sleeping next to another warm body. Sexual activation also occurs during REM for most mammalian species. This activation can be seen as nothing more than a by-product of brainstem activation during REM or as an opportunistic function given the assumption that the individual does not sleep alone. When sexual partners co-sleep their brains and bodies and their biological rhythms become intertwined and resonant as do co-sleeping babies and mothers. In the infant several forms of nighttime signaling such as crying, sucking, nursing, smiling, grasping, twitches, cooing, babbling, and other vocalizations influence the mother's sleep/wake patterns as well as daytime attachment processes. All of these behaviors are more likely to either occur in, or to emerge from, REM than NREM sleep. Co-sleeping with the parent influences number and duration of night waking episodes in the infant (McKenna et al., 1990; 1993; 1994) as well. In general, bed-sharing infants are more likely to nurse and, in turn, more likely to awaken more frequently during the night to feed.

In ancestral communities children very likely grew up co-sleeping as well. When children reached maturity they graduated into sleeping with sexual partners and/or with extended family members. It is only in the last hundred years or so that human beings began to sleep alone in a minority of rich countries in Europe and North America. Throughout human history sleep has been a social behavior.

Other indications of the social nature of human sleep include the fact that sleep deprivation is associated with diminished emotional expressivity, impaired emotion recognition, and increased emotional reactivity (Beattie et al., 2015). Emotion is the glue or the currency of social

Table 1.4 Social isolation and sleep

Gemignani et al., (2014) studied the effects of social isolation in a simulated spaceflight environment in six healthy volunteers who lived in the spaceship simulator Mars (MARS500) for 105 days. Volunteers were sealed in the spaceship simulator for 105 days and studied at five specific time-points of the simulation period. The researchers found that although cortisol levels were within normal limits, higher cortisol levels were associated with fragmented sleep in the form of shorter sleep durations, increased numbers of arousals and reduced REM latencies; reduction of delta power and enhancement of sigma and beta in NREM N3. Social isolation, even with cortisol fluctuations in the normal range, significantly alters sleep structure and sleep EEG spectral content.

interactions. There also appears to be a generally altered tendency to perceive and evaluate one's own and other's emotions as more negatively toned than they are, after sleep deprivation. Without the ability to accurately read the emotions of others and to express one's own emotions, social interactions will break down. The neuroscience basis of these effects of sleep deprivation appear to be a disconnection between prefrontal cortex and the amygdala induced by sleep deprivation. Sleep deprivation results in a 60 percent increase in activation of the amygdala and a threefold greater extent of activation of the amygdala volume relative to control group values. Functional connectivity is disrupted after sleep deprivation between the amygdala, the medial prefrontal cortex, bilateral orbitofrontal cortex, and left fusiform gyrus. The amygdala mediates emotion while the medial and orbitofrontal prefrontal cortices help to regulate amygdalar reactivity. The fusiform gyrus mediates face perception (a bearer of emotional expression). Given this set of results regarding the effects of sleep deprivation on expression and processing of emotions as well as the fact that there is a global epidemic of sleep deprivation (summarized earlier), we must conclude that some portion of the negativity we all experience during social interactions can be attributed to chronic sleep deprivation. It would not be hyperbole to claim that broad promotion and an international health effort to introduce simple sleep hygiene techniques to the world's people would constitute something of a social revolution, as many daily social interactions would not carry the extra burden of emotional processing breakdowns that accompany even temporary episodes of sleep deprivation.

1.3.6 Quiescent State

Quiescent state simply means reduced physical activity relative to the resting waking state. So imagine your most relaxed, resting state during waking life and then reduce physical activity even more and eventually you will arrive at the quiescent state. Quiescence does not require complete cessation of physical activity. You can observe some minor movement during the different phases of sleep. In REM you can observe the eyeballs moving around rapidly under the closed eyelids while the rest of the body is mostly motionless. The earlobes and other parts of the body might occasionally twitch during REM but mostly the body is motionless because of the paralysis typically associated with REM. In NREM sleep you can observe the eyeballs slowly rolling back and forth under the closed eyelids while the rest of the body twitches slightly.

1.3.7 Perceptual Disengagement

One of the most striking characteristics of a sleeping animal or person is that they do not respond normally to environmental stimuli. If you open the eyelids of a sleeping mammal the eyes will not see normally – they are functionally blind. Some visual information apparently gets in but it is not processed normally as it is truncated or attenuated. The same is the case with the other sensing systems. Stimuli are registered but not processed normally and they fail to rouse the individual. Perceptual disengagement presumably serves the function of protecting sleep so some authors do not count it as part of the definition of sleep itself. But insofar as sleep would be impossible without it, it seems essential to its definition. Nevertheless, many animals (including humans) use the intermediate state of drowsiness to derive some benefits of sleep without total perceptual disengagement. In the drowsiness state the eyelids are half closed and eyes continue to process visual stimuli normally. Micro-sleeps, where the animal dips fleetingly into deep sleep and then quickly arouses again into drowsiness, happen continuously under drowsiness.

1.3.8 Species-Specific Posture

In most terrestrial mammals sleep occurs at a specially constructed sleep site with the animal in a recumbent position and with eyes closed. Animals construct sleep nests in order to protect against the cold and predators, and to co-sleep with a sleeping partner or set of partners, but it is unclear why most animals sleep with their eyes closed. Is it because closing the eyes protects sleep? If your eyes are closed you are less likely to see things that will wake you up. But many animals sleep with their eyes only half closed (ruminants) or with one eye open (some aquatic mammals and some birds). Some people actually can sleep with their eyes open, so the purpose of eye closure during sleep may not be due solely to the need to protect sleep.

In birds and in some aquatic mammals (like dolphins and whales) sleep occurs in one brain hemisphere at a time. The open eye in these species is usually contralateral to the hemisphere that is asleep and thus it is reasonable to assume that the open eye is transmitting information primarily to the awake hemisphere rather than the asleep hemisphere. It is possible that some information from the pathway from the open eye to the awake hemisphere leaks over to the pathway to the asleep hemisphere. In any case, unilateral eye closure (or keeping one eye and hemisphere awake) functions to allow the animal to "sleep on the wing." By this I mean that aquatic mammals can continue to swim while one hemisphere sleeps and birds can continue to fly.

Most terrestrial animals sleep in a protected site in a recumbent position. They lay down in their sleep nest and then fall asleep. Laying down presumably conserves energy but conservation of energy cannot be the whole story as the brain is very highly activated during sleep, thus precluding energy conservation as a major causal factor in sleep recumbency. It may be that animals lie down to sleep simply because any other posture is incompatible with the muscle atonia and paralysis associated with REM. Ruminants like cows can sleep while standing. Not surprisingly they exhibit very little REM. Sea otters, on the other hand, prefer to sleep floating on the ocean's surface. Bats sleep while hanging upside down from a cave wall. Many juvenile mammals sleep next to siblings or to mothers, thus deriving heat comfort and protection from these relatives. Sleep is not a passive process in mammalian juveniles as they can grasp, suck, and snuggle while asleep. Sleep in the juvenile rat, for example, "expects" a social environment and appears to be adapted to sleeping in groups near a mother who provides heat, protection, and nutrients. Adult rodents sleep curled up in groups within a hidden niche or a burrow.

Sleep sites vary systematically with social organization in primates (Anderson, 1998). Social relationships among individuals in a group influences arrangements of sleeping clusters in primates. Kin relations, reproductive status, and dominance relations influence spatial and huddling relations during sleep. Fruth and McGrew (1998) and Fruth and Hohmann (1993) have noted that among the great apes a number of filiative and cooperative interactions such as play, grooming, sexual encounters, and mother–infant nursing take place in the nests at sleep sites. This suggests that sleep processes themselves are intimately shaped by social factors in the primates.

1.3.9 Elevated Arousal Thresholds

One of the defining features of sleep is that it is difficult to arouse the sleeping animal with sensory input that does not exceed a threshold of touch, or loudness or light, etc. The sensory input has to go beyond that threshold to wake someone up. The brain employs protective mechanisms to keep you asleep once you are asleep. If a noise occurs within the room you are sleeping in, the brain will take that information and suppress it so that it does not wake you up. The brain uses neuronal inhibitory mechanisms to prevent the sound information from reaching arousal centers of the brain. Those inhibitory mechanisms are sometimes indexed by so-called k complexes and sleep spindles, which I will discuss more fully shortly.

We have now completed our review of the key terms in our definition of sleep. It is worth mentioning, however, a couple of other behavioral phenomena that are intimately related to sleep as they will help to bring out potential functional aspects of sleep.

1.3.10 Yawning

In primates, yawning may be contagious such that if I see or hear you yawning I will experience an irresistible urge to do so myself. Yawning may be contagious because it can function as a signal to conspecifics that can help synchronize sleep times among these conspecifics. For example, once one monkey yawns within a troop other monkeys begin to do so and then a suite of behaviors kick in: searching for a suitable sleep site; construction of a sleep site; ritual circling of the sleep site; choosing partners to sleep with, then bedding down, etc. At an individual level yawning is associated with attempts to change brain state either from quiescence into more alert states or from alert states into quiescence. Yawning appears to occur in all mammals, in some birds, and may even occur in reptiles. Yawns often involve involuntary openings of the mouth, inspiration of a breath, closing of the eyes, and stretching of torso and limbs. Like REM sleep, yawning is associated with cholinergic excitation and dopaminergic inhibition. Oxytocin and testosterone infusions can induce yawns as well. Interestingly, when oxytocin is injected into the paraventricular nucleus or the hippocampus it induces both yawning and penile erections (Argiolas and Gessa, 1991). REM sleep is associated with erections too. Yawning even occurs in the fetus. The yawn's wide taxonomic distribution in the animal kingdom suggests an ancient lineage as well as important functional relationships with sleep states.

1.3.11 Hibernation and Torpor

Hibernation is an adaptation that allows some warm-blooded animals to engage in a period of prolonged inactivity with dramatically reduced needs for food and warmth. The animal finds a well protected site like a cave or constructs a burrow or rest site and then hunkers down for a day or two in the case of torpor, or for the winter in the case of hibernation. It looks like the animal is sleeping, but it is not. The hibernating animal reduces its core body temperature and metabolic activity and enters a period of immobility but it periodically arouses and enters into slow wave sleep as if it is catching up on sleep. Hibernation allows the animal to survive periods like long winters when food is scarce and when there is no benefit to expending the calories looking for it. Torpor does the same for animals like squirrels but these animals only need to be in torpor for short periods of time, not the entire winter. While the animal in torpor can drastically reduce its need for food and water and warmth it cannot reduce its need for sleep, so it must periodically arouse and engage in sleep. When an animal arouses out of torpor it immediately goes into slow wave activity (SWA) as if to make up for lost sleep. But the amount of slow wave sleep the animal engages in appears to be tied to its body and brain temperature rather than sleep need per se, as the lower the temperature of the brain, the greater the SWA is immediately following the arousal.

Bears are the great hibernators. Hibernation in the bear is triggered by a gradual waning of their circadian rhythms of sleep and wake. Bears actually regulate their body temperatures by shivering and increasing their metabolic rates. They show mostly non-REM sleep and REM sleep with brief episodes of wake throughout the hibernation season.

1.4 Comparative Sleep

1.4.1 Introduction

Some form of sleep is found in all mammals and birds and may be present in reptiles and even in invertebrates. Particularly important for an analysis of sleep's evolutionary history is the identification of changes in sleep patterns as a function of divergences between species in evolutionary pathways. Modern mammalian and avian lineages, for example, are thought to have diverged from their reptilian ancestors about 250 million years ago. Modern extant forms of reptiles may retain some of the sleep characteristics of their ancestors who flourished before the rise of the mammals and we mammals in turn may inherit some of the features of reptilian sleep. Thus, studies of modern reptiles may reveal the form of sleep from which mammalian and avian sleep evolved.

1.4.2 Reptiles

The sleep processes of mammals and birds appear more alike than do the sleep processes of either of these with reptilian sleep. This fact is surprising given that birds are more closely related to reptiles than they are to mammals. Yet clear unequivocal electrophysiologic signs of both REM and NREM sleep states have been identified in birds and mammals but not as clearly or unequivocally in reptiles until recently. High voltage slow waves (HVSW) or high-amplitude spikes and sharp waves appearing in tandem with clear behavioral signs of sleep (e.g., eye movement patterns or arousal thresholds) in reptiles have been proposed as reptilian precursors of slow wave activity (SWA) found in the sleep of mammals. The equation of reptilian HVSW with mammalian SWA is supported by findings of compensatory rebound of sleep-related processes including EEG spikes after sleep deprivation (SD) in some reptiles. Karamanova (1982) argued that some reptiles evidenced these electrophysiologic precursors to REM and NREM sleep. More recently, Shein-Idelson and colleagues (2016) identified in the Australian dragon lizard, Pogona vitticeps, electrophysiologic signs of REM and NREM sleep states that are similar to those seen in mammals and birds. What was most interesting in this report was that the lizard's REM and NREM sleep phases alternated one another just as they do in mammals. A phase characterized by low frequency/high amplitude sharp waves (homologous to mammalian slow wave sleep) alternated with a phase characterized by awake-like brain activity and rapid eye movements (homologous to mammalian REM). In Pogona, SWS and REM alternate regularly throughout the night with a short period (~80 s), generating up to 350 SWS-REMS cycles (compared with four to five ninety-minute cycles in humans). Shien-Idelson et al. also recorded coordinated activity of the lizard's cortex with the dorsal ventricular ridge during slow wave sleep. Similar coordinated neural activity occurs in mammals between the cortex and the hippocampus and may underlie memory consolidation processes in mammals.

Thus, it is looking more and more like reptiles, birds, and mammals all have developed two major sleep processes that can legitimately be called REM and NREM. The ubiquity of REM and NREM among these three taxa may be due to all three sharing a common ancestor who lived around 320 million years ago and developed the two-phase sleep process. In that case, sleep as we know it, is an extremely ancient physiologic process. Alternatively the similar sleep processes of reptiles, birds, and mammals may be due to convergent evolution. Convergent evolution would suggest that the similar sleep patterns observed in these three taxa were due to these animals developing similar solutions to common evolutionary challenges.

1.4.3 Avian Sleep

Birds show the same EEG characteristics of NREM and REM sleep as do mammals but REM sleep periods typically last only a few seconds in birds (though there are many of them in any given sleep period). The percent of total sleep time occupied by REM in birds is less than half that of mammals. Birds may be able to sleep on the wing during periods of migration. When the migratory white crowned sparrows are studied under laboratory conditions they show "migratory restlessness." When they begin to show migratory restlessness they dramatically reduce the time they spend in sleep (only 13 percent of day activities spent in sleep), suggesting that they also do so when on the wing.

As in aquatic mammals, unilateral eye closure and unihemispheric slow wave sleep or USWS also occurs in birds (reviewed in Rattenborg, et al., 2000; 2009). In USWS only one hemisphere sleeps at a time and there is some evidence that birds in migratory formations sleep this way while flying. Slow wave sleep (SWS) in birds does not appear to be homeostatically regulated. SWS in NREM sleep in pigeons does not decline in the course of the dark period suggesting that SWS in these animals is not building up some chemical that was depleted during waking. Unlike mammals, sleep spindles are absent during NREM in birds. In addition to conventional SWS, birds also display sleep states that simultaneously combine features of both wakefulness and SWS.

Monotremes

Composed of three extant species (two species of echnida and the duck-billed platypus), these mammals are thought to have diverged from the main mammalian line prior to the divergence of marsupials and placental mammals. While initial studies of the short-beaked echnida (*Tachyglossus aculeatus*) suggested unequivocal SWS, no EEG signs of REM were noted. Follow-up work revealed that REM could be characterized by concurrent cortical activation, reduced tonic EMG activity, and rapid eye- movements in short-beaked echidnas under low, thermo-neutral, and high-ambient temperatures. Apparently irregular reticular discharge patterns during SWS in the short-beaked echnida constitutes a kind of mixture of REM and NREM. Rapid eye movements were also later recorded in the duck-billed playtypus despite no overt EEG signs of REM. Thus, the mono-tremes appear to exhibit a mixed, indeterminate form of sleep containing elements of both REM and NREM mammalian sleep states. It is possible that mammalian sleep states emerged out of this primordial hybrid state of indeterminate sleep with SWS and REM segregating into independent brain states dependent on the central nervous system or CNS organization of the animal.

1.4.4 Aquatic Mammals

Sleep in marine mammals like the bottlenose dolphin, the whale, mana-tee, walrus, and seal is remarkably different from sleep in terrestrial animals (reviewed in Lyamin et al., 2008). Like many avian species and unlike terrestrial mammals, marine mammals tend to exhibit unihemi-spheric sleep wherein one hemisphere of the brain sleeps at a time. That sleeping hemisphere engages in NREM but not REM sleep. As in birds, unihemispheric sleep in aquatic mammals is associated with keeping one eye open during sleep – typically the eye contralateral to the hemisphere that is asleep. When in the water, fur seals always use unihemispheric sleep, but when on land, they, like other terrestrial mammals, show bilateral hemispheric sleep.

Although EEG signs of REM are absent, cetaceans show other behav-ioral signs of REM including rapid eye movements, penile erections, and muscle twitching. The two main families of Pinnipeds, Otariidae (sea lions and fur seals) and Phocidae (true seals), show both unihemispheric and bihemispheric forms of sleep. Phocids sleep *under* water (obviously holding their breath) while both hemispheres exhibit either REM or SWS. Amazonian Manatees (*Trichechus inunguis*) also sleep while under water, exhibiting three sleep states: bihemispheric REM, bihemi-spheric SWS, and unihemispheric SWS. Both hemispheres awaken to surface and breathe. Whales (*Delphinapterus leucas*) and dolphins (*Tur-siops runcates*) show only USWS. Northern fur seals and sea lions (family Otariidae) are aquatic and terrestrial. While in water these animals have USWS, like cetaceans, but on land they have both USWS and BSWS. It is unclear whether cetaceans have REM sleep, whereas Otariidae have REM sleep on land, and it is always bilateral.

Sleep deprivation in an animal exhibiting unihemispheric sleep may evidence unihemispheric sleep rebound, prompting some authorities to claim that sleep serves a primary function for selected portions of the brain rather than the body. It appears that sleep rebound effects may occur only for local regions of the forebrain. The data on unihemispheric sleep in marine mammals also suggests that REM and NREM serve distinct functions, as animals without full polygraphic REM can survive.

The fact that SWS can be expressed in one hemisphere raises the question of whether that is the case for REM as well. To my knowledge REM can only be expressed bihemispherically. It may be that one hemisphere or brain region cannot support REM. In addition, when REM occurs in marine mammals it is always bihemispheric. The bilateral nature of REM may be considered one of its costs and the brain structure of certain marine mammals, apparently, cannot bear these costs. During unihemispheric slow wave sleep or USWS, one hemisphere has high-amplitude slow wave activity (1.2–4 Hz), while the other hemisphere has desynchronized EEG activity, which is typically deemed wake or REM. What happens if we attempt to prevent USWS? That hemisphere and that hemisphere alone incurs a sleep debt and will evidence rebound (increased amount and intensity of USWS) once the hemisphere is no longer prevented from entering USWS. This fact, that sleep rebound occurs in only one hemisphere in these species, implies that the homeostatic need for sleep accumulates *independently in each hemisphere.* If homeostatic need is hemisphere-specific then the thing that gets depleted with wake has to be in that hemisphere. In a recent study (Lyamin et al., 2016) of USWS in northern fur seals (*Callorthinus ursinus*), levels of histamine, norepinephrine, and serotonin during USWS were not higher in the desynchronized (awake) hemisphere compared to the contralateral hemisphere with USWS. On the other hand, acetylcholine release in the cortex was lateralized and tightly linked to the hemisphere that was awake. Therefore, whatever is getting depleted in the awake hemisphere during wake is not these classical neurotransmitter levels.

1.4.5 Terrestrial Mammals

Moving from the oceans onto the land, now we come to the sleep of terrestrial animals. The sleep of terrestrial mammals varies tremendously. Average total daily sleep duration ranges between three hours in the donkey (*Equus asinus*) to twenty hours in armadillos (*Chaeto-phractus villosus*; Affani, Cervino, and Marcos, 2001), while average sleep cycles vary from six minutes in the chinchilla (*Chinchilla lanigera*) to ninety minutes in humans and chimpanzees (*Pan troglodytes*). Comparative studies of sleep quotas/values in terrestrial mammals suggest that NREM and REM sleep quotas increase in tandem with one another. That is, whenever there is an evolutionary increase in NREM duration, REM too will increase its duration (Capellini, Barton, et al., 2008). Both REM and NREM sleep durations are lower when animals sleep in more exposed and vulnerable sites and have a more herbivorous diet suggesting that total sleep time is constrained in species that experience higher predation risk.

1.4.6 Primates

Sleep in primates is reviewed in Nunn et al., 2010. While living primates are divided into two groups, the Strepsirhini (lemurs and lorises) and the Haplorhini (monkeys, apes, and the tarsier), we are primarily interested in the Haplorhines – the line that gave rise to humans. Haplorhines include two groups, the Platyrrhini and the Catarrhini. Platyrrhines are monkeys that are native to the New World. Catarrhines include both Old World monkeys and the apes.

Non-human primates exhibit two major sleep phases: REM and NREM. In some apes NREM exhibits two subphases as well: a phase of light sleep and deep sleep characterized by slow wave activity. Owl monkeys, cotton top tamarins (*Saguinus oedipus*), and mouse lemurs (*Microcebus murinus*) exhibit average total sleep time per day from thirteen to seventeen hours. The short sleepers (averaging between eight and eleven hours total sleep) include humans, the chimpanzee, a handful of cercopithecine monkeys, a lemur, and some New World primates. Time devoted to REM sleep among primates varies from a little over thirty minutes per day in the vervet monkey (*Cercopithecus aethiops*) to two hours per day in the chimpanzee and human. Relative to other primates, humans have exceptionally shorter sleep times but a significantly higher proportion of REM (Samson and Nunn, 2015).

In general, primate sleep is characterized by (1) *Consolidation of sleep into a single long bout*, or two relatively long bouts possibly to achieve greater sleep intensities; (2) *Reductions in total sleep times among diurnal primate species including humans*, which could reflect a number of different advantages or constraints associated with diurnality (or being active in daylight); (3) *Increased sleep intensity*, possibly associated with differentiation of NREM sleep stages into lighter and deeper stages of sleep; and (4) *Maintenance of social contact during sleep*, which likely has advantages in terms of infant care, predation risk, and thermoregulation.

1.4.7 Ancestral Human Sleep

There is an ongoing debate about the normal human sleep pattern with some scholars claiming that humans sleep for a few hours during the night and then take a long nap in the late afternoon. This is called the "bimodal sleep pattern." Other scientists claim that that bimodal pattern occurs during the dark period which is split up into two bouts of sleep with a period of wakefulness during the night. Yet other scholars claim that humans sleep in one long bout during the dark period, i.e., that there is no bimodal sleep pattern at all. Historians and anthropologists have presented extensive evidence that a bimodal pattern was common in preindustrial societies. Ekirch, 2005 notes that traditional peoples often refer to "first" and "second" sleep. He provides the example of the Asante and Fante on the West African coast, for whom the phrase in their native Tshi language "woadá ayi d. fã" signifies "they lie in the first sleep," whereas "wayi (or wada) d. biakō" reads "he has slept the first part of the night." The bimodal pattern allows traditional peoples to engage in numerous social interactions during the dark period, from tending to children to forming social alliances and keeping watch against nighttime predators (Yetish et al., 2015).

1.4.8 Conclusion

Sleep in the form of regularly occurring periods of quiescence and some amount of sleep rebound can be found in even the simplest of organisms from earthworms and fruit flies to nonhuman primates and human beings. We do not see evidence, however, of the emergence of distinct sleep states until we come to the reptiles. Birds and aquatic mammals also evidence distinct sleep states including the phenomenon of unihemispheric sleep, which allows these animals to sleep while flying or swimming. REM may only occur bihemispherically. The presence of high voltage slow waves as well as REM-like brain activation patterns in reptiles, birds, and mammals suggests that the biphasic, REM, and NREM sleep phases we find in humans is a very ancient adaptation indeed and that its benefits outweigh the risks associated with quiescence and reduced responsiveness to the environment.

Review Questions

- Delta brain waves indicate the intensity with which we sleep. Why do you think that these waves are strongest over the frontal lobes during sleep?
- Slow wave sleep can occur in only one brain hemisphere at a time. REM sleep, on the other hand, never occurs unihemishperically as far as we know. Why do you think REM sleep requires both hemispheres to manifest?
- Why do you suppose some birds and some aquatic mammals like dolphins sleep with only one hemisphere at a time?
- What strengths and weaknesses do you see with the scientific claim that sleep is social?

Further Reading

Lyamin, O. I., Manger, P. R., Ridgeway, S. H., Mukhametov, L. M., & Siegel, J. M. (2008). Cetacean sleep: An unusual form of mammalian sleep. *Neuroscience and Biobehavioral Reviews*, 32, 1451–1484.

Rattenborg, N. C., Amlaner, C. J., & Lima, S. L. (2000). Behavioral, neurophysiological and evolutionary perspectives on unihemispheric sleep. *Neuroscience and Biobehavioral Reviews*, 24, 817–842.

Rattenborg, N. C., Martinez-Gonzalez, D., & Lesku, J. A. (2009). Avian sleep homeostasis: Convergent evolution of complex brains, cognition and sleep functions in mammals and birds. *Neuroscience and Biobehavioral Reviews*, 33, 253–270.

Siegel, J. M. (2008). Do all animals sleep? *Trends in Neuroscience*, 31(4), 208–213.

(2005). Clues to the functions of mammalian sleep. *Nature*, 437, 1264–1271.

CHAPTER 2

From Biological Rhythms to the Sleep Cycle

Learning Objectives

- Describe how the sleep-cycle fits into the larger twenty-four-hour circadian cycle
- Identify the regulatory functions of the master biological clock: the suprachiasmatic nucleus (SCN)
- Identify the causes and consequences of major disorders of biological rhythmicity
- Identify the major electrophysiologically defined sleep stage components of the sleep cycle

2.1 Introduction

All terrestrial animals live their lives embedded in the twenty-four-hour hour light-dark cycle. Their challenges and opportunities also appear and disappear regularly in tandem with that twenty-four-hour light-dark cycle. For example, challenges for human beings include the appearance of predators (e.g., big cats) that operate most effectively during the dark cycle. Opportunities include the easy availability of some food sources, and in-group social interactions including pursuit of reproductive opportunities, many of which occur more easily during the dark half of the twenty-four-hour cycle. It is no surprise then that all animals have developed adaptations that allow them to avoid predators and capitalize on reproductive opportunities linked to the twenty-four-hour cycle.

Sleep is no exception to the rule. It is firmly embedded in the twenty-four-hour light-dark cycle that is called the circadian rhythm. We sleep primarily during the dark phase of the cycle, yet we are descended from primates who slept mainly during the light phase. The shift from nocturnality (active during the dark cycle) to diurnality (active during the light phase) within the primate order was associated with dramatic changes in ecology and behavioral capacities including the gradual consolidation of sleep into the dark cycle. The shift to a diurnal lifestyle was associated with a move out of the trees, with key lineages becoming more terrestrial, thus allowing them to move into more open habitats where it paid to be active during the light phase (Nunn et al., 2010). With the exception of owl monkeys in the genus *Aotus*, all monkeys and apes, including humans, are now diurnal-active during the day and at least partially quiescent at night.

How does the sleep cycle fit into the larger twenty-four-hour or circadian cycle? The current belief is that a brain-based circadian pacemaker or master clock is synched up with, or entrained to the light-dark cycle such that it sends chemical messages to the rest of the brain and body signaling changes in the daily light-dark cycle. As light turns to dark and dark turns to light the master clock sends the appropriate chemical messenger into the appropriate brain regions that turn sleep on and off. A homeostatic process linked to the pacemaker region regulates (with the help of pacemaker genes) or influences the amount and timing of sleep, possibly via accumulation of adenosine or some other neuroendocrine or neurochemical substance that signals sleep need and sleep debt. Adenosine accumulates as the individual goes about his waking day and with it the urge to sleep increases until sleep occurs and adenosine levels reset. The circadian pacemaker regulates release of adenosine and related chemical messengers via its control of the neuroendocrine hypothalamic region that contains the master clock.

The master clock is believed to be housed in the hypothalamus and is usually identified with the suprachiasmatic nucleus (SCN). For example, the SCN of the hypothalamus receives information from the visual system that tells it whether the individual is entering a light or dark phase, and then based on that information the SCN will release melatonin (that is synthesized in the pineal gland) that will then trigger termination or initiation of sleep. We will discuss this process in more detail shortly, as its dysfunction results in several types of sleep and circadian rhythm disorders.

2.2 Circadian Rhythms and Sleep

2.2.1 Introduction

The brain region which appears to act as the master circadian clock in humans is the suprachiasmatic nucleus (SCN). The SCN is located above the optic chiasm and at the bottom of the hypothalamus. It receives direct input from the retina via the retinohypothalamic tract. The retinohypothalamic tract transmits light information from the optic nerve in the eye to the geniculate nucleus of the thalamus, and thence to the visual cortex and the SCN. The core SCN cells receive light information from ganglion cells in the retina that contain the unique photosensitive pigment called melanopsin. When light information arrives at the SCN cells within the core of the SCN they entrain their firing patterns with the light and dark cycle. Another group of cells surround the core cells of the SCN. These are called the shell cells and they are involved in regulation of melatonin release.

Melatonin is a hormone produced in the pineal gland and is linked to onset of seasonal estrus in seasonally reproducing animals. It is released primarily during the night in both diurnal and nocturnal animals and thus it can be used by seasonal breeders as a measure of day length. As day length increases in the spring, the longer light period inhibits melatonin production leading to shorter durations for nighttime peak values. These changes in nocturnal melatonin levels then disinhibit release of gonado-tropins, bringing the animal into reproductive mode.

In humans, melatonin release begins to increase at around 10 P.M. with central nervous system or CNS levels peaking around 3 A.M. (when REM predominates) and then declining to very low levels by 8 A.M. Daytime levels are almost undetectable. Circulating levels of melatonin decrease dramatically in prepubertal children and may contribute to disinhibition of gonadotropins and to development of nocturnal-entrainment of release of these gonadotropins. When melatonin is administered to humans its primary effect is to increase sleepiness.

Melatonin is synthesized and released from the pineal gland, which sits between the cerebral hemispheres and is connected to the brain by a small stalk. However, the neural connection to the pineal does not go through that stalk. Cells from the shell of the SCN project to a nearby region in the hypothalamus called the paraventricular nucleus. Connections from this nucleus to the SCN then help to regulate melato-nin release. Once melatonin is released from the pineal it comes under the control of SCN, thereby helping the clock to entrain physiologic processes with the twenty-four-hour light-dark cycle.

2.2.2 The REM-NREM Cycle

Sleepiness is triggered by SCN-related melatonin activity. Once an indi-vidual mammal is asleep another cyclic process is activated within the overall twenty-four-hour circadian cycle called ultradian cycle. This ultradian cycle involves the alternation between REM and NREM sleep states. We will discuss brain mechanisms of sleep onset and offset shortly, but for now we just wish to note that the REM-NREM cycles in humans with a period of about ninety minutes during the dark phase of the circadian cycle. In other words, about every ninety minutes one undergoes a period of REM and a period of NREM sleep. In the adult human the ultradian cycle involves sleep onset through NREM sleep stages and sleep offset through REM sleep stages, with NREM sleep states predominating in the first third of the night and REM sleep periods predominating in the last third. Most of us awaken from an REM rather than an NREM episode. This ninety-minute ultraradian sleep cycle takes years to develop in the human.

Now let us look a little more closely at how this sleep cycle works during a single night of sleep in an average adult man or woman. We enter sleep through non-REM or phases N1, N2, and N3, or slow wave sleep (SWS). After about an hour of non-REM sleep, we leave deep SWS as sleep lightens and we briefly pass back up through stages 2 and 1. EEG amplitude declines and the wave form gets faster and faster, almost resembling waking activity. The slow, rolling eye movements, characteristic of N3 begin to show periodic spikes with the eyes darting back and forth under the closed eyelids. Muscle tone is lost and we are unable to move. Heart rate increases and the sexual system becomes activated with penile erection in males and clitoral engorgement in females. All of these dramatic changes signal the onset of the first episode of REM sleep of the night. Once we enter this first REM episode we will have undergone one full NREM to REM cycle. While this first REM period will last about only ten to twenty minutes, by the time morning comes these REM episodes will last about thirty to forty minutes. After the first full NREM to REM cycle we begin to cycle again back down into slow wave sleep. We "descend" from REM through brief phases of N1 and 2 into N3 with slow wave activity on EEG, increased muscle tone, slow rolling eye movements, no sexual activation, and regular breathing and heart patterns, and after about an hour, the EEG again returns rapidly through stages 2 and 1 to another episode of REM sleep and so on throughout the night.

When we use a graphic representation, called the hypnogram, to portray the changes in EEG and arousal states over the NREM-REM cycle, we can see the changes in the distribution of REM and NREM sleep times across a single night of sleep. Time is on the horizontal axis, and sleep state is on the vertical axis. We call the resulting picture of sleep over a single night the sleep architecture. In Figure 2.1 the new nomenclature for sleep states will assimilate stage 3 and 4 into one stage, N3.

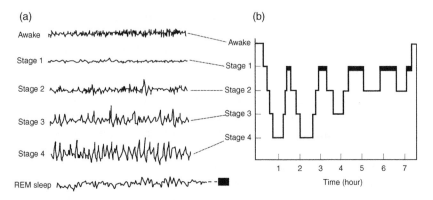

Figure 2.1 Human sleep architecture (Hypnogram)

2.2.3 What Triggers the Ultradian Sleep Cycle?

In the mid-1990s, Saper and colleagues (reviewed in Saper et al., 2005) argued that there was a sleep switch in the anterior hypothalamus. Neurons within the anterior hypothalamus increase their activity just before the transition into sleep. Gamma-aminobutyric acid, or GABA neurons project to all the brain stem wake-promoting neurons and turn them off. Interestingly, the GABA sleep promoting neurons in the anterior hypothalamus and related neurons within the hypothalamus such as histaminergic neurons, hypocretin neurons, and the sleep-on neurons receive inputs directly or indirectly from the nearby suprachiasmatic nucleus (SCN), which as we noted transduces light signals from the retina into hormonal and neuronal messages concerning the dark-light circadian cycle. In short, what triggers the NREM-REM sleep cycle is messages coming from the retina to the SCN in the hypothalamus that signal that the dark period has commenced. Then messages from the SCN to the anterior thalamus activate GABAergic sleep-on neurons in the anterior hypothalamus that send inhibitory signals to neurons in the brain stem that maintain wakefulness, basically instructing them to turn off, and thus sleep onset commences. When sleep has finished and the light phase of the daily cycle commences this information is sent from the SCN down to hypocretin neurons in the hypothalamus and these neurons then send excitatory signals down to the wake-*promoting* nuclei in the brainstem, which send inhibitory signals back to the hypothalamic sleep-on cells at the same time they are activating the cortex.

2.2.4 The Role of Adenosine

The chemical signal that tells the brain that it is time to sleep is very likely adenosine. Adenosine levels in the brain accumulate slowly throughout the day. As adenosine levels rise so does sleepiness. Caffeine blocks the cumulation of brain adenosine and thus sleepiness. Sleepiness appears to be tied directly to lack of energy. Energy is stored as glycogen in the glial cells of the brain. As sleep deprivation or wakefulness continues, energy supplies in the brain diminish and eventually the brain starts to tap its glycogen reserves. As the glycogen reserves diminish, adenosine is released and the induction of sleepiness and sleep occurs. Injections of chemicals that mimic the actions of adenosine promote sleep with onset of slow wave or delta power activity in the brain.

2.2.5 The Interaction of Circadian Rhythms with Sleep Rhythms: The Two Process Sleep Regulation Model

The most dramatic effect of sleep deprivation in every mammalian species studied thus far has been the phenomenon of "compensatory rebound," or the increase over baseline of sleep times and intensity, where intensity is measured by higher arousal thresholds, enhanced slow wave activity, enhanced rapid eye movement frequencies per unit time, and "deeper" and longer sleep cycles (Borbeley, 1980; Borbeley et al., 1984). After sleep deprivation mammalian animals attempt to make up for lost sleep by enhancing the intensity and duration of subsequent sleep. During the wakefulness or deprivation period some neurochemical, possibly adenosine (Strecter et al., 2006; Blanco-Centurion et al., 2006) accumulates in proportion to the length of the wake period. As its levels increase in a sleep center (possibly the basal forebrain) they exert an inhibitory effect on neurons in the brainstem and forebrain that promote arousal, thus increasing sleepiness. During sleep adenosine stops accumulating and existing stores begin to dissipate at a rate depending on sleep intensity until they return to baseline. When the individual awakens he will once again need to cumulate adenosine throughout the day in order to successfully initiate sleep.

Borbely (1982) first formalized the insight that mammalian sleep was involved in a balance between sleep amount and sleep intensity and that sleep was therefore under homeostatic control. In his "two-process" model of sleep regulation a sleep need factor called Process S (presumably associated with adenosine levels) increases during waking (or sleep deprivation) and decreases during sleep. This part of the model indexes restorative aspects of sleep and explicitly predicts that sleep is required for some restorative process of the brain or the body or both. Process S is proposed to interact with input from the light-regulated circadian system (Process C) that is independent of sleep and wakefulness rhythms. Slow wave activity (SWA) is taken as an indicator of the time course of Process S because SWA is known to correlate with arousal thresholds and to markedly increase during the previous waking period and during the rebound period after sleep deprivation in all mammals studied. Once a threshold value of Process S is reached (i.e., once the appropriate amount and intensity of SWS is reached), Process C will be activated. Simulations using the model's assumptions show that the homeostatic component of sleep falls in a sigmoidal manner during waking and rises in a saturating exponential manner during sleep.

This simple two-process model has allowed investigators to model real-life sleep disturbances by simply modulating one of the basic components or parameters of the model. For example, insomnia or sleep deprivation can be modeled by diminishing or deleting the S process when it interacts with C. Thus, if Process S does not result in enough adenosine to effectively inhibit arousal centers then the individual will not sleep or sleep well. To account for cognitive effects of sleep deprivation investigators have used nonlinear bidirectional interactions between the circadian C and the homeostatic S processes instead of the unidirectional effect of C on S processes as captured by the original model. Attempts have also been made to incorporate the ultraradian NREM-REM cycle within the overarching two-process C vs. S model.

The two-process model does not address homeostatic aspects of REM. REM, evidences rebound after sleep deprivation, but here the intensity component is likely to be some process associated with frequency (density) of rapid eye movements per unit time. Regardless, both REM and NREM are under homeostatic control and enhancements of sleep intensity over baseline addresses the homeostatic need for sleep. In short, *sleep intensity indexes functional need.*

Although the elegant simplicity of the two-process model captures normal functioning of the sleep-wake cycle, multi-oscillator models have been developed to capture more complex interactions of sleep cycles with other behavioral variables. In a multi-oscillator model two or more mutually interacting oscillators create the cycles of each of the behavioral variables being modeled. For example, one oscillator might be the suprachiasmatic nucleus (SCN) – the master clock. The SCN, in turn, drives temperature rhythms and melatonin rhythms. A second oscillator might be the controller for sleep-wake rhythms, perhaps centered on the ventrolateral preoptic nucleus (VLPO). This drives REM-NREM cycles. Recent discovery of a so-called flip-flop switch in the VLPO has prompted development of flip-flop models of sleep-wake state regulation. A flip-flop switch refers to the mechanism wherein whenever the switch is in one position (sleep) the other position (wake) is prevented and vice versa. In one recent flip-flop model it is assumed that sleep active neurons within the VLPO (S-R) oppose wake active neurons within the hypothalamus and brainstem, which fire during wakefulness and reduce firing during REM (W-A neurons); a third group of neurons that fire during REM within the extended VLPO region and a final fourth group of neurons within the basal forebrain that fire during both wake and REM (W-R group of neurons) interact with the first two group of neurons. The four interacting groups of neurons promote a flip or switch of brain state when sleep promoting substances (e.g., adenosine) accumulate during wake and activate S-R neurons and then dissipate during sleep. A second kind of sleep promoting substance (possibly a hormone like somatostatin or growth hormone) accumulates during wake and during NREM. It then would activate W-R neurons of the extended VLPO and then dissipate during REM.

2.2.6 Social Modulation of Biological Rhythms

Both the ultradian and the circadian rhythms are exquisitely sensitive to social cues in nonhuman primates and of course in human beings. The amount and quality of social interactions exert a profound influence on the body's rhythms. Social rhythms and light cues are known to act as powerful "zeitgebers" or timekeepers or signals that entrain bodily rhythms to regularly occurring social events. These social zeitgebers do so by preparing individuals to take advantage of regularly occurring opportunities (e.g., for social meals, formation of social alliances, social negotiations, reproductive opportunities, etc.) or threats in the environment. It may be that "morningness" and "eveningness" (Are you a morning person or a night person?) developed in response to the extent to which individuals are sensitive to differing social cues or zeitgebers. Morning people usually prefer to rise between 5 A.M. and 7 A.M. and retire between 9 P.M. and 11 P.M. Evening people tend to prefer both a later wake up (9 A.M. to 11 A.M.) and a later bed time (11 P.M. to 3 A.M.). Circadian and sleep cycles tend to be less variable in morning people.

Another regularly occurring sleep-related phenomenon called the "post-lunch dip" or the daytime "siesta" period is also exquisitely sensitive to social cues. The siesta period is a period of increased sleepiness and sluggishness and decreased alertness that strikes most people between 1 p.m. and 4 p.m. in the afternoon. In offices and factories all over the world people start to fall asleep at their desks or they begin to make small errors when their attention lapses and they become sleepy. During the siesta period body temperature declines significantly as if the body was preparing for sleep. This siesta period is consistent with the idea that the ancestral human sleep pattern is bimodal, with a long bout of sleep at night and a short bout in the late afternoon that in the modern era has become a siesta period instead of a napping period. The fact that what was once a daytime sleep period has become a mere siesta period in most cultures (and no rest at all in many cultures) demonstrates the extent to which sleep is influenced by social norms and that at least some amount of sleep is non-obligate or plastic.

2.2.7 Rhythm Disorders (see Table 2.1)

About a quarter of people who complain of difficulty sleeping or non-restorative sleep very likely actually have a disorder of biological rhythms. That is, their twenty-four-hour sleep-wake schedules have been desynchronized with their social zeitgebers or social obligations. In the so-called delayed sleep phase disorder (DSPD), sleep-wake schedules are advanced at least two hours later than habitual or conventional sleep times. So if most people in the local culture go to sleep by midnight, sleep onset times at around 2 a.m. would be considered possible DSPD. The individual with DSPD has tried to go to sleep earlier but typically cannot, and even when he does manage to sleep earlier he still wakes up later than the cultural norms. Therefore his sleep schedule conflicts with the demands of the society he lives in. He must awaken earlier than his body wants to awake. He therefore is constantly incurring a sleep debt so he walks around sleepy and fatigued all the time. DSPD sometimes runs in families so there may be a genetic component to the disorder. Its onset is typically in adolescence.

Advanced sleep phase disorder (ASPD) is the counterpart to DSPD. While the DSPD patient prefers to go to sleep later than others, the ASPD patient prefers to go to sleep substantially earlier than others. ASPD patients become sleepy early in the evening and prefer early morning wakings. Even when they try to sleep in, they can't – they spontaneously wake in the early morning.

To treat the delayed sleep phase patient we can expose them to bright light in the morning and reduce light exposure in the evening in order to

Table 2.1 Disorders of biological rhythms

Disorder	Symptoms	Pathophysiology and Treatment
Shift work and jet lag	Fatigue, sleepiness, confusion, listless, low energy, GI ailments	Individual's biorhythms are out of phase or sync with social group's rhythms and activities (e.g., due to shift work or skipping time zones due to air travel). Treatment: After travel across time zones it takes a week to adjust to local time schedules. Melatonin administration can help reset internal clock.
Seasonal affective disorder or SAD	Mood dysfunction and depression during dark months	Reduced day length or duration and intensity of sunlight during fall and winter alters SCN output and disrupts circadian organization. Treatment involves phototherapy (exposure to varying light intensities to reset SCN), and antidepressants medications.
Bipolar 1 disorder	Cycling between periods of extreme manic episodes lasting about one week and depressive episodes also lasting about one week. During manic phases there are feelings of euphoria and elation. There is disinhibition, agitation, sleeplessness, and occasionally delusional beliefs. During the depressive phase there is major depression (sadness, despair, anhedonia, etc.).	Causes are unknown but clock genes expressed in the SCN have been implicated. Treatment: antipsychotics, mood stabilizers, antidepressants.
Delayed sleep phase wake disorder	The individual's sleep-wake times are two or more hours ahead of the social reference point.	Cause is unknown but one possibility is that the delayed sleepiness represents an exaggerated reaction to the normal shift in the internal clocks that is seen in adolescents after puberty Treatment: phototherapy with bright light exposure in the morning, melatonin.
Advanced sleep phase wake disorder	Individual goes to sleep earlier and awakens earlier than the social reference point.	Treatment: bright light exposure in the evening and melatonin in the morning.

reset the master clock (which is normally entrained via daylight) so as to be entrained with conventional sleep-wake schedules. In addition, melatonin can be administered six hours before desired sleep time so as to shift the master clock backwards and get it more aligned with conventional rest-activity schedules. An opposite course is followed for ASPD patients: bright-light exposure in the evening to delay sleep and melatonin release.

We all know what jet-lag disorder is. When we fly across time zones our normal sleep-wake schedules get disrupted such that our circadian rhythms become out of phase with local social schedules. Your timing for sleep is out of phase with the locals as is your meal time and rest times. Therefore, your entire physiology has to adjust to local time if you are to interact normally with the locals. Seasonal affective disorder (SAD) is a subvariant of major depressive disorder dubbed depressive mood with seasonal pattern. People with SAD become depressed, sleepy, and inactive during dark winter months and their spirits lift with the return of sunlight and springtime. In bipolar 1 disorder, mood swings significantly within a day or across several weeks. The patient can cycle between manic episodes of sleeplessness and frenetic activity that can last several days and then suddenly crash into episodes of dark depression, sleepiness, and inactivity. During a manic episode the patient can go without sleep for days at a time and exhibit a rapid, pressured form of speech. They are flooded with ideas, easily excitable, and sometimes hypersexual. When, however, the depression returns, there is a crash; they tend not to want to talk and there is little if any ideation. They are self-critical and depressed and appear to be somnolent – though quality sleep may elude them. SAD and bipolar 1 disorder can be treated effectively with antidepressants and mood stabilizers. Chronotherapy, or the selected use of bright light exposure can effectively reset circadian rhythms and thus treat phase disorders and perhaps even SAD.

2.2.8 Conclusion

The ultradian NREM-REM sleep cycle is embedded within the larger twenty-four- hour circadian cycle. The sleep cycle interacts with the circadian cycle, which in turn is controlled by the SCN master clock within the hypothalamus. The two-process model captures interactions between the circadian process and the sleep cycle. Disorders of biological rhythmicity such as delayed sleep phase syndrome and manic depression have significant but treatable effects on sleep. In the next chapter we will learn that sleep expression also changes in remarkable ways across the lifespan.

Review Questions

- What is the probable role of adenosine in regulation of the sleep cycle?
- What is the evidence that manic depression/bipolar disorder is a sleep-related disorder of biologic rhythms?
- What are two ways that social processes modulate biological rhythms?
- How does the two-process model describe the interactions of the circadian cycle with the sleep cycle?
- Why do you suppose we enter sleep via NREM stages rather than REM?

Further Reading

Alloy L. B., Ng, T. H., Titone, M. K., & Boland, E. M. (2017). Circadian rhythm dysregulation in bipolar spectrum disorders. *Current Psychiatry Reports*, 19(4), 21. doi: 10.1007/s11920–017–0772-z. Review. PMID:28321642.

Borbely, A. A. (1982). A two process model of sleep regulation. *Human Neurobiology*, 1, 195–204.

Czeisler, C. A., & Gooley, J. J. (2007). Sleep and circadian rhythms in humans. *Cold Spring Harbor Symposia on Quantitative Biology*, 72, 579–597.

Saper, C. B., Scammell, T. E., & Lu, J. (2005). Hypothalamic regulation of sleep and circadian rhythms. *Nature*, 437(7063), 1257–1263.

CHAPTER 3

Expression of Sleep across the Human Lifespan

Learning Objectives

- Identify the relevance of several mid-level evolutionary theories (attachment theory, parent-offspring conflict theory, heterochrony, etc.) for the expression of sleep characteristics across the lifespan
- Evaluate evidence for the claim that REM sleep is crucial for brain development
- Describe the significance of changes in proportion to REM and NREM sleep states across the lifespan
- Identify the impact of sleep on longevity

3.1 Introduction

How should we study the typical development and expression of sleep patterns in people? The most straightforward way to do so would be to simply observe the development of sleep states in people as those people develop into maturity, reproduce, age, and die. But who, what peoples, should we study in order to get a picture of the typical human pattern?

Unfortunately, the vast majority of studies of sleep development and expression across the lifespan have been conducted on only a single class of people. Beebe (2016) has called them "Western, Educated, Industrialized, Rich, and Democratic (WEIRD)" peoples. Thus, the evidence on what sleep scientists have regarded as normal lifespan sleep patterns is based largely on one small and unrepresentative slice of the human family (most of the world's population is not rich, for example): WEIRD samples. That would be OK if sleep was known to be unaffected by social or cultural factors, but that simply is not the case. Sleep IS strongly affected by social and cultural factors, so basing our understanding of sleep development on a single sample that is not typical of the rest of the human family is problematic. For example, in non-WEIRD societies co-sleeping is the norm at all stages of life from infancy to old age, whereas co-sleeping is not universal in WEIRD societies, even for mother-infant pairs. Thus, the reader needs to keep these considerations in mind when perusing the information and data presented in this chapter concerning norms of sleep expression across the human lifespan (Peña et al., 2016).

We also need to understand the evolutionary context in order to fully understand developmental sleep schedules across the human lifespan.

3.2 Evolutionary Background to Sleep Development

3.2.1 Heterochrony or Changes in the Timing of Neurodevelopmental Processes

McNamara (1997) and others (e.g., Burns, 2007) have noted that *hypermorphosis* or the extension of growth times (relative to our primate ancestors) within each normal phase of development (infancy, childhood, adolescence, and maturity, etc.) captures the unique character of human development across the lifespan. We have long drawn out growth phases *within* each of the classical periods of primate lifespan development. That means that the brain grows larger during infancy and childhood simply because it grows for a longer period of time within the infancy and childhood phases (again relative to our nearest evolutionary relatives). Because hypermorphosis characterizes human developmental schedules, we can expect that human sleep cycles will necessarily be affected. For example, if sleep functions in part to promote brain development then sleep cycles may operate more intensely during the period of life where most brain development occurs – infancy and childhood. Hypermorphosis implies that during infancy and childhood sleep cycles have had to either (1) become longer or (2) become more intense than they are in other primates or at other times of the lifecycle. It turns out that relative to other primates, humans have exceptionally *shorter* sleep times but a significantly higher proportion of REM (Samson and Nunn, 2015), suggesting that we opted to increase sleep intensity in the form of REM quotas to support longer brain development times. There is in fact growing evidence to support the idea that REM enhances brain development during infancy and childhood. Sleep intensity is also very high in adolescence, another period that is extended in the human family relative to our primate relatives.

3.2.2 REM Promotion of Brain Development

Dumoulin, Bridi, et al. (2015) presented evidence that REM sleep in early life promotes brain development by facilitating the release of a kinase critical for neuronal plasticity, so-called extracellular signal regulated kinase, or ERK. Kinase phosphorylation in the primary visual area of the cortex, area V1, requires REM sleep, because it will not occur in sleep-deprived animals. REM-induced ERK phosphorylation is essential for plasticity changes in the visual region of the brain. REM sleep deprivation after monocular deprivation (suturing one eye shut) profoundly and selectively inhibited ERK phosphorylation in V1 in kittens. Preventing rapid eye movement sleep after monocular deprivation reduced ocular dominance plasticity (normal visual development) and inhibited activation of ERK, the kinase critical for this plasticity.

Formation of new neuronal circuits in the brain is accomplished by experience-dependent selective pruning and elimination of an initial exuberant overgrowth of synapses during development. REM deprivation prevents selective pruning and elimination of neuronal synapses. Li et al. (2017) have shown that REM sleep promotes pruning of newly formed postsynaptic dendritic spines of layer 5 pyramidal neurons in the mouse motor cortex during development and motor learning. Dendritic calcium spikes arising during REM sleep are important for this pruning and strengthening new spines (Li et al., 2017).

In birds paradoxical/active sleep (REM is sometimes called paradoxical sleep or "PS" in nonhuman species) appears to be required for some aspects of song learning (Margoliash et al., 2005). REM sleep may also mediate certain aspects of sexual learning in birds. The total amount of time spent in PS sleep, as well as the number of PS episodes, increase significantly following a sexual imprinting session in the laboratory. Mirmiran et al. (1983; Mirmiran 1995) found that masculine sexual responses (mounts and ejaculations) were significantly impaired in rats that had been treated early in life (when neonates) with REM suppressant agents (e.g., clomipramine). Vogel and Hagler (1996) demonstrated that administration of the REM suppressant and antidepressant drugs clorimipramine, zimeldine, or desipramine to neonatal rats produced abnormalities at maturity including depressive symptoms and sexual dysfunction. To test whether the causative factor was REM per se, Vogel and Hagler administered iprindole to neonates. Iprindole is an antidepressant drug that does not produce REM sleep deprivation or RSD. When the iprindole-treated rats matured they evidenced no sexual dysfunction or depressive symptoms.

While it is increasingly clear that REM is important for brain development, REM's role in brain development needs to be appreciated within the organism's overall developmental schedules that are aimed at optimizing long-term reproductive fitness calculations. There are several evolutionary forces operating upon human developmental schedules that will need to be considered in order to understand the role of sleep within these developmental schedules. The relevant evolutionarily informed theories are parent-offspring conflict, life history, and attachment theory.

3.2.3 Parent-Offspring Conflict

Postnatal sleep states in the infant develop in the context of mother–infant interactions. Development of mother–infant interactions, in turn, occur within the broader context of conflict between mother and child over amount and quality of resources to be invested in the infant. This conflict over provisioning of, or investment in the infant is driven by the contrasting genetic interests of the mother versus those of the infant. The infant wants more resources than the mother can, or is willing to give, and thus the struggle ensues.

Trivers (1974) pointed out that parents are related to their offspring by a coefficient of relatedness of 0.5. That is, the child carries only half of the maternal genomic complement. Consequently, the genetic interests of mother and child are not identical and offspring will tend to want more from their parents than their parents are willing or able to give. Offspring in mammals, furthermore, may not share the same father and thus their genetic interests will diverge significantly from those of their siblings. Even if they do share the same father, they are related to siblings only by 0.5 and thus their interests are not identical to those of their siblings. Offspring should therefore attempt to monopolize extraction of resources from the mother regardless of consequences to the mother or to siblings. The infant's strategies to obtain more resources from the caregiver include vocalizations, grasping, smiling, crying, wailing, and suckling to name a few. Sleep represents a period of relief for the mother unless the infant suckles while asleep. Thus, night waking, in particular, become a battleground between the mother/caregiver and the infant. We will see shortly that infantile night wakings are related to the type of attachment bond created between mother and child.

3.2.4 Life History Theory

According to life history theory (Stearns, 1992), life cycle traits such as gestation length, size, and number of offspring, age at first reproduction, lactation/weaning period, ongoing reproductive strategy, and length of life are all influenced by local ecologic and social context and contribute to reproductive fitness. Individuals develop mechanisms or biobehavioral strategies that help them solve problems of infant survival, childhood growth, adult development, and reproduction across the life-span. Perceptual-emotional information about current environmental conditions (e.g., local mortality rates) is used to make (unconscious) decisions about optimal allocation of limited resources.

Trade-offs have to be made between time and energy devoted to "somatic effort" (i.e., investing in growth and development of the body) versus time and energy devoted to "reproductive effort" (i.e., funneling effort toward producing and raising offspring). Since sleep functions in part to regulate energy budgets, sleep quotas (time devoted to sleep) will vary, to some extent, depending on somatic or reproductive aims. Repro-ductive effort has two further components: mating effort (locating, courting, and retaining a suitable mate) and parenting effort (i.e., gestat-ing, giving birth, and engaging in postnatal care). Given the impact of developmental sleep processes on brain development, it is possible that sleep processes may figure in unconscious decisions concerning somatic development as well as development of behavioral strategies to support reproductive effort (parent-offspring relations and mating strategies).

Those unconscious decisions concerning developmental schedules very likely rest on an intuitive grasp of one's own genetic inheritance as well as one's current experience of the social environment. Some investigators (e.g., Belsky, Chisholm, 1999) have suggested that for the neonate and the juvenile, making a bet on future social-ecologic conditions must be based on their inherited genetic profile and on their current experience of their caregivers. If the caregivers invest only minimal resources in the child then the child concludes that local social and ecologic conditions are adverse and he sets developmental schedules accordingly: "Grow up fast, sleep little and sire many kids as you will be dead soon." If on the other hand caregivers invest quality time and resources into the child then the child gets the message that the social and ecologic context is favorable; the child will opt for a slower developmental schedule, longer or more intense sleep cycles, and a longer lifespan. "Grow up slowly, sleep intensely, invest heavily into one or two kids and live longer." In short the child's experi-ence of the parents is crucial in setting developmental sleep-wake sched-ules and that child's experience of the parents can be operationalized under the concept of "attachment."

3.2.5 Attachment Theory

Bowlby (1969) and Ainsworth (Ainsworth et al., 1978) developed attach-ment theory. The basic idea behind attachment theory is that between birth and eighteen months infants develop a particular bond of emotional trust with the caregiver. Bowlby regarded the attachment system as a biobehavioral regulatory process that adjusted physical and emotional closeness between caregiver and child. The attachment system expects the optimal bonding style called "secure attachment" wherein the infant is consistently cared for by the caregiver and therefore develops closeness and comfort with leaving the caretaker's immediate physical presence to explore.

Through her "strange situation procedure" (SSP), Ainsworth was able to identify insecure attachment orientations. A child with inconsistent parenting develops an insecure-anxious orientation that is evidenced by inability to tolerate separation from caregivers without emotional crisis. These kids are difficult to console after separation and prefer to continually seek proximity to the caregiver. A child with insecure-avoidant orientation on the other hand prefers to avoid interactions with the caregiver and appears emotionally inhibited.

Similar attachment orientations occur in adults and such attachment orientations are conceived as cognitive working models capturing perspectival relations between the self and the attachment object (see Table 3.1).

Table 3.1 Attachment orientations as a function of internal working models of self vs. other

		Self is perceived as	
		Positive	Negative
Attachment target is perceived as	Positive	**Secure** Individual is comfortable with both self and attachment target; wants to be in relationship and is comfortable in relationship.	**Preoccupied** Individual has negative view of self and an overly positive view of attachment target. Individual is anxious to be in relationship.
	Negative	**Dismissive** Individual has an overly positive view of self and an overly negative view of the attachment target. Individual claims low need for intimacy.	**Fearful** Individual has negative view of both self and attachment target. Individual is anxiously avoidant of relationships.

That is, each of us cognitively represent attachment relations as representation of relations between self and other. Adults with secure orientations tend to have positive views of themselves and their attachment targets and are comfortable with intimacy and independence. Individuals with insecure-ambivalent or preoccupied orientations overly value their attachment targets while devaluing themselves and are uncomfortable with independence. Individuals with insecure-avoidant orientations have negative views of themselves and their attachment targets but are comfortable with independence. Individuals with dismissive orientations have inflated views of themselves and negative views of their attachment objects. There is increasing evidence that these internal working models of self and other are formed during REM dreaming. I will return to this issue in a later chapter on dreams and attachment themes. For now we are focused on the interrelationships between developmental schedules, social attachment processes, and sleep.

The attachment relationship is crucial for development of sleep-wake schedules. If the neonate/child can form a secure emotional attachment to the mother, the child will "conclude" that the local environment will support adequate resources and a long-term reproductive strategy of delayed maturity and high investment in a few high-quality offspring. In that case infantile sleep intensity should be high, while night waking, nightmares, and other sleep disturbances should occur infrequently. We will see shortly that recent studies support these predictions.

3.2.6 Fetal Sleep

All mammals studied to date exhibit a period of spontaneous and mixed brain activity in utero known as indeterminate sleep that slowly differentiates into distinct sleep states by the middle of the pregnancy. Beginning at approximately twenty-eight to thirty-two weeks gestational age (ga) two forms of sleep, quiet sleep (QS) and active sleep (AS), develop out of this "indeterminate sleep." At about twenty-eight weeks ga discrete periods characterized by REMs and respiratory movements begin alternating with periods of sustained motor quiescence with no or very low numbers of eye movements. A REM-like active sleep state appears between thirty and thirty-two weeks ga and increases in amount until it comprises approximately 90 percent of fetal sleep. REM remains at about 90 percent of sleep until about one to two weeks of postnatal life and then it begins a relatively rapid decline toward adult values. No one knows why the developing fetus spends most of its time in REM, though this fact is consistent with the idea that REM functions to support brain development.

3.2.7 Neonatal Sleep

Newborns sleep about sixteen hours a day. In contrast to the adult pattern of entering sleep via an NREM episode, normal, full-term newborns enter sleep through a REM-like state rather than an NREM-like state. Infant sleep is equally divided between AS and QS, which alternate in a fifty-minute cycle. That is, there are typically six to eight regularly occurring sleep periods in a twenty-four-hour day for a typical newborn. Significant variability exists, however, so that some newborns, for the first few days after birth, sleep for eighteen to twenty hours while others sleep for only ten to twelve hours in a twenty-four-hour period (Burnham et al., 2002). Within the first month following birth, sleep-wake state organization begins to adapt to the light-dark cycle and to social cues.

The infantile precursor sleep states (AS and QS) begin to approximate adult forms of REM and NREM by about three to six months. With increasing maturity, the proportionate amount of time in REM sleep diminishes. The two- to three-year-old child spends approximately 35 percent of sleep time in REM sleep, while the adult spends about 20 percent in REM sleep. After three months of age, REM periods continue to recur with a periodicity of fifty to sixty minutes. However, the amount of REM sleep in each cycle begins to shift. REM sleep predominates in the later sleep cycles of the night and NREM sleep predominates during the earlier cycles, especially NREM stage N3 sleep. By three years of age, the temporal organization of sleep during the night resembles that of adult sleep except for the sleep cycle periodicity, which does not lengthen to the ninety-minute periodicity of adults until adolescence.

Studies of the effects of maternal separation on developing rats (Hofer and Shair, 1982) and monkeys (Reite and Short, 1978; Reite et al., 1976) provide a dramatic illustration of how AS/REM values are linked with infant-mother contact. These studies have conclusively shown that measures of AS/REM sleep (but not NREM or SWS) are selectively influenced after maternal separation. There is an initial increase in AS/REM times and then a dramatic reduction after separation.

In contrast to REM where the maturation of electrographic features are quite prolonged (e.g., PGO waves are not present in the kitten until three weeks postnatally) the maturation of NREM brain activity (slow waves in the delta bands 0.5–4.0 Hz and sleep spindles at 7–14 Hz) is completed in a relatively short time. EEG slow waves are generally reported to develop as isolated slow waves in a burst suppression EEG

Table 3.2 Sleep changes from neonatal to adult period

	Infant	Adult
%REM/NREM	50/50	20/80
REM/NREM cycle	50–60 minutes	90–100 minutes
Sleep onset state	REM	NREM
Temporal organization of sleep states	REM/NREM cycles equally throughout sleep period.	NREM predominates in first third of night; REM predominates in last third of night.
Sleep architecture	1 NREM stage	3 NREM stages

---

pattern, called "trace alternant" in the human infant. This pattern in turn is replaced later with a more continuous slow wave pattern during the course of development. Sleep spindles appear later as well.

3.2.8 Attachment and Infant Sleep

Burnham et al. (2002) reported significant variability in number of night waking/arousals in the infant. At one month, infants woke an average of 4.12 (SD = 2.57) times, with a range from one to eleven times. At twelve months, infants were waking an average of 2.62 times (SD = 2.03), with a range of zero to ten times. Evolutionary theory predicts that night waking should vary with attachment status. When nighttime awakenings are followed by an infant signaling episode such as crying they are more likely to elicit a maternal intervention than when no signaling occurs after an awakening. Several forms of nighttime signaling can influence attachment processes including crying, sucking, nursing, smiling, grasping, twitches, cooing, babbling, and other vocalizations. All of these behaviors are more likely to either occur in, or to emerge from, REM rather than NREM sleep (see McNamara, 2004 for review).

Consistent with evolutionary theory, night wakings are known to be sensitive to attachment status. In a study of twenty infants judged insecurely attached to mother, Benoit et al. (1992) reported that 100 percent of these children evidenced severe sleep disorders. When Sagi et al. (1994) studied the effects of sleeping arrangements in Israeli kibbutzim (communal vs. home) on attachment security, they found that 52 percent of communal-sleeping infants (i.e., those who slept away from their parents' home) and only 20 percent of home-sleeping infants were later classified as insecurely attached. Scher (2001) reported that securely attached infants awaken once per night, and stay awake for about eleven minutes. Forty-three percent of "dependent secure" (i.e., B4: secure infants who nevertheless exhibit some ambivalence as well) and 23 percent of the mothers of secure infants reported that their infants had settling difficulties. Infants with frequent night awakenings scored higher on contact-maintenance in the Strange Situation than non-night-waking infants. Beijers and colleagues (2011) found that infants that were classified as insecure resistant, or insecure-anxious, evidenced the most frequent number of night waking at six months of age whereas insecure-avoidant infants evidenced the least. McNamara and colleagues (2003) reported a similar pattern with insecure anxious/resistant infants evidencing more and longer night wakings than insecure avoidant infants at fifteen months. Morrell and Steele (2003) also found that insecure-anxious or insecure resistant attachment in twelve-month-olds was associated with frequent night waking and predictive of persistent sleep problems in a one-year follow-up. Taken together, these studies suggest that insecure-anxious attachment in infants is associated with disproportionately high number of night waking, between six and eighteen months while infants with insecure-avoidant and secure orientations tend to evidence night waking much less frequently in that time period. Why is that? If night waking functions to extract greater resources from the mother then infants with secure orientations will not need to utilize that behavior as they perceive themselves to be adequately provisioned. Insecure avoidant infants do not signal as often as insecure-anxious/resistant as they have adopted the avoidant strategy. We will see shortly that these infantile night waking patterns make sense within an evolutionary context.

3.2.9 Infant Sleep and Genetic Conflict

Every new parent knows that it is exhausting to be a new parent. Your baby keeps you awake all night with frequent night waking and loud "vocalizations" or crying episodes. There is a huge industry composed of supposed experts on infant sleep that advise new parents on how to get their baby to sleep through the night so that parental sleep patterns can return to normal. Why would Mother Nature produce such a seemingly maladaptive pattern of sleep in the neonate? It does no one any good if neither the baby nor the parents get any sleep and are chronically sleep deprived. Haig (2014) and Blurton Jones and da Costa (1987) argued that infant night wakings function to prolong interbirth intervals via nursing-induced suppression of ovulation. That is, if the mother nurses the infant she cannot get pregnant (nursing induces suppression of ovulation). If the mother does not have another baby while the current baby is struggling to survive the first couple of years of life then that baby will get more resources from the mother and thus its chances for survival will increase. We have seen that it is the infants with insecure-anxious/resistant orientations that experience the greatest number of night waking. Presumably these infants night waking's result in nursing episodes that suppress ovulation in the mother and so the infant can monopolize maternal resources for a while. If night waking declines over time at a slower rate for insecure resistant vs. avoidant infants then the point at which maximal benefits of contraceptive suckling are obtained may differ for infants dependent upon attachment orientation.

Optimal interbirth intervals or IBIs may differ for mother-infant dyads depending on both attachment status and social-ecologic context. In environments with high mortality rates parents pursue an opportunistic reproductive strategy aimed at greater numbers of offspring appearing at shorter IBIs and receiving lower levels of investment (e.g., reduced nursing), resulting in fewer night wakings and greater numbers of avoidant attachment orientations.

3.3 Sleep, Genetic Conflicts, and the Human Lifespan

Belsky, Steinberg, and Draper (1991), Stearns (1992), and Chisholm (1999) noted that local mortality rates may act as a proximal environmental cue that directs people toward different developmental/reproductive schedules and strategies. When mortality rates are high in an area, the optimal reproductive strategy should be to start early and maximize current fertility rates. When local mortality rates are low, the best strategy involves deferred long-term reproduction in which fewer offspring are given better and more long-term care. Genetic conflict as described may not only occur during the fetal and early infancy periods. The human lifespan itself may be influenced by the ways in which developmental schedules, including sleep-wake schedules, are set early in life.

Telomeres are repeating sequences of DNA found at the ends of chromosomes that protect DNA strands on the chromosomes, thus reducing chances for harmful mutations. One of the most frequent ways to get a harmful mutation is by losing pieces of information from each end of the chromosomal strand. Each time the DNA makes a copy of itself, its telomeres get shorter, thus increasing chances that information will be lost through the ends of the strand. The telomeric caps at the ends of the strands prevent this loss of information and therefore prevent accumulation of mutations over time. The longer the telomeric cap, the longer the individual will be protected against mutational accumulation and therefore, theoretically, the longer he or she will live. In sum, short telomeres increase chances for mutation accumulation over time because they eventually will wear away to nothing while longer telomeres protect against this effect (Aviv and Susser, 2013).

But there is a major exception to this telomere shortening effect: sperm. In fact, the telomeres in sperm-producing stem cells not only resist wearing away, they actually grow. This growth may be due to the fact that sperm are bathed in the telomere-repairing enzyme telomerase. Thus, the older the man, the longer the telomeres in his sperm will be. This telomere lengthening effect in sperm of older men can be passed on along the paternal line from father to son and grandson (Eisenberg et al., 2012). Therefore, the age at which a man conceives his offspring increases that offspring's chances to live a long life and increase his (and the whole lineage's) reproductive fitness.

But wait a minute! You might be asking yourself, "What about all those studies that show deleterious effects of older paternal age on offspring?" Older dads tend to have kids with greater health risks of all kinds right?

Yes and no. Some studies show negative effects of paternal age on offspring while other studies show positive effects (Janecka et al., 2017). Advancing age of the mother certainly is associated with negative effects on offspring but less so for the dad – though there is no doubt that some negative effects are there and well documented. Aging is associated with de novo mutations and thus you get the association between parental age and offspring defects. Nonetheless, this negative effect of aged parents on offspring is diluted or muted for older dads with longer telomere lengths, though the issue is exceedingly complex as the effects of paternal age on offspring are likely mediated by many factors from age of the mother, birth order effects in the family, and economic status of the dad. Most importantly, however, is that effects of paternal age on offspring should differ as a function of gender of offspring. Effects (both negative and positive) of paternal age on offspring are likely to be gender specific simply because (as noted) telomere length is inherited down the paternal line.

But what does all this have to do with sleep? It has been demonstrated that both too much sleep and too little sleep is associated with short telomere length (Jackowska et al., 2012). You need optimal sleep amounts in order to have longer telomere length. Interestingly, the same holds true for semen quality: You need optimal sleep amounts for optimal semen quality (Chen et al., 2016). Too much or too little sleep will result in reduction in semen counts and quality in a dose response manner. It is possible that the effects of restricted sleep durations on semen quality is related to sleep effects on telomere length. *In any case, nonoptimal sleep duration carries a higher fitness cost for males than for females given that semen quality and telomere length declines after nonoptimal sleep.*

So, we know the following: (1) telomere length may increase longevity and fitness via protection against harmful mutations; (2) sperm is protected against short telomeres and is associated with growth in telomere lengths; (3) telomere length can be inherited down the paternal line from an older dad; and (4) you need optimal sleep durations in order to have longer telomere lengths and better sperm quality.

Eisenberg and Kuzawa's (Eisenberg, 2011; Eisenberg and Kuzawa 2013) work on the evolutionary theory of paternal age effects notes that in order to optimize reproductive fitness, parents need their kids to be prepared for whatever environment they find themselves in. That was the spirit of Haig's theory concerning optimal interbirth intervals and how differing IBIs affect night wakings in infants. In environments with high mortality rates parents should pursue an opportunistic reproductive strategy aimed at greater numbers of offspring appearing at shorter IBIs and receiving lower levels of investment (e.g., reduced nursing) resulting in fewer night wakings and greater numbers of avoidant attachment orientations. In short, if a child is born into a chaotic environment with high mortality rates its best genetic strategy may be to grow up fast and reproduce fast. The fast schedule, however, results in shorter lifespans. You live fast and die young. If, on the other hand, the environment is more stable, then the optimal reproductive strategy is to grow more slowly and reproduce later in life. In this scenario offspring will tend to live longer. But for this slower strategy to work parents and kids need to know about environments *in the future* – when their kids will be born and grow into their maturity. The parents (and kids) need to use currently available information to make bets on how the future will turn out. But how can potential parents (or growing kids) peer into the future? What information can parents and kids use *now* to plan for the future?

Eisenberg et al. (2012) suggested that *paternal age at reproduction* is a very reliable signal of environmental stability. If you have men who are living into older age brackets and reproducing at those ages, then that is very good evidence that things are stable enough to support slower growth and reproductive schedules. But how will an individual kid/

parent know that older dads are occurring reliably? They will know because they inherit the long telomere from an older dad. *Interestingly, only certain kids will be able to use the information about older dads.* Only the boys (and to some extent the girls) born to older dads have the information in their genome (in the form of long telomeres) that tell them what the environment is likely to be like when their children will be born. They therefore have extremely valuable fitness-related information no one else in the group will have. As Eisenberg and Kuzawa (2013) put it (page 2): "Thus, the lineages of men with the ability to extend sperm telomere lengths with age and to transmit these modified telomeres to offspring might have increased Darwinian fitness because their offspring were better able to calibrate their reproductive and maintenance expenditures across the likely duration of their lifespans within the variable environments that human populations have confronted."

The offspring of older dads will have in their genomes the information concerning long term stability of the environments that will allow those kids to plan optimally for the future, and thus increase their fitness. While receiving the "long telomeric inheritance" signals optimism for these kids, we have seen that restricted sleep amounts will partially negate these beneficial effects – especially for males. As mentioned, nonoptimal sleep duration carries a higher fitness cost for males than for females given that semen quality and telomere length declines after nonoptimal sleep. Given this differential cost of restricted sleep for males should become a battleground between the sexes (mothers versus sons), particularly during early development.

3.3.1 Sleep in Childhood

From toddler hood up through early teens children begin to sleep about ten hours a night. Of course, that is only an average and there is great variability around this average. Children quickly go into N3 stage slow wave sleep for about an hour, then briefly arouse, are cognitively confused ("confusional arouals") turn over in bed, perhaps emit vocalizations, and then return back into N3, skipping altogether the first REM period. When they do go into their first REM period it lasts about twenty minutes and then they normally cycle between REM and NREM for the rest of the night. The amount and intensity of SWS peaks around age four in humans. This is interesting as age four is the traditional weaning age in humans. It is certainly easier for a mother to wean a child if the child is asleep and not demanding attention. It is also around this age that night terrors may occur. Night terrors can occur between ages three and twelve but they peak at around age four. They involve confusional arousals out of N3 slow wave sleep. The child may sit on the side of the bed and scream bloody terror. Their eyes may be wide open but they may be unresponsive to others during the episode. It takes a lot to shake them awake.

We have seen that infant sleep is embedded within the social context of mother–infant genetic conflict and social attachment patterns. Attachment orientation in the child continues to influence childhood sleep patterns during the years of childhood. Specifically attachment security predicts sleep patterns into adolescence and vice versa suggesting that secure attachment promotes more stable sleep patterns. Troxel and colleagues (2013) reported that children rated high in negative emotionality in infancy (negative emotionality is often linked to insecure attachment in infancy), evidenced stronger associations between their attachment orientations and sleep patterns in toddlerhood. Keller (2011) reported that mother–child attachment security was predictive of decreased subjective sleepiness during the day for both boys and girls. Among boys, increased physical restlessness at night (indicating short arousals/awakenings) as measured by a wrist actigraph in third grade predicted a decrease of mother–child attachment security in fifth grade. Additionally, a boy's emotional distress about his parent's marital relationship in third grade predicted sleep problems in fifth grade.

3.3.2 Sleep in Teens

Adolescence is associated with a decline in percentage of total sleep time composed of SWS. Sleep scientists generally agree that teens need about ten hours of sleep per night but get only eight or less. Sleep-deprived teens make more impulsive decisions, are involved in more accidents, and generally are more moody than non-sleep-deprived teens. Sleep loss in teens appears to be related to school demands and social pressures. The widespread use of smartphones and other electronic devices with brightly lit screens is also having a negative impact on sleep times in teens. Adjusting school schedules so that teens get the sleep they need has demonstrated positive results but the trend has not caught on.

Adolescence of course is associated with the onset of puberty and this biological storm both influences and is influenced by sleep. The onset of puberty is triggered by hypothalamic-initiated release of the gonadotropin-releasing hormone (GnRH), luteinizing hormone (LH), and follicle-stimulating hormone (FSH). Under the influence of these hormones, secondary sexual characteristics emerge including voice changes, height gains, breast development, genital development, and cellular changes in sexually dimorphic brain regions such as the amygdala and the hypothalamus. The pulsatile release of these hormones may be influenced to some extent by melatonin and sleep cycles. Virtually all of the growth hormones released during these years occurs during sleep and many of the hormones controlling onset of puberty are also influenced by sleep processes.

REM deprivation early in life is associated with later impairment in sexual functions in the adult, at least in the rat and the monkey. REM is also associated with cyclic occurrence of penile erections in men and vaginal lubrication, clitoral engorgement, and pelvic thrusting in females. Total times (mean of 190 minutes) spent in tumescence peaks in teenaged boys. Nocturnal emissions begin to occur during adolescence, probably during the REM period.

3.3.3 Sleep in Adulthood: Women

Women's sleep is influenced by the menstrual cycle. While there are no reported differences in percent of time spent in specific sleep stages women report subjective changes in feelings of sleepiness. Progesterone release induces sleepiness in most women and this could account for the subjective sense of greater sleepiness. Pregnancy is associated with dramatic increases in the action of gonadal steroids, estrogen, and progesterone, and the pituitary hormones, prolactin, and growth hormone on the maternal brain and the developing fetus. Fetal sleep influences maternal sleep and vice versa. The steady rise of progesterone activity levels over the course of the pregnancy up to term is associated with an increase in NREM and a decrease in REM sleep (as well as an increase latency to REM) in the mother. The placenta stimulates an increase in estrogen and cortisol activity, particularly at term, which tend to inhibit REM. Prolactin enhances slow wave sleep with levels peaking four to six hours during delivery. Prolactin also promotes lactogenesis. Oxytocin interacts with melatonin activity during labor to promote uterine contractions. Levels of the placental growth hormone (GH) in the mother's blood increases throughout pregnancy and peak around week thirty-five of gestation. GH in turn is known to stimulate slow wave sleep.

From the point of view of sleep state biology, pregnancy is, of course, a unique physiologic process wherein the sleep states of two genetically distinct individuals may interact. Haig (1993) has called attention to the fact that the placenta is genetically part of the fetus and not of the mother, and thus there is potential for a divergence of genetic interests between the fetus and the mother. Abnormal triploid fetuses with a double set of the father's genes and a single set of the mother's have a very large placenta, while abnormal fetuses with a double set of the mother's genes and one of the father's have very small placentas and show a retardation of growth. Modeling of genetic strategies of parents and their offspring suggests that with respect to the maternal-fetal interaction, the fetus is selected to extract as much resources from the mother as possible, while the mother is selected to moderate attempts to extract her resources. Her genetic interests lie not just in the present child but in whatever future children she may bear. She needs to be discriminative when it comes to investment of valuable resources in the current child. Future offspring of the mother, therefore, are in direct competition with the current fetus for resources, and the fetus thus attempts to extract as much as it can from its mother. The interplay between maternal and fetal sleep processes and growth of the fetus over the course of the pregnancy may be influenced by this genetic background (Table 3.3).

During the first ten weeks of pregnancy, human chorionic gonadotropin (hCG) levels secreted from the trophoblast of the embedded zygote maintains the corpus luteum and its secretions of estrogen and

Table 3.3 Sleep in pregnancy

	First Trimester	Second Trimester	Third Trimester	Labor/ Delivery	Comments
Sleep measures relative to prepregnancy baselines	Increased total sleep time but decreased percentage of SWS.	Decreased total sleep time; vivid dreams of baby animals, etc.; decreased SWS.	Increased total sleep time but decreased sleep efficiency and decreased SWS and REM; vivid dreams and occasional anxiety dreams and nightmares.	Decreased REM; increased delta waves with labor onset.	

progesterone. These sex steroids together with prolactin (secreted from the pituitary) foster the profound physiologic changes and growth in both the mother and the fetus throughout the pregnancy. Increased levels of progesterone, furthermore, dampen or prevent uterine contractions. HCG falls in the second trimester as the placenta itself increases its production of placental lactogen (PL), progesterone (P), and estrogen (E). PL is very similar in structure and function to GH. GH is a hormone whose release in males and to a lesser extent in females is intimately dependent on sleep: 95 percent of daily production of GH occurs in SWS during development. The relation between GH release and SWS is not merely temporal. The SWS state itself stimulates release of the hormone. SWS in females likely plays a similar role but stimulates release of other growth factors in addition to GH.

3.3.4 Sleep in the Elderly

The most consistently reported change in the sleep architecture of healthy elderly persons is a decline in percentage of sleep composed of delta wave indexed-slow wave sleep (SWS; Bliwise, 2000). In some cases SWS may occupy only 5 to 10 percent of total sleep. While there is great variability, REM percentage tends not to decline with age. Women experience the loss of NREM sleep indices about ten years after men. Elderly women evidence twice as many N2 sleep spindles relative to aged-matched men. Despite these objective differences in the sleep patterns of elderly men and women, women report poorer sleep quality than do men, particularly coincident with menopause.

3.3.5 Conclusions

Figure 3.1 sums up some of the main lifespan trends in sleep discovered to date. The time it takes to fall asleep (latency) declines until midlife and then remains about the same into old age. Time spent awake after initial sleep onset (WASO) declines across the lifespan but its proportion of total sleep period increases. That is, people tend to have a greater number of awakenings as they age. REM percentages decline with age but the proportion of total sleep spent in REM remains about the same. The same is the case with N2 stage light sleep and N1 transitional sleep; these proportions remain about the same or slightly increase as people age. Finally, N3 slow wave sleep undergoes a steady decline with age until it almost completely disappears in old age. Throughout the lifespan sleep evidences intimate and possibly bidirectional causal associations with socio-emotional attachment

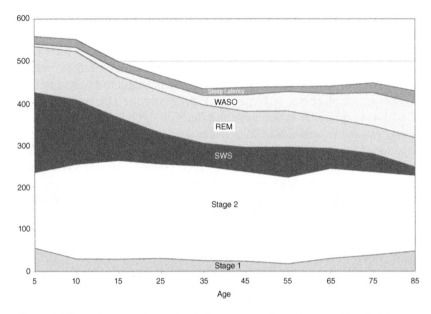

Figure 3.1 Age-related trends for stage 1 sleep, stage 2 sleep, slow wave sleep (SWS), rapid eye movement (REM) sleep, wake after sleep onset (WASO) and sleep latency (in minutes). (from Ohayon et al., *Sleep, Vol. 27, No. 7, 2004*)

processes between child and parent during the developmental phase and then between sexual/romantic and close friends during the adult phase. These relationships between sleep processes and attachment processes once more underline the social nature of sleep.

We have now completed our survey of the ways in which sleep is expressed across the lifespan and the ways in which evolutionary forces shape that expression. We turn next to a detailed examination of the biobehavioral and neurological characteristics of each of the major sleep states: NREM and REM.

Review Questions

- What is the significance of the differences in sleep patterns in children with insecure attachment orientations as opposed to children with secure attachment orientations?
- What is the significance of the differences in sleep patterns in adults with insecure attachment orientations as opposed to adults with secure attachment orientations?

- Why does the proportion of slow wave sleep/total sleep decline with age?
- What are the strengths and weaknesses of the evidence for social influences on sleep across the lifespan?

Further Reading

Beattie, L., Kyle, S. D., Espie, C. A., & Biello, S. M. (2015). Social interactions, emotion and sleep: A systematic review and research agenda. *Sleep Medicine Reviews*, 24, 83–100. doi: 10.1016/j.smrv.2014.12.005.

Carskadon, M., & Dement, W. C. (2000). Normal human sleep: An overview. In M. H. Kryger, T. Roth, & W. C. Dement (eds.), *Principles and Practice of Sleep Medicine* (3rd edn, pp. 15–25). Philadelphia: Saunders.

Keller, P. S. (2011). Sleep and attachment. In M. El-Sheikh (ed.), *Sleep and Development* (pp. 49–77). New York: Oxford University Press.

Troxel, W. M. (2010). It's more than sex: Exploring the dyadic nature of sleep and implications for health. *Psychosomatic Medicine*, 72(6), 578–86. doi: 10.1097/PSY.0b013e3181de7ff8. Epub 2010 May 13. Review. PMID: 20467000.

CHAPTER 4

Characteristics of REM and NREM Sleep

Learning objectives

- Describe the electrophysiologic characteristics of each of the non-REM sleep stages
- Describe the electrophysiologic and biobehavioral characteristics of REM sleep
- Identify the key brain activation and deactivation patterns associated with NREM sleep
- Identify the key brain activation and deactivation patterns associated with REM sleep

4.1 Introduction

Non-rapid eye movement sleep or NREM is composed of three EEG stages, N1, N2, and N3. N1 is a drowsy state transitional from wake to sleep. N2 is a light sleep stage with characteristic electrophysiologic signals called "sleep spindles" and "k complexes" measured by the EEG. N3 is a deep sleep state characterized by slow wave forms and abundant delta activity. Delta (δ) activity (0.5–4 Hz) becomes increasingly dominant during the progress from light to deep sleep. Delta waves have the largest amplitudes, normally between 20–200μV. Over the course of a single night of sleep there is a progressive decline in delta power (and an increase in REM). Sleep therefore promotes dissipation of whatever brain process delta power indexes. There is less and less of a need for delta power as sleep progresses. The magnitude of the delta power seen in sleep is partially dependent on the amount (and intensity) of wakefulness prior to the onset of sleep. One way that "intensity of wakefulness" has been measured by researchers is via the amount of frontal lobe-dependent executive control and social cognitive tasks engaged in during the waking period. Executive control cognitive tasks involve things like working memory, paying close attention, vigilance tasks, crunching numbers, and so forth. Social cognitive tasks involve things like attempting to read the minds of others or gauge their intentions and so forth. The link between delta power during sleep and engagement of frontal lobe processes during waking has suggested to some (e.g., Harrison et al., 2000; Anderson and Horne, 2003) that slow wave sleep functions in part to restore frontal lobe functions. While that supposition is likely true, sleep, including N3 SWS, also very likely has multiple functions – not just the restoration of frontal lobe functions.

4.2 Characteristics of NREM

4.2.1 Succumbing to Deep Sleep

Eventually we all MUST succumb to sleep – this odd, undignified, helpless period of behavioral inactivity that is composed of a bizarre mixture of oblivion and the hyperconsciousness that comes with dreaming. NREM encompasses that phase of sleep where we come closest to oblivion while still nonetheless remaining alive. If we follow a typical individual's path down to deep sleep, we find that we each enter into oblivion via a state of relaxed wakefulness or drowsiness. During this period, the EEG changes from the fast, desynchronized wave pattern of alert wakefulness to a slower, more regular wave pattern at a frequency of 8–12 Hz known as alpha activity. The alpha waves are replaced by low-amplitude, mixed frequency theta waves with a predominance of activity in the 4–8 Hz range, which characterize the N1 stage. N1 lasts only a few minutes. Next, the hapless individual headed toward oblivion alights at stage N2 non-REM sleep. During stage N2, the individual experiences a form of light sleep. He is easily aroused from this stage of NREM. His EEG shows occasional bursts of higher-frequency oscillations that are called sleep spindles and K-complexes, which are very high amplitude spikes. Sleep spindles are low amplitude 7–14 Hz synchronous waveforms that often precede the so-called K-complex waveform during stage N2 non-rapid eye movement (NREM) light sleep. K-complexes occur randomly throughout stage N2 sleep, but may also occur in response to auditory stimuli. Spindles, on the other hand, occur in all stages of sleep but "prefer" stage N2 NREM. They propagate in thalamocortical networks and exert strong depolarizing effects on projection targets in the neocortex.

Another EEG pattern that occurs in NREM is the so-called cyclic alternating pattern or CAP (Terzano et al., 1985). This periodic activation pattern appears to occur every twenty to forty seconds with input-associated alternations of activation dubbed A events (A) and then generalized background (B) periods against which A events occur. A phases can come in three forms: A1, A2, and A3. A1 exhibits purely slow wave constituents (e.g., K-complexes and slow wave groups) with little autonomic and muscle changes but with signs of high homeostatic pressure. A3 exhibits the traditional arousal pattern with desynchronized fast activity, increased autonomic signs, and increases in muscle tone. A2 is a mixture of A1 and A3 features. Topographic brain mapping studies of the CAP reveals that spectral components with anterior frontal prevalence are typically present in A1 type (0.25–2.5 Hz) events, while those in the A3 type (7–12 Hz) events have a different prevalence over the parieto-occipital areas.

Building on the distinctions between slow oscillations and delta activity and the fact that 1–4 Hz waves reflect thalamic clock-like delta activity and cortical delta activity, while the < 1 Hz component of slow wave activity during NREM is solely of cortical origin and reflects different physiological processes, Halasz et al. (2014) suggested that there were two types of slow wave activity, an instant reactive form and a more long-term non-reactive form – though both forms likely act to protect sleep and frontal lobe activity as well as cognitive functions. The quick-acting slow wave homeostatic form includes electrophysiologic events like K-complexes and spindles that compensate for any potentially sleep disturbing events by providing instant "delta injections" to maintain the nightly delta level, thus protecting sleep and cognitive functions mediated by the frontal lobes.

N2 spindles and K-complexes, however, index more than just protection of sleep via suppression of incoming sensory information. Spindles arise from recurrent inhibition of cortical-projecting thalamic neurons by reticular thalamic neurons. Spike bursts in thalamocortical neurons entrain cortical populations in spindle oscillations. The depolarizing effects of phasic synchronous bursts of spindling activity facilitate an influx of calcium ions (Ca^{2+}) into pyramidal neurons, a well recognized and highly potent trigger for plastic events that potentiate synaptic sensitivity (Sejnowski and Destexhe, 2000). The fast influx of Ca^{2+} triggers an upregulation of calcium-calmodulin-dependent protein kinase II, leading to phosphorylation of new post-synaptic plasticity-related protein receptors. Consequently, glutamatergic transmission is enhanced, leading to increased excitability within that circuit, and thus long term potentiation (Walker, 2005; Walker & Stickgold, 2006). Long-term potentiation or LTP is an electrophysiologic neuronal marker for memory and learning. Thus, it appears that spindles may also index sleep-related memory and learning capacities.

Consistent with the plasticity-related effects of spindling activity on neocortical neuronal networks are reports of strong associations between spindling activity and memory, and learning performance in both humans and nonhuman animals. Building on both the physiologic and behavioral findings, Fogel et al. (2007) have argued that spindling activity indexes an individual's overall memory or general learning capacity. A reduction in sleep spindling activity is, in fact, associated with a variety of neurodegenerative disorders including Alzheimer's disease, Creutzfeldt–Jacob disease, progressive supranuclear palsy, and dementia with Lewy bodies (Clawson et al., 2016).

Topographic EEG (electroencephalogram) analysis of N2 electrophysiologic events in humans reveals two different spindle types, a slower type that typically manifests over central-frontal regions and a faster type that typically manifests over parietal regions (Table 4.1). The two types of spindles are differentially affected by aging, sleep deprivation, and pharmacologic agents, with the frontal type more strongly affected by sleep deprivation, aging, and dopaminergic agents than the parietal type, and more strongly related to declarative and verbal learning materials than the parietal type. Given the sleep protective and plasticity-related effects associated with N2 sleep spindles it is certain that sleep spindles will receive intensive investigation by sleep scientists in the near future.

After spending several minutes in N2 light sleep, the wayfarer then descends into the promised oblivion of deep sleep wherein *"the death of each day's life ... knits up the ravell'd sleave of care'"* (Shakespeare, *Macbeth*, Scene 2, Act 2). Now the EEG shows the characteristic delta waves of slow wave sleep in the band of 0.5–4.5 Hz. It becomes almost

Table 4.1 Two spindle types

	Slow	Fast
Frequency	12 Hz	14 Hz
Topographic location	Frontal	Parietal
Neuropharmacology	Dopaminergic	Serotoninergic
Sleep deprivation	Very sensitive	Less sensitive
Aging	Very sensitive	Not affected
Cognitive correlates	Effortful processing, social cognition, motor and verbal learning, declarative memory	General mental ability, performance IQ

impossible to arouse the individual who is for all intents and purposes dead to the world.

If the individual does begin to arouse without first passing back up the three stages of sleep in reverse order (N3 to N2 to N1, etc.) you will see the strangest parasomnias emerge. For example, the individual may engage in complex motor and goal directed behaviors despite being completely unconscious. Somnambulism (sleep walking), somniloquy (sleep talking), night terrors, sleep paralysis, and "sleep sex" all might occur if the individual partially arouses toward awakening or REM without first passing through N3, N2, and N1. In sleep walking the individual may navigate through all kinds of barriers with apparently normal eyesight even though the brain still records slow wave activity. Some individuals go to the kitchen and eat huge amounts of food and then later fully awaken puzzled by the bloated feeling they then experience. In sleep talking, individuals can carry on long conversations with an invisible interlocutor. Night terrors typically occur in children who sit up on the side of the bed and scream bloody terror. Even though the child's eyes are open wide they appear unable to see you as their brain is still in slow wave sleep. In sleep sex the individual attempts to initiate sex with a bed partner even though both he and his partner are asleep.

4.2.2 Brain Mechanisms in NREM

NREM is initiated after adenosine levels in the basal forebrain activate GABA-ergic efferents that project to cortical sites that ultimately dampen activation levels in these cortical sites. In addition, thalamic efferents to cortical sites begin to fire rhythmically until they entrain cortical neurons, ultimately resulting in slow rolling waves across the cortex during N3 slow wave sleep (SWS). Most areas of the brain at this point begin to relax metabolic activity and blood flow decreases slightly relative to waking. During N3 slow wave activity (SWA) predominates over frontal areas (Finelli et al., 2001) and travel (propagate) backward to posterior areas of the brain. Beyond this variability, slow waves seem to systematically recruit various brain regions. The power density of delta waves (1–4 Hz) during NREM sleep is negatively correlated with cerebral blood flow in the network of the social brain – the ventromedial prefrontal cortex, the basal forebrain, the striatum, the anterior insula, and the precuneus (Dang-Vu et al., 2005). Subcortically, slow waves originate in the insula and cingulate gyrus, and propagate up through the precuneus, the posterior cingulate, ventrolateral, and medial frontal areas. Why these brain regions? Interestingly, all of these regions are

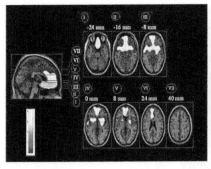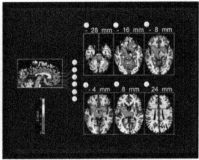

Figure 4.1 Functional neuroanatomy of normal human non-REM sleep, assessed by H2 150 PET (left panel). Brain areas in which regional cerebral blood flow (rCBF) *decreases* as a function of delta power during non-REM sleep (stages 2–3). Image sections are displayed on different levels of the z axis as indicated on the top of each picture. The color scale indicates the range of Z values for the activated voxels. Displayed voxels are significant at P < 0.05 after correction for multiple comparisons (right panel). Brain areas in which rCBF *decreases* during non-REM sleep as compared to wakefulness and REM sleep. Note the similarity of the regional blood flow distribution between left and right panels.
(Reprinted with permission from Dang-Vu, T. T., Desseilles, M., Petit, D., Mazza S., Montplaisir, J., Maquet, P. (2007). "Neuroimaging in Sleep Medicine." Sleep Medicine, 8, 349–372; page 350.)

associated with the network of structures that have been designated the "social brain network." Note that not all the brain regions implicated in NREM sleep overlap with or are included in the social brain network. But the interesting fact is that most are included. This network, then, is preferentially and slowly taken off-line (*decreases* in activation) during NREM sleep phases (Figure 4.1). We will see when we discuss REM that this same network is then reconnected and taken back online during REM phases.

4.2.3 Slow Wave Sleep and Growth Hormone

Slow wave sleep of NREM is associated with a major surge in Growth Hormone (GH) release (Steiger, 2003) – at least during the first N3 period in adults. It may persist beyond the first N3 period in children. When Growth Hormone Releasing Hormone or GHRH levels rise in blood they stimulate onset of NREM sleep, while conversely somatostatin (SS) inhibits NREM while enhancing REM. SS also interacts with GH. Physiologic and growth-promoting effects of GH in the rat and in the human depend on pulsatile release of GH. But pulsatile release of

GH, in turn, depends on somatostatin activity. SS is released in a sinus-oidal pattern. When GHRH is released during a trough period of SS release, it induces pulsatile release of GH, while a rise in SS release reduces GH release to baseline levels, thus allowing a new cycle of GH-SS interactions to begin. Fluctuating levels of SS release are therefore required to sustain pulsatile release of GH which in turn influences NREM onset.

4.2.4 Slow Wave Activity and Memory

A number of important studies in the 1990s and early 2000s (reviewed in Walker and Stickgold, 2004) demonstrated that SWS was crucially important for acquisition and consolidation of certain types of new memories into long term memory stores. For example, Plihal and Born (1997) demonstrated that learning of paired associates (word pairs like cat-dog that are semantically related to each other) and visual-imaginal, mental rotation tasks are dependent on obtaining a bout of NREM (early sleep) rather than REM (late morning sleep) after learning the task.

In addition to the role that whole bouts of NREM play in facilitation of memory processing, specific electrophysiologic events within NREM are also associated with memory and learning. For example, Huber, Ghilardi, Massimini, and Tononi (2004) showed that localized increases in slow wave activity (SWA) within NREM is associated with improved performance on tasks mediated by the frontal lobes. These sorts of findings imply that sleep homeostasis has a local component, which can be triggered by a learning task involving frontal brain regions. Interestingly, the local increase in SWA over frontal regions after learning correlates with improved performance of the task *after* N3 sleep. Benington and Frank (2003) point out that activation of T-type calcium (Ca^{2+}) channels in non-REM sleep may promote either long-term neuronal depression or long-term potentiation, both processes that have been linked to hippocampal memory functions. Sleep-associated consolidation of information gathered during the wake state appears to depend on hippocampal-cortical interactions that occur during both NREM slow wave sleep (SWS) and REM and involve some sort of replay during REM sleep of learned associations acquired while awake. Wilson and McNaughton (1994), for example, showed that hippocampal cells that are active when rats learn a new maze are also active during subsequent sleep.

4.2.5 Special Role of N3 Slow Wave (SWS) Sleep in Children

Given the cumulating evidence that N3 appears to facilitate learning and memory functions, one might expect that SWS plays a critical role in boosting brain plasticity or learning during childhood development. The percentage of total sleep that N3 SWS composes is very high in developmental years of children and it gradually declines as a percentage of total sleep over the adult years until it disappears almost entirely in old age. This developmental profile of N3 is prima facie evidence that it is important for development and especially important for brain development given that a disproportionate amount of metabolic effort is funneled into brain development in humans. Anderson and Horne (2003) have demonstrated that N3 sleep deprivation differentially impairs frontal lobe functions. It is difficult to selectively deprive people of N3 SWS sleep as when we do so we inevitably also disrupt REM sleep that occurs downstream from N3 in the nightly sleep cycle. You can partially selectively deprive people of N3 by sounding a tone loud enough to disrupt N3 but not so loud that subsequent REM is disrupted. Recovery sleep from this sort of selective N3 deprivation involved making up N3 sleep first and then some REM. There is proportionally greater amounts of recovered N3 in the first few minutes and hours of N3 recovery than in the later minutes and hours of N3 recovery sleep. The fact that you can selectively deprive people of some portion of their SWS without dramatically altering REM increases our confidence in Anderson and Horne's results concerning the effects of N3 deprivation on frontal lobe functions. Frontal lobe functions include things like working memory, attention, language fluency, planning, executive control, self-regulation, and personal reflection and insight. Obtaining enough SWS during childhood may be critical for normal acquisition of these frontal lobe related skills.

4.2.6 Bodily Changes during NREM

To fully understand NREM phenomena we need to briefly touch on its ancillary effects on the body. During NREM the parasympathetic sub-branch of the autonomic nervous system is more active than the sympathetic nervous system. Heart rate, blood pressure, temperature, and metabolic rate all decrease slightly from daytime baseline levels during NREM. Infectious challenges such as getting the flu or some other infection can cause an increase in N3 sleep duration as well as delta wave activity. Sleep deprivation, on the other hand, increases vulnerability to infection. These latter facts will be discussed more fully but they point to a crucial function for NREM – immune system maintenance.

4.2.7 Fatal Familial Insomnia (FFI)

Knowledge concerning NREM-related sleep disorders will help fill out the picture concerning NREM characteristics. Both the NREM parasomnias and NREM-related sleep disorders like sleep terrors will be discussed shortly. Here I want to briefly discuss an extremely important NREM disorder that appears to underline the fact that if you go without sleep (at least NREM sleep) for too long you will most certainly die. Fatal familial insomnia (FFI) is an extremely rare autosomal dominant hereditary disease caused by a mutation (missense coding at codon 178) of the prion protein gene (PRNP) (Lugaresi et al., 1986). Current knowledge suggests that only a few hundred families/patients in the world have the disease. The disease is characterized by loss of NREM sleep and very probably loss of some REM as well, though patients appear to be enacting REM dreams. Onset is typically in middle age and patients die typically within a year of diagnosis. After disease onset there is a progressive insomnia, somnolence (dreamy sleepiness), a kind of apathetic stupor, motor activation (possibly REM dream enactment behaviors), and recurrent stereotypical behaviors resembling daily activities like hair combing, greeting nonexistent persons, handling objects, etc. When patients are asked about these behaviors they say they were dreaming them. After disease diagnosis, polysomnographic studies reveal fragmentation and progressive reductions in NREM spindle and delta activity until they disappear completely. Then stage N1 and short bursts of REM appear sporadically, lasting only thirty to forty seconds and are the only signs of sleep that occur for the final weeks or months of the patient's life. Postmortem analyses of the brains of FFI patients reveal degeneration and loss of cells in the thalamus and in mesio-orbital areas of the frontal lobes. This terrible disease once again underlines the apparent functional connections between NREM sleep and the frontal lobes in humans.

Having completed our review of NREM sleep characteristics we turn next to REM sleep. We will see that REM sleep is in many ways an opponent process to NREM. While the parasympathetic system is activated in NREM, the sympathetic system is activated in REM. While mesio-prefrontal systems are taken off-line during NREM, they undergo gradual activation in REM. While metabolic, cardiovascular, and sexual systems are all stable in NREM they are all unstable and fluctuating in

REM. While we dream of everyday friendly interactions in NREM, we dream of aggressive and bizarre interactions in REM.

4.3 Characteristics of REM

4.3.1 The Biobehavioral Characteristics of REM

REM sleep accounts for about 22 percent of total sleep time in humans. It is that form of sleep associated with vivid dreaming and with rapid eye movements under the closed eyelids – thus the name. Brain activation levels within the limbic system (the emotional brain) can be higher than they are in waking state. REM is composed of tonic and phasic events. Tonic aspects of REM are the processes that occur more or less constantly during REM and phasic aspects of REM occur intermittently. REM's tonic characteristics are a desynchronized electroencephalogram (EEG), sexual activation (penile erections/clitoral engorgement), and atonia of the antigravity muscles. Its phasic characteristics include bursts of rapid eye movements under the closed eyelids, myoclonic twitches of the facial and limb muscle groups, increased variability in heart rate, respiration, blood pressure, and autonomic nervous system discharges. The phasic aspects of REM tend to occur in association with some mammals with bursts of pontine-geniculo-occipital (PGO) waves. These PGO waves are essentially electrical spikes in visual centers of the brain. In addition some mammals also exhibit a theta rhythm in the hippocampal formation during REM. The hippocampus is an important structure for formation of memories. REM is also associated with autonomic nervous system instabilities that become more extreme as duration of REM episodes increase across the night. Like NREM sleep, REM deprivation results in a rebound phenomenon indicating that a certain amount of REM is required and must be made up if lost. Interestingly, after total sleep deprivation NREM sleep is made up before that of REM.

4.3.2 REM-on and REM-off Cellular Networks

REM is initiated via action of REM-on cells near the ventrolateral preoptic nucleus of the hypothalamus. Neurons in the extended VLPO area promote REM via GABAergic inhibition of nearby hypothalamic and thalamic arousal systems. In addition, cholinergic neurons originating within the laterodorsal tegmental (LDT) and pedunculopontine tegmental (PPT) nuclei (LDT/PPT) initiates REM once inhibition is lifted from these neurons. That inhibition is coming from noradrenergic (NA) and serotonergic (5HT) neurons in the locus ceruleus and dorsal raphe nucleus (DRN/LC), respectively. Activation of REM occurs after removal of inhibition exerted by these aminergic efferents on cholinergic cells in the LDT/PPT. The release of acetylcholine (Ach) from terminals of LDT/PPT cells triggers the onset of REM. As REM proceeds, cholinergic excitatory effects trigger activation of brain regions that control various components of REM including brainstem sites, hypothalamus, limbic, amygdala, and the basal forebrain. When these activation levels reach a threshold their continuing firing results in a feedback inhibition on REM-on cells of the LDT/PPT, thus ending the REM period. In sum, REM expression is regulated by antagonistic cellular groups with aminergic cell groups inhibiting expression of REM and cholinergic groups promoting expression of REM. When cholinergic REM-on cells are activated aminergic REM-off cell groups are inhibited and vice versa.

4.3.3 Brain Mechanisms in REM

Recently a number of positron emission tomography (PET) and functional Magnetic Resonance Imaging (fMRI) studies of the sleeping brain have revealed that REM (relative to the waking state) is associated with high activation in extra-striate visual regions, limbic, limbic striatum, paralimbic, anterior insula, Brodmann's Area 10 in prefrontal cortex, the ventromedial prefrontal cortex, and temporal regions and relative hypoactivation in inferior and middle frontal gyrus and inferior parietal regions (reviews in: Dang Vu et al., 2010; Maquet et al., 2005). In addition, the motor and premotor cortices are also very active during REMS (Maquet et al., 2004). Interestingly, the superior frontal gyrus, the medial frontal areas, the intraparietal sulcus, and the superior parietal cortex are not less active in REMS than during wakefulness (Maquet et al., 2005). In addition, hippocampal outflow to the cortex is blocked during REM. Instead, the hippocampus receives information from cortical networks.

Some authors (Domhoff, 2011; Pace-Schott and Picchioni, 2017) have noted that the collection of structures activated and deactivated during REM overlap to a significant extent with the so-called default mode network (DMN). The DMN includes posterior cingulate, praecuneus, retrosplenial cortex, inferior parietal, superior temporal, hippocampal formation, and medial prefrontal cortex. These brain regions collectively are always active when the individual is at rest and simply thinking, letting his/her mind wander or daydreaming. Pace-Schott and Picchioni argue that the DMN is composed of at least two major subsystems: one

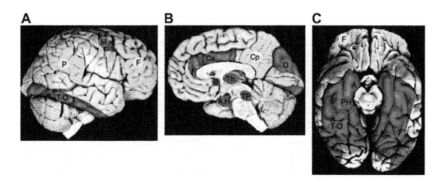

Figure 4.2 Functional neuroanatomy of normal human REM sleep, integrating data from PET and fMRI. Regions colored in red are those in which there is a relative increase in neural activity associated with REM sleep; those in blue correspond to relative decreases in neural activity associated with REM sleep. (A) lateral view; (B) medial view; (C) ventral view. A, amygdala; B, basal forebrain; Ca, anterior cingulate gyrus; Cp, posterior cingulate gyrus and precuneus; F, prefrontal cortex (middle, inferior, and orbito-frontal cortices); H, hypothalamus; M, motor cortex; P, parietal cortex (inferior parietal lobule); PH, parahippocampical gyrus; O, occipital-lateral cortex; Th, thalamus; T-O, temporo-occipital extra-striate cortex; TP, pontine tegmentum.
(Reprinted with permission from Dang Vu, T. T., Desseilles, M., Petit, D., Mazza, S., Montplaisir, J., and Maquet, P. (2007). "Neuroimaging in Sleep Medicine." Sleep Medicine, 8, 349–372; page 351.)

centered on the medial temporal lobe and the hippocampus (the simulation system) and the other centered on the medial prefrontal cortex (the self-referential system). The simulation system is operative when we imagine future or past states of affairs while the self-referential system computes or handles information about the self, including of course emotional information. Both are operative during dreaming. In NREM, slow wave sleep brain nodes in the DMN are disconnected, but in REM they transiently reconnect with the simulation system displaying more stability during REM than the self-referential system. In short, the anterior portions of the DMN are reconnected during REM but these structures, in turn, are part of the larger social brain network discussed in Chapter 1. REM appears to involve the reconnection of the interrelated set of structures that make up the social brain network after it is disassembled or disconnected during the NREM phases of sleep. We will return to the issue of the activation of the social brain network during dreaming in the next section. First we need to continue our survey of REM phenomenon/characteristics.

4.3.4 REM and Motivational Reward

Perogamvrosa and Schwartz (2012) present what they call their "Reward Activation Model" (RAM) of sleep and dreams. The authors integrate recent neurophysiological, neuroimaging, and clinical findings that point to significant activation of the mesolimbic dopaminergic (ML-DA) reward system during both NREM (N2 in humans, SWS in rats) and REM sleep. With regard to REM, dopamine bursting activity within the ventral tegmental area is elevated during REM. This is significant because this is precisely what occurs in the waking brain when it is processing stimuli, particularly social stimuli, that carries reward value.

4.3.5 REM-Related Physiologic Phenomena

REM is associated with very unusual physiologic and cognitive phenomena. In REM you get a very highly activated brain, but the body is paralyzed; the autonomic nervous system erupts in periodic discharges or storms; thermoregulatory reflexes are reduced or absent but the sexual system is activated, and of course you get intense dreams. Needless to say, it is not at all clear why Mother Nature would, every ninety minutes or so during sleep, intensely activate your brain and your sexual system, paralyze your body, and force you to watch these things we call dreams! Let us discuss a bit more fully some of these strange characteristics of REM.

4.3.6 REM Dream Content

People dream in both REM and NREM sleep states but some scientists believe that the dreams associated with REM awakenings are very different in kind from dreams associated with the other sleep states. REM dreams tend to be more intense, more story-like, more aggressive, more emotional, and contain vivid visual detail, unpleasant emotions, and occasional bizarre and improbable events. Some dream researchers believe that most of these differences disappear when you control for number of words per dream as well as time of the night when a dream occurs. As morning draws near the body's arousal systems begin to activate and so dreams are more vivid when they occur towards morning. While the debate is not yet closed on whether the differences between REM and NREM are real, the bulk of the evidence appears to be consistent with the claim that the REM-NREM dream content differences are marked, stable, dramatic, and real.

4.3.7 REM Sleep and Autonomic Nervous System Storms

Relative to the waking state, sympathetic activity rises dramatically during phasic portions of REM. These sympathetic discharges or storms increase in intensity over the course of the night until they peak in the early morning hours. During late morning REM there is severe reductions in ventilation (alveolar hypoventilation) when oxygen desaturation levels are maximal and Cheyne–Stokes-like breathing patterns predominate. REM-related autonomic nervous system or ANS storms are therefore linked to cardiopulmonary crises that can occur during REM. For example, heart rate, arterial blood pressure (BP), pulmonary BP, and intracranial arterial BP all exhibit increased variability during REM-related ANS storms in the early morning hours and there is, not surprisingly, an increased risk for cardiac arrest during the late morning hours coincident with the final REM period before waking (Verrier et al., 1996).

4.3.8 REM-Related Lapse in Thermoregulation

Thermoregulatory responses such as sweating and panting do not occur reliably in REM. Some authors have suggested that REM involves a reversion to a poikilothermic state.

4.3.9 REM-Related Motor Paralysis

One of the most paradoxical features of REM is that phasic eye movements and muscle twitches occur upon a background of paralysis in the antigravity musculature including the jaw, neck, and limbs. When we are in REM sleep, we are essentially paralyzed. The motor neurons that go to our muscles and cause them to contract are inhibited; they are shut down. The most common functional explanation for this strange phenomenon is that the paralysis prevents us from acting out our dreams. Why else would Mother Nature allow us to become so vulnerable to predation every night during a REM episode except to preserve us from injury if we acted out our dreams? Support for this view comes from experiments with cats whose brainstem neurons responsible for REM-related paralysis are experimentally destroyed. When that procedure is done the cats appear to act out their dreams. In addition, REM Behavior Disorder is associated with destruction of cells responsible for REM paralysis and when loss of REM atonia occurs, patients exhibit very clear dream enactment behaviors.

But if the REM atonia functioned to prevent dream enactment it becomes difficult to understand why we don't have atonia associated with NREM sleep. After all we have very complex, vivid dreams during NREM sleep as well. If as some dream researchers believe that NREM dreams are no different from REM dreams in terms of vividness of content and emotionality, then it follows that dream enactment behaviors should occur in NREM N2 sleep – but they do not. Either REM dreams ARE dramatically different from N2 dreams and that accounts for the need for REM atonia, or the muscle atonia associated with REM is not there to prevent dream enactment behaviors. Unfortunately no one at present has any convincing theory for REM atonia, even though most sleep researchers believe that REM atonia is there precisely because it prevents dream enactment behaviors.

4.3.10 Sexual Activation in REM

Every REM period is associated with penile tumescence in males and clitoral engorgement/pelvic thrusting in females. The REM-related erections apparently even occur in infants. They persist throughout the lifespan but are not reliably associated with erotic desire in dreams. REM-related sexual activation in women manifests as clitoral engorgement, vaginal lubrication, uterine contractions, and pelvic thrusting – all signs of sexual desire. It is surprising that desire is not reliably reflected in mental content, i.e., in dreams. If mental content is reducible to brain processes, then one would expect sexual desire to be reflected in mental images, but it is not when it comes to dream content. Of course, occasionally people do experience intense sexual desire and feelings during dreams but the point here is that REM is invariably associated, every night and several times a night with intense sexual activation and yet most people report only a few sex dreams per month. REM-related erections have been observed in all mammalian species where they were looked for, with the interesting exception of the nine-banded armadillo (Affani, Cervino, and Marcos, 2001). In this armadillo, penile erections occur but not in association with REM. It is not clear why sleep-related erections or SREs are NREM-related rather than REM-related in this species. One possibility is that the armadillo differs from most other mammals in terms of its reproductive behaviors. Armadillos exhibit a rare reproductive phenomenon or strategy called polyembryony, which results in offspring that are genetic clones of one another. Among other things, polyembryony should reduce genetic conflict between siblings.

One potential evolutionary function of REM-related erections is that they function as a signal of fitness. In other species newborns and juveniles may be killed by their parents unless they signal their fitness. This can be done via behavioral displays like crying, begging, smiling, vigorous muscular activity, etc. or via physiologic displays like coloring, hormonal levels, or other behavioral phenomena. Penile erections could function as a signaling device in infants. While this "fitness hypothesis" would explain the existence of nocturnal erections in male juveniles it does not explain why sexual activation during REM occurs in tandem with REM or why the phenomenon persists into adulthood. One possibility is that they occur in tandem with REM and persist into adulthood because of a continuing need to produce behavioral displays of fitness during sleep. Every animal is vulnerable to predators and to conspecifics during sleep. Many male animals display erections during aggressive interactions with conspecifics in order to display dominance or to protect territory. Perhaps sexual activation during REM sleep functions to signal conspecifics that the sleeper is reproductively fit. Admittedly this is a very speculative hypothesis. Unfortunately sleep scientists have not yet produced any convincing theories concerning the function of REM-related sexual activation.

4.3.11 REM Sleep and Sexual Signaling

REM-related erections and clitoral engorgement are not the only pieces of evidence linking REM and sex. REM deprivation early in life is associated with later impairment in sexual functions in the adult, at least in the rat and the monkey. Velaquez-Moctezuma et al. (1996) reported that even when effects of the stress associated with the REM deprivation or REMD procedure in rats are controlled, sexual behavior is radically impaired in male rats after selective REMD. When compared to control rats, REMD rats evidenced an increase in mount, intromission, and ejaculation latencies and in mount frequency as well. There was also a decrease in ejaculation frequency. Some sex hormones may increase in association with REM. For example, prolactin (PRL) release is related to REM with its levels rising rapidly at sleep onset and peaking around 3–5 A.M. when REM predominates. Finally, cognitive content associated with REM (i.e., dreams) appears to reflect sex differences in mating strategies. When men have sexual dreams they report content involving multiple anonymous sexual encounters while women report sex involving a familiar partner (Brubaker, 1998).

4.3.12 REM Properties and REM Functions

The aforementioned inventory of REM sleep properties present to us is a kind of paradox. On the one hand REM is associated with reward and sexual function but on the other hand it involves several harmful physiologic properties. REM-related PGO waves, activation of the amygdala, ANS storms, cardiovascular instabilities, respiratory impairment, and thermoregulatory lapses, suggests that REM is risky for one's health. Indeed, increased REM sleep durations (relative to the population norm) and sleep complaints are significantly associated with increased risk for mortality, even after adjusting for age, gender, mental illness, and "medical burden" or physical health status (Kripke, 2011). Dew et al. (2003) were able to analyze measures of sleep architecture in relation to risk for mortality. They reported that three measures of sleep architecture best predicted mortality: (1) sleep latencies of greater than thirty minutes; (2) poor sleep efficiency; and (3) an unusually high or low percentage of REM sleep.

This inventory of the basic properties of REM tells us what needs to be explained in any theory of REM function. Approximately every ninety minutes while we sleep, access to external sensory information is reduced, the brain becomes highly activated – particularly networks supporting socio-emotional functions – and the body is essentially paralyzed. As the night progresses these REM periods become more and more violent, eliciting autonomic nervous system storms and serious fluctuations in heart rate and respiratory functions. In addition, the dreamer finds himself a central participant in a series of hallucinatory dream-dramas that vary from the prosaic to the epic and bizarre. Sometimes banal and sometimes frightening, experience of these dreams is involuntary – we are compelled to participate whether we like it or not. Finally, to add a note of the absurd to the whole affair, the male experiences an erection, regardless of dream content and the female may experience uterine contractions and even pelvic thrusting – again regardless of dream content.

4.3.13 Conclusions: REM vs. NREM Sleep

It is difficult to imagine what the function of REM sleep might be, given the odd constellation of traits we have just summarized. Its biobehavioral characteristics are paradoxical in that its physiologic correlates appear to be injurious to the health of the organism while its brain correlates suggest social-emotional functions. Unlike REM, NREM biobehavioral characteristics are slightly less paradoxical but still enigmatic. NREM's physiologic functions may be related to immune system function while its electrophysiologic properties are clearly related to the restorative functions of sleep. Both REM and NREM sleep likely participate in memory processing but so does the waking state. The fact that NREM appears to be associated with the gradual deactivation of a select group of brain structures that are then reactivated during REM suggests that the two sleep states either work in harmony with one another to maintain optimal brain function or that NREM undoes something that REM instantiates. To understand the peculiar functions of REM or NREM and whether they operate in harmony or in opposition to one another, we will need to assemble one more set of facts concerning disorders associated with REM and NREM sleep, and it is those facts we review next.

Review Questions

- What is the significance of the two major spindle types associated with stage N2 NREM sleep?
- What is the Reward Activation Model (RAM) of REM sleep and why is it significant?
- What is the motor paralysis associated with REM and why is it significant?
- Why do you think paralysis does not occur with NREM?
- What is the significance of the sexual activation that occurs in REM?

Further Reading

Clawson, B. C., Durkin, J., & Aton, S. J. (2016). Form and function of sleep spindles across the lifespan. *Neural Plasticity*. doi: 10.1155/2016/6936381. Epub April 14, 2016.

Halász, P., Bódizs, R., Parrino, L., & Terzano, M. (2014). Two features of sleep slow waves: Homeostatic and reactive aspects – from long term to instant sleep homeostasis. *Sleep Medicine*, 15(10), 1184–95. doi: 10.1016/j.sleep.2014.06.006. Review. PMID:25192672.

Jouvet, M. (1999). *The Paradox of Sleep: The Story of Dreaming*. Cambridge, MA: MIT Press.

Perogamvrosa, L., & Schwartz, S. (2012). The roles of the reward system in sleep and dreaming. *Neuroscience and Biobehavioral Reviews*, 36, 1934–1951.

CHAPTER 5

Sleep Disorders

Learning Objectives

- Describe the two main families of sleep disorders
- Describe the major dyssomnias
- Describe the major parasomnias
- Describe the significance of brain state transition failures in parasomnias

5.1 Introduction

Sleep disorders can be divided into two very broad classes: dyssomnias and parasomnias. Dyssomnias involve changes in sleep duration such that the patient gets too much or too little sleep. Parasomnias involve partial arousals from within a REM or NREM sleep state. A third class of *sleep-related* disorders involve changes in the circadian pacemaker system such that the daily sleep period is displaced (delayed or advanced) from its normal slot within the twenty-four hour day. Since I discussed circadian-related sleep disorders in another chapter I confine discussion here to the dyssomnias and parasomnias.

Dyssomnias involve a change in sleep amount from normal reference values. Hypersomnolence is too much sleep and insomnia is too little sleep. Insomnia and excessive daytime sleepiness are, in fact, the most common disorders of sleep. Changes in sleep duration, furthermore, are associated with significant risks to both physical and mental health. Persons with longer REM sleep durations (relative to the population norm), for example, experience greater risks for various medical conditions (e.g., cardiovascular disease, obesity, etc.) and mortality. They are also at greater risk for depression. Moreover, it has become increasingly clear in recent years that the restorative or homeostatic properties of sleep are dependent on an interaction between sleep amounts and sleep intensity parameters, as formalized in Borbeley's original two-process model of sleep regulation (Borbeley, 1982) and its more recent emendations (Achermann and Borbeley, 2003). When deprived of sleep, mammals typically exhibit a sleep rebound proportional to the amount of sleep lost, indicating that the amount of sleep, or some specific intensity component of sleep reflected in "amount of sleep" is physiologically obligatory. Thus, "sleep amount or duration" is a strictly regulated physiologic need for the organism and any deviation from the amount required must be considered a disorder. Too much or too little sleep will have dire consequences for the organism. Too little sleep is a more common complaint than too much, so we begin with a discussion of insomnia, the most common dyssomnia.

5.2 Dyssomnias

5.2.1 Insomnia

Insomnia is defined as difficulty initiating sleep or staying asleep or both. Insomnia is very common, with over 95 percent of the population claiming to have experienced it at least once in their lives. For the vast majority of these people the sleeplessness lasts just a few nights. For about 10 percent of the population, however, the insomnia can be persistent, resulting in very significant hits to health and well-being. The daily fatigue and exhaustion that is associated with chronic insomnia undermines all other aspects of a person's life, making them irritable, unhappy, and vulnerable to all kinds of minor and major health complaints. Insomnia, in short, is a major public health crisis in the world today.

There are two forms of insomnia: primary and secondary insomnia. Primary insomnia is sleeplessness due to intrinsic sleep-related causes while secondary insomnia is sleeplessness due to non-sleep related causes such as anxiety or an illness or stress, etc.

5.2.2 Primary Insomnia

The paradigm case of a *primary* insomnia is fatal familial insomnia (FFI), a prion disease that damages the thalamic neurons that keep the brain awake. A "prion" is a tiny protein that gets misfolded and entangled up in the metabolic machinery of certain neurons that are important for maintaining wakefulness and sleep. Accumulation of enough of these proteins in the wrong places in neurons creates significant brain dysfunction. In FFI the prion disease affects mostly those regions of the brain that inhibit the thalamic alerting neurons. Thalamic alerting centers of the brain can no longer be effectively inhibited and thus the individual can no longer transition into non-alertness and sleep. FFI results in death in about eighteen months post-diagnosis but it is a very rare disease. After diagnosis progression is rapid as sleeplessness persists. First there is inability to concentrate, then confusional states ensue, then panic attacks and hallucinations, and finally loss of weight. The individual fluctuates between stage NI and REM in a kind of dreamy twilight state until death intervenes.

Aside from FFI most sleep scientists are not in agreement as to whether there are any other intrinsic or primary insomnias. Interestingly, an individual can believe that they are not sleeping at all or sleeping well, but when we bring them into the sleep lab to test their sleep it turns out that they are in fact sleeping perfectly well. These "insomnia" cases are sometimes called "sleep state misperception." About 4 percent of people who report insomnia are actually suffering from sleep state misperception. Most sleep clinicians believe that these individuals maintain a highly aroused baseline state of vigilance or anxiety and therefore their brain systems never fully relax into sleep, even though the EEG unmistakably demonstrates deep sleep.

5.2.3 Secondary Insomnia

Most cases of insomnia are in the secondary insomnia category; the cause of the insomnia is usually not something intrinsic to the sleep-wake brain systems that normally regulate transitions into and out of sleep. In cases of secondary insomnia there are usually medical issues, emotional issues, or everyday stress or work-related issues that keep the person awake at night. Many medical conditions can impair sleep, such as chronic pain, restless legs syndrome, and drug side effects. In addition, medical conditions such as hyperthyroidism (too much thyroid hormone) and hypercortisolemia (too much of the adrenal hormone cortisol) can lead to chronic hyperarousal and therefore difficulty falling asleep or maintaining sleep. By far the most common secondary cause of insomnia is psychological or emotional problems. The everyday worries and chronic anxiety people experience on a daily basis is the enemy of deep restorative sleep.

The major psychiatric syndromes like major depression, schizophrenia, and bipolar disorder are also associated with major disruptions of sleep including severe insomnia. During the manic phase of manic-depressive illness, for example, the individual can stay awake for sometimes days at a time before collapsing due to exhaustion. During active psychotic states associated with schizophrenia individuals do not sleep normally and during major depressive episodes sleeplessness and early morning awakenings are common and are sometimes used to diagnose depression.

5.2.4 Major Depression

Depression is almost always associated with complaints of insomnia – specifically early morning awakenings. Major depressive disorder is associated with a range of symptom clusters including the hallmark symptoms of persistent sadness and anxious and hopeless feelings. When sleep does occur dreams are recalled as intensely unpleasant experiences with elevated levels of scenes of aggression by unknown strangers against the dreamer/self. Reduced REM sleep latency and increased REM density and REM time are commonly observed in depressed patients. REM sleep deprivation can temporarily alleviate depressive symptoms (Vogel et al., 1975). Most antidepressant drugs reduce REM sleep and degree of REM suppression is correlated with a degree of symptomatic relief in responders. Thus, signs of enhanced REM sleep pressure in some depressed patients may reflect a primary symptom of the disorder rather than a mechanism compensating for the affective disturbance. Depressed people may use their dreams to work through unpleasant affect (Cartwright, 1999).

5.2.5 Sleep Apnea

Sleep apnea is a very common disorder that prevents sleep because the individual's airway is blocked during sleep. About 24 percent of men and 9 percent of women develop sleep apnea, particularly as they age. Sleep apnea is responsible for 50,000 premature and preventable deaths each year from accidents, heart attacks, and strokes. The airway is blocked often because there is simply too much fat in the neck so the collapse of the airway during sleep cuts off airflow to the lungs and the individual who suddenly cannot breathe awakens briefly to catch his breath. This brief arousal or apnea episode stimulates a return to wakefulness. These brief arousals happen hundreds of times during the night and thus the individual's sleep architecture becomes extremely fragmented. Loud snoring usually accompanies the sleep of the patient with sleep apnea because they cannot breathe normally through the mouth. In the morning all the individual knows is that he does not feel fully rested and during the day he is fatigued and very sleepy.

There are two types of sleep apnea: central sleep apnea and obstructive sleep apnea (OSA). Central sleep apnea occurs when the problem is located within the central nervous system such that the respiratory muscles do not respond normally. The most common cause of sleep apnea, however, is obstruction of the airflow. The barriers to airflow are the soft tissues of the mouth and nasal cavities and the throat. These tissues can begin to occlude the airway if the musculature of the jaw and chin is such that it promotes occlusion. By far the most common cause of occlusion is that fat deposits begin to build up in the soft tissues of mouth and nasal cavities and the throat, thus making them more prone to closure. Obesity is one of the strongest predictors of OSA.

The severity of an individual's OSA can be quantified by an apnea hypopnea index (AHI) – the number of apneas and hypopneas terminating in arousals across the night divided by the number of hours of sleep. Mild OSA is defined as an AHI between 5 and 15; moderate, between 15 and 30; severe, between 30 to 45; and extremely severe, above 45.

The most common treatment for OSA is Continuous Positive Airway Pressure or CPAP. When the patient goes to bed, he or she wears a face mask that directs positive pressure airflow into the nose. This positive pressure prevents collapse of the air passageway leading up to the trachea and allows normal breathing to continue during sleep. Most people, however, do not enjoy sleeping with a mask on, and the airflow can dry out the nasal passages.

We have now discussed the major sleep disorders involving too little or loss of sleep. Disorders of hypersomnolence or too much sleep include narcolepsy and Kleine-Levin syndrome.

Hypersomnia is excessive daytime sleepiness not attributed to lack of sleep or transient disruptions of sleep that often occur to each of us. It is a sleepiness that has more unusual causes. People with hypersomnolence have to fight or work hard during the day just to stay awake. Hypersomnolence can often be attributed to depression. When depression is the root cause of the hypersomnolence, placing the patient on antidepressants typically solves both the mood disorder and the hypersomnolence. Often daytime sleepiness can be attributed to an underlying sleep apnea. When the sleep apnea is appropriately diagnosed and treated the daytime sleepiness lifts. If we rule out all of these potential causes of excessive daytime sleepiness – depression, sleep apnea, commonplace and transient sleep disruptions, etc., and if we rule out other well-studied hypersomnias like narcolepsy and Kleine-Levin Syndrome (KLS), then we are left with "idiopathic hypersomnia" or excessive daytime sleepiness of unknown origin. Idiopathic hypersomnias can be effectively treated even though we do not know the causes. Treatment typically involves stimulant medications.

Kleine-Levin Syndrome is a periodic hypersomnia characterized by recurrent episodes of prolonged sleeping or hypersomnia and other behavioral and cognitive symptoms. It mainly affects teenage boys, who display the pattern of sleeping most of the day and night for weeks at a time. The International Classification of Sleep Disorders diagnostic criteria for KLS include: (1) episodes of excessive sleepiness lasting more than two days and less than four weeks, occurring at least once a year; (2) episodes intermixed with long intervals of normal alertness, mood, cognition, and behavior lasting usually months to years; (3) episodes recurring at least every year interspersed with long periods of normal sleep; and (4) episodes not better explained by a sleep disorder, a neurological disorder (e.g., idiopathic recurrent stupor, epilepsy), a mental disorder (e.g., bipolar disorder, psychiatric hypersomnia, depression), or the use of drugs (e.g., benzodiazepines, alcohol). In addition to these recurrent episodes of hypersomnia, KLS patients should experience at least one of these symptoms: hyperphagia (overeating), hypersexuality, odd behavior, or cognitive disturbances (e.g., confusion, feeling of derealization, or hallucinations). Arnulf et al. (2005) reviewed the literature on 108 cases and found that many reported marked apathy, exhaustion, memory problems, temporal disorientation, derealization, dreamy state, and impaired speech among other cognitive and perceptual symptoms.

5.2.6 Narcolepsy

Narcolepsy is another major disorder where affected individuals complain of too much sleepiness. It is characterized by (1) excessive daytime sleepiness; (2) hypnogogic hallucinations (vivid images at sleep onset); (3) "sleep attacks" or sudden paralysis (cataplexy) following a strong emotional stimulus like laughing or an intense emotion; and (4) sleep paralysis or paralysis during the transition from sleep to wake or from wake to sleep. In the sleep to wake transition the paralysis normally associated with REM sleep has not yet ceased even though the patient is conscious or awake. Affected individuals may also exhibit reduced hypocretin in the cerebrospinal fluid, and sleep-onset REM (SOREM) on the EEG. Recall that the normal pattern is to enter sleep via NREM. SOREM indicates that the individual skips the NREM sleep stages and goes right into REM while falling asleep. Hypocretin (sometimes also called orexin) is a neuromodulator that is a peptide manufactured in the hypothalamus. Hypocretin receptors in the thalamus appear to be crucially important for activation of the awakening circuit centered on the thalamus. They are partially destroyed in narcolepsy but it is unclear what agent or process destroys these orexinergic cells.

There is some evidence to suggest that narcolepsy may be an auto-immune disorder wherein the immune system selectively attacks certain neurons in the brain or cells in the body. In the case of narcolepsy postmortem examination of the brain of narcoleptics revealed damage to orexin/hypocretin-producing neurons in the hypothalamus. Genetic studies of narcoleptic individuals have revealed that narcoleptics often (though not always) share an HLA gene variant called DQB1*0602.

Let us examine the symptomology associated with narcolepsy a little more closely as it teaches us that components of REM sleep may be affecting a patient's waking behaviors. With respect to the excessive daytime sleepiness narcoleptics fall asleep several times a day. The "sleep attack" is usually for a few minutes at a time but it can occasion-ally last up to an hour or two. After these "naps" or sleep attacks, the feeling of excessive sleepiness subsides for a few hours but then returns. Patients also experience microsleeps when they transiently fall into a sleep state but it is brief, and the patient is generally unaware of it. Patients can generally sense when they have a "sleep attack" coming. They feel a buildup of irresistible sleepiness and then sleep suddenly overcomes them. The cataplexy symptom involves sudden paralysis during wakefulness, usually triggered by strong emotions like laughter, surprise, or fear. They can occur during other experiences involving strong emotions such as watching a movie, having sex, or exercising. Cataplexy does not occur in all narcoleptics but when it does it typically looks like seizure activity in that it comes on fast and the patient becomes immobilized and loses consciousness. In an attack the patient feels a sudden weakening in the knees, the sagging of facial muscles, head dropping forward, and arms flopping to the sides. These are all signs associated with the normal paralysis associated with REM sleep. It seems as if the patient is experiencing an irruption of REM physiology into waking life. Consistent with this thesis is the fact that patients also report an intense dream-like state during sleep attacks as if they are dreaming. When studied in a sleep lab most narcoleptics demonstrate signs of REM pressure. Latency to REM is very short and patients report that they are immediately immersed in vivid dreams after they fall asleep. When vivid dreams and images occur in the transition from waking to sleep these dreams are called hypnogogic hallucinations. When they occur in the transition from sleep to wakefulness they are called hypnopompic hallu-cinations. When muscle paralysis occurs in one of these transitional states we call it sleep paralysis because the mind is awake but the body remains in REM paralysis. Thus the patient is awake and is aware that he or she cannot move. They may see or hallucinate some residual dream imagery – typically frightening imagery. There is a sense of threat and of an evil presence in the room yet the patient cannot move to protect him or herself.

About one-quarter of narcoleptics experience the classic tetrad of symptoms: excessive daytime sleepiness, cataplexy, hypnogogic or hypnopompic hallucinations, and sleep paralysis. The majority of narcoleptics experience at least two of these symptoms. The Multiple Sleep Latency Test (MSLT) assesses the extent to which an individual when given the chance, transitions into sleep quickly or slowly. The test also assesses whether the first sleep state the patient enters is the normal entry via NREM sleep or the abnormal entryway via REM. The MSLT can facilitate (though not definitively) diagnosis of narcolepsy if the patient falls asleep within eight minutes and preferentially enters sleep via REM. This profile is called sleep-onset REM period or SOREMP. SOREMP is characteristic of narcolepsy, depression, and some other neuropsychiatric disorders.

Treatment for narcolepsy currently involves use of stimulants such as Ritalin and Modafinil to combat daytime sleepiness and clomipramine and imipramine (which historically were used as tricyclic antidepressants) to treat cataplexy.

5.3 Parasomnias

5.3.1 Introduction

Parasomnias are disruptions of behavior or consciousness during sleep. They typically occur in between brain states, for example during the transition into or out of sleep, or in the transition between sleep states, for example between NREM and REM. They are divided into REM sleep parasomnias and non-REM sleep parasomnias.

5.3.2 Non-REM Parasomnias Sleepwalking

Somnambulism is the most common NREM parasomnia. Sleepwalking, which is most prevalent in children, is also seen in adults. It typically emerges when the individual transitions from N3 SWS to N2 light NREM sleep. About 20 percent of children experience at least one episode of sleepwalking up to about eleven or twelve years of age and about 4 percent of adults occasionally sleepwalk. A family history of sleepwalking is the strongest predictor that an individual will sleepwalk.

Thus, sleepwalking likely has a genetic basis though no genetic profile has been found yet to characterize sleepwalkers. Sleepwalkers can accomplish very complex behavioral acts including preparing meals or searching for objects, even though they are only semiconscious and are likely hallucinating if their eyes are open. Efforts to wake them up frequently result in a state of agitated, confused arousal that might even involve aggressive or violent acts. There is typically disorientation such that the sleepwalker is confused as to where they are. In addition, there is typically no memory for the sleepwalking episode. Occasionally a sleepwalker develops a habit of getting out of bed, stumbling to the kitchen, and preparing and eating favorite dishes. This is called sleep-related eating disorder.

The EEG of sleepwalkers demonstrates unstable delta activity and frequent arousals during the early part of the sleep period and it is out of these arousals that a sleepwalking episode begins. Sleepwalking can be treated effectively with clonazepam or alprazolam (Xanax).

5.3.3 Sleep Sex

As in the case of sleepwalking, sleep sex is a condition that involves sexual activity while asleep or in a confusional arousal out of NREM sleep that exhibits nonstable delta activity. Sleep sex can occur when the sleeper is alone or with a bed partner. It can involve a very wide variety of sexual behaviors including masturbation, touching, fondling, sex talk, and outright intercourse. Interestingly, there is typically no kissing. Sometimes these sleep sex behaviors can involve overpowering the bed partner, which then becomes dangerous. Thus, sleep sex is a clinically significant problem and potentially a legal issue when the sleeper over-powers his bed partner. There is little reliable data on the disorder probably because most people with the disorder are ashamed to talk about it. From what little we know most patients (80 percent) with sleep sex disorder are men. Many also exhibit sleepwalking behaviors. The sleep sex is typically robotic because the initiator is asleep. If you wake him up he is confused and disoriented and sometimes ashamed or angry. There is often amnesia for the act. This disorder is associated with major personal and sometimes legal consequences for the patient. Bed partners of these patients are often perplexed and sometimes shocked by the patient's behaviors. When the sex is forced, of course, there are legal consequences. If the patient is in a new relationship the bed partner will be shocked by the unconsciously initiated and often aggressive sleep sex.

5.3.4 Night Terrors

Like sleepwalking and sleep sex, night terrors emerge when the patient (typically a child) is attempting to arouse out of N3 SWS. There is unstable delta activity and frequent arousals usually in the first couple of sleep periods. The child sits upright and screams as if in terror. Night terrors run in families. Night terrors may not be recalled however and it is very difficult to awaken the child. Episodes can last between a few minutes and a half hour and there is amnesia for the episode after awakening.

Sleep-related binge eating involves an individual awaking from an NREM episode and then going to the kitchen in a somnambulant state and bingeing on some sweets or very rich foods. Most cases (75 percent) of sleep-related binge eating involve girls or women. Risk factors for development of this NREM disorder include a family history of sleepwalking or other sleep disorders and a history of eating disorders (e.g., anorexia or bulimia). Although it appears to be an NREM parasomnia, an arousal can begin in an NREM state but then switch into a REM state while the patient is bingeing. Level of consciousness can vary during a bingeing episode, with some patients having no awareness and no memory of the episode and others being partially awake but feeling no control over their behavior. Often the binge eating co-occurs with a classic sleep walking disorder and both disorders run in families. The binge eating episodes can occur regardless of whether or not the patient had had a full meal before bedtime and regardless of hunger. In the morning there is always a feeling of being bloated and not hungry. The foods the patients choose to binge on are typically high-carbohydrate foods but mixed with very unusual items reflecting the clouded consciousness they operate under during an episode. For example, patients have reported eating raw meat and bacon, salt sandwiches, soap or hand cream, dog food, coffee grounds, ketchup, and mayonnaise. Patients may also go through elaborate food prep rituals and attempt to cook these items and then forget to turn off the stove. Other negative consequences of sleep-related binge eating are not surprising: weight gain, increased risk of food poisoning, daytime appetite changes, dental, and other health complications.

5.3.5 Sleep Talking

Although the available data suggests that sleep talking can occur in any stage of sleep it may be that like sleepwalking, sleep sex, sleep-related bingeing, and sleep terrors, sleep talking typically begins as a confusional arousal out of N3 slow wave sleep after some unusual delta activity and then proceeds to unfold in a hybrid or mixed form of REM sleep. About 50 percent of children sleep talk and some 4 percent of the adult population sleep talks on a consistent basis. Like the other NREM parasomnias, sleep talking runs in families and typically co-occurs with one or more of the other NREM parasomnias. The content of sleep talk is typically mundane. It most often involves interactions with hallucinated or dreamed interlocutors. The speech is most often linguistically well formed and grammatical but its semantic content can often be meaningless. Bilinguals most often prefer to sleep talk in their native first learned tongues. Interestingly, when two sleep talkers sleep in the same bed they can often carry on largely meaningless conversations, all while they are asleep! As in the other NREM parasomnias there is typically amnesia for the sleep talking event in the morning. Although sleep talking is harmless in and of itself it can sometimes weakly predict (in a middle-aged adult) later onset of a neurodegenerative disorder like multiple system atrophy.

"Exploding head syndrome" is a real disorder! It is characterized by a sense of a flashbulb sound or explosion going off inside your head. Typically it occurs in the transition from waking into N1 sleep and the explosion sound wakes you up. The explosion is usually experienced as deep within in the center of the brain but there is no pain. It lasts a second and disappears upon awakening. It typically occurs only a few times in a lifetime in most people but may be more common in the elderly. Aside from being startled there are no apparent negative clinical effects of the experience. Nobody knows what causes this sleep-related experience.

5.3.6 REM Parasomnias

The major parasomnias of REM sleep are nightmares, REM behavior disorder (RBD), and isolated sleep paralysis.

5.3.7 Nightmares

The DSM-5 defines Nightmare Disorder (DSM-5 307.47 (F51.5)) as a parasomnia involving repeated awakenings from extremely frightening dreams that do not occur in the context of some other mental disorder. Upon awakening the individual is oriented and alert and has clear recall of the content of the dream, which in turn is associated with clinically significant distress and impairment in daytime functioning. Similarly, the 2016/17 ICD-10-CM Diagnosis Code F51.5 defines nightmare disorder as a sleep disorder characterized by the repeated occurrence of frightening dreams which precipitate awakenings from sleep. Upon awakening, the individual becomes fully alert and oriented and has detailed recall of the nightmare, which usually involves imminent danger to the individual.

Nightmare disorder typically involves distressing nightmares that occur at least once a week for a month or more. Epidemiological studies indicate that 2–6 percent (about 15 to 20 million people) of the adult American population experience nightmares at least once a week. Between one-half and two-thirds of children experience recurrent nightmares. Recurrent nightmares in children significantly predict later adolescent and adult risk for psychosis. If we can effectively treat nightmares in children we may be able to prevent later onset of psychosis in at least some of these kids. Indeed, experience of frequent nightmares in both children and adults is associated with a host of neuropathological and neuropsychiatric risk factors and disorders including anxiety, depression, stress, and suicidal ideation (Spoormaker, Schredl, and van den Bout, 2006). Severely distressing and repetitive nightmares are a hallmark of PTSD (post-traumatic stress disorder), REM Behavior Disorder (RBD), and several other chronic and disabling neuropsychiatric syndromes. Development of an effective treatment for nightmare disorders will improve treatment outcomes of nightmare-related distress in these other disorders as well.

Nielsen and Levin (2007) proposed that dreaming normally functions to extinguish fear memories. Dreaming allows the individual to effectively handle emotionally disturbing memories by decontextualizing the fear memories, thus making them more amenable to being encoded into long-term memory systems. If you separate the emotion from the context that elicited or caused the emotion then you can better cope with that emotion in new unrelated contexts. Dreams provide an ever changing sequence of contexts that can be paired with the intense negative affect and fear-related elements (e.g., a danger of threat or trauma) encoded within a fear memory. These novel pairings of unrelated contexts with particular affect loads and fear elements of particular fear memories function to decontextualize the memory, thus making it more amenable to consolidation. Bad dreams are thought to be examples of successful dreaming wherein fear levels associated with the original fear memory are reduced or extinguished, while nightmares are thought to be examples of failed fear extinctions. The memory never gets decontextualized and therefore never gets encoded into long term memory, so it sits in short-term memory circuits that get reactivated during dreaming such that the individual experiences the repetitive, scary dreams we call nightmares.

Many events can contribute to failed fear extinction during dreaming, including too high a level of fear or arousal associated with the original memory. In addition, the natural circadian rise of cortisol during late REM sleep may both increase physiologic arousal as well as influence consolidation of emotional memories. Disturbance of this system may contribute to failed extinction memories during dreaming. Given that the alpha-1 adrenergic receptor antagonist Prazosin has proved remarkably effective in ameliorating nightmares, it follows that high physiologic arousal levels associated with increased noradrenergic tone during REM contributes to failed extinction memories during dreaming in REM.

While failed fear extinction may contribute to the formation of nightmares, it does not explain their maintenance over time as in recurrent nightmares or their content features crucial for clinical distress. To explain these latter features of nightmares, Spoormaker (2008) proposed that information about the storyline of a recurrent nightmare is represented in the memory as a fixed expectation pattern: a script. This script describes a typical sequence of events or dream images that automatically follow one another once triggered but that can also allow for variability. For instance, a person with recurrent nightmares in which he/she is chased may be chased by different attackers in different settings during different dreams. The nightmare script contributes specifically to nightmare maintenance (recurrence) and content, and therefore the distress associated with nightmares. Nightmare scripts can be activated whenever a dream produces an element or character that matches or is related to an element or character in the script. A normal dream of someone walking fast, for example, could trigger the chase script. This replay of the chase script strengthens the nightmare script, a process mediated by the emotional intensity of the nightmare. Other factors that would influence activation of the script according to Spoormaker might be interpretive bias and accessibility of the script. An anxious person or a person operating in a dangerous environment would be more prone to interpret neutral dream elements in threatening ways, thus enhancing accessibility of the script and so on. The nightmare script is theorized to be strongly connected with adverse emotions when activated, most commonly intense fear.

Strategies to cognitively avoid the fearful dream make the nightmare script that much more difficult to extinguish. Cognitive avoidance makes memory integration of the nightmare script into the (autobiographical) memory less probable. Studies of cognitive restructuring approaches to nightmare treatment suggest that direct exposure and working with the images involved in the script, as is the case with imagery rehearsal therapy (IRT), can neutralize the fear memories associated with the script.

Cognitive-restructuring techniques such as IRT very likely work by restructuring the nightmare script. IRT (Krakow and Zadra, 2010) is a technique in which participants are instructed to change a recurrent nightmare any way they wish, which they then have to rehearse in imagination. The introduction of non-fear provoking, nightmare-incompatible elements into the nightmare script may reduce the affect/ stress load associated with the script and thus promote fear extinction. In addition, introducing a different ending or goal into the script may break down the expectation pattern of the script. IRT has demonstrated reduction in nightmare frequency and distress in randomized trials.

5.3.8 REM Behavior Disorder

REM sleep behavior disorder (RBD) is characterized by loss of the atonia normally associated with rapid eye movement or REM sleep. Patients therefore often act out dreams normally associated with REM sleep. They appear to experience visual and auditory hallucinations in association with violent themed dream narratives. RBD may herald by decades the onset of one of the synucleinopathies such as Parkinson's disease (PD), Lewy body dementia (LBD), or multiple system atrophy (MSA). Dream enactment can last for minutes and be quite violent, with the individual physically doing battle with imaginary foes. These patients exhibit complex exploratory and often defensive motor activities during REM sleep, usually in association with dreams. Common behaviors include screaming, punching, grasping, kicking, or jumping out of the bed in pursuit of or in flight from a supernormal or monstrous foe. Fantini, Corona, Clerici, and Ferini-Strambi (2005) studied the REM sleep dreams of forty-nine patients with polysomnographic-confirmed RBD and seventy-one healthy controls. Compared to controls, patients with RBD reported a striking frequency of aggression wherein the dreamer was threatened or assaulted by monstrous beings or unfamiliar strangers with intent to harm the dreamer or his family. This signature RBD dream interaction was captured by various standardized Hall/Van de Castle dream content indicators, including a higher percentage of *dreams with at least one aggression* (66 percent vs. 15 percent), an increased *aggression/friendliness interactions* ratio (86 percent vs. 44 percent), and an increased *aggressions/characters (A/C)* ratio (0.81 vs. 0.12).

Whence comes all this aggression in REM dreams of patients with RBD? We know that the amygdala is intensely activated while the dorsolateral prefrontal cortex is down regulated during REM. The amygdala is known to specialize in mediation of threat detection, fear conditioning, and emotional function. It maintains reciprocal feedback loops with the anterior insula, temporal lobes including primary auditory cortex, inferior, and superior parietal lobes, and the medial, orbital, and dorsolateral prefrontal cortex (DLPFC). Cortical hypoactivity in frontal cortex is strongly associated with amygdala hyperactivity and that may be what we see in RBD. Without prefrontal cortical modulation of amygdala reactivity, amygdala mediation of perceived threat in dreams would no longer be effectively modulated.

5.3.9 Sleep Paralysis

Isolated sleep paralysis (ISP) is a relatively common experience typically characterized by an inability to move or speak after waking up as well by the eerie sense that someone or something is in the room with you who is somehow evil or malignant and threatening you. The individual/patient is really still in REM sleep although he might believe he has fully awakened, or at least that his mind is awake. It is legitimately categorized as a dream because the individual often experiences both auditory and visual hallucinations as well as the muscle atonia or paralysis that normally accompanies REM.

The experience is caused by fragmentation of the brain state associated with REM such that one does not move entirely out of REM when one transitions from REM to wake. The potential causes of the failure to completely transition out of REM into waking consciousness are multiple. They include stress, disease, injury, illness, chemical imbalances, and sleeplessness among many other causes. Cheyne (2002) of the University of Waterloo has collected some data on the phenomenology of these sleep paralysis dreams/visions. He used a survey to tabulate the frequency with which these various features occur in these experiences. Of 2,397 respondents, the mean age of onset was seventeen, but the experiences can happen at any age. About one-quarter report experiencing sleep paralysis weekly or more frequently. Almost 80 percent experienced a sensed presence; that is, when they are awake but paralyzed they sense that someone or something is in the room with them and usually intends them harm. So the individual attempts to scream for help but cannot. Approximately 60 percent reported auditory and visual hallucinations, whereas only 41 percent reported tactile hallucinations. They hear the sensed presence breathing or moving towards them and can actually feel them touching or pressing in on them. One-third (33.4 percent) of respondents were able to assign a sex to the sensed presence. Of these, most (82 percent) perceived the presence to be male, with women significantly more likely than men to see the sensed presence as male. Slightly more than half of the auditory hallucinations involved hearing voices. Approximately two-thirds of respondents reported feelings of pressure. Almost as many reported feeling that they might die. Forty to thirty percent of respondents reported out of body experiences or OBEs where they could see themselves from a point above their bodies, while only about 20 percent reporting spinning sensations or autoscopy (seeing a double). Almost 100 percent (96 percent) of respondents reported fear. But substantial percentages also reported feeling erotic feelings and even bliss.

Parker and Blackmore (2002) used the Hall/Van de Castle dream content scoring system to quantitate the characteristics of ISPs that differentiate them from standard dreams. In ISP reports there were four times as many references to the body than in standard dream reports. In addition there were higher levels of physical aggression against the individual than that found in run of the mill dreams. Unlike dreams that depict a variety of emotions, fear predominated in ISP reports. Parker and Blackmore found that the typical ISP "takes place in a familiar, indoor setting (the bedroom). Often a presence or person not known to the dreamer is present. The presence is more often male (if gender is reported), but most common of all is that a sexless 'creature' or 'form' is sensed. Interactions with the presence are predominantly aggressive (although men do attempt to befriend it more often than women do). 'Dreamers' often feel victimized by these interactions. They also report a much greater awareness of their body, particularly torso, which is accompanied by increased reports of negative emotion (fear). They often struggle to overcome the situation (paralysis) and meet with equal degree of success or failure (sometimes they are able to overcome the paralysis or not)" (Parker and Blackmore, 2002, page 57).

How might we explain this extraordinary phenomenology? I know of no convincing explanations of ISP phenomenology in the scientific literature. In speaking with other sleep scientists about ISP phenomenology most believe it represents a release of innate threat-protection behaviors. The release of these innate behaviors/cognitions is due to

Table 5.1 Sleep disorders and the law

Can someone perform all of the complex acts of killing another person while "asleep"? Rosalind Cartwright is a sleep scientist who has studied the issue and testified in court cases concerning sleepwalking and homicide. Cartwright says that in rare cases this is possible. In her 2010 book *The Twenty-Four Hour Mind* she presents in detail the tragic case of Scott Falater's murder of his wife of many years. A neighbor heard the cries of the wife and saw Falater pushing the body of the bloodied woman into the family pool. Falater had stabbed his wife dozens of times and then calmly left the scene of the murder (apparently to place the bloodied knife and clothes into a Tupperware container), then returned to the body to push it into the pool. After pushing the body into the pool Falater apparently went back into the house. Cartwright thinks Falater went back into the house to go back to bed/sleep, just as most other sleepwalkers do unless they are awakened by a loud sound. Falater was convicted of murder despite the defense's claim that the defendant had been sleepwalking. Cartwright claims that a genuine sleepwalker who engages in complex criminal acts while asleep is utterly amnestic for the episode in the morning and attempts no cover-up of the deed. There is an individual and family history of sleepwalking and then after the tragedy there is intense grief, remorse, and efforts to cooperate in the investigation. Siclari et al. (2010) suggest other factors that can be used to establish a sleep disorder as a causative factor in sleep-related violence. First, as Cartwright says, there should be medical evidence (e.g., from an polysomnographic sleep study) of an underlying sleep disorder as well as a family or individual history of sleep symptoms. Next the violent act itself should conform to other independently established norms concerning sleep-related violent acts. For example, most such acts occur without apparent motivation and they are bitterly regretted upon awakening. There must also be precipitating factors to trigger a parasomnia such as prior sleep deprivation and thus increased homeostatic drive (see summary).

Presence of an underlying sleep disorder
- Presence of solid evidence supporting the diagnosis
- Previous occurrence of similar episodes

Characteristics of the act
- Occurs on awakening or immediately after falling asleep
- Abrupt onset and brief duration
- Impulsive, senseless, without apparent motivation
- Lack of awareness of individual during event
- Victim: coincidentally present, possible arousal stimulus on return to consciousness
- Perplexity, horror, no attempt to escape Amnesia for event

Table 5.1 (cont.)
Presence of precipitating factors
• Attempts to awaken the subject
• Intake of sedative/hypnotic drugs
• Prior sleep deprivation
• Alcohol or drug intoxication precludes the use of disorder of arousal in forensic cases

the parasomnia – the incomplete transition out of REM. The idea seems to be that REM biology encodes behaviors and cognitions (in the form of innate images that become the ISP hallucinations) that would alert the individual to danger in the form of an intruder. But this explanation would require that REM biology not only encodes basic engrams for protection against threat but in addition encodes with extreme detail "images" that relate to smell, sense of touch, and sense of the "presence" itself. How is it possible for memory images encoded into REM to produce the extraordinarily elaborate images and sensory experiences associated with ISP? For an innate threat detection system to produce something as elaborate as the ISP, phenomenology would require a virtual revolution in our understanding of REM and indeed of innate brain capacities. Nor can the innate threat detection theory explain the fact that the patients/individuals who experience ISP *are awake* with relatively clear consciousness. They can and do reflect on what they are experiencing. They have insight. They question its reality. The experience cannot be dismissed as mere hallucinatory phenomena. The patients/individuals who experience ISP do not only report victimization. Some report bliss and out of body experiences. The phenomenology is more akin to perceptual experiences than to hallucinations. Whatever the ultimate explanation of ISP will be, it will not be possible to describe it or understand it as mere hallucination.

5.3.10 Conclusions

The neuroscience of sleep and dreams teaches us that there are three basic brain states: waking, REM, and NREM sleep. What determines or creates and maintains each of these three states is a differing mixture or profile of brainstem-generated neurotransmitter (aminergic and cholinergic modulation) activity levels as well as differing forebrain activation and deactivation patterns, which were discussed in previous chapters. The three different brain activity profiles that give rise to the three different brain states must be thought of as probabilistic profiles. Each brain state's profile can be fully engaged or only partially engaged. Most importantly for understanding the experiences associated with parasomnias, the transitions between the brain states can also be complete or only partial. When one state ends another state begins if the transition between states is complete. But because the mechanisms that control brain states are probabilistic, transitions between states are virtually never entirely complete. When transitions between states are partial we get a hybrid brain state, for example, a mixture of REM and waking or a mixture of NREM and waking or REM with NREM. When these hybrid states occur we get the classic parasomnias.

For example, sleep paralysis represents a hybrid of REM and waking. The patient is conscious and awake but he is paralyzed and cannot move because the muscle atonia associated with REM is persisting into the wake state. In addition, the patient hallucinates an intruder possibly because many REM dreams are about potential threats and so on. Similarly, lucid dreams (to be discussed later) are a hybrid of REM and waking states because the dorsolateral prefrontal cortex is partially activated in lucid dreaming. In normal REM, the dorsolateral prefrontal cortex is deactivated. But when it is activated during REM the individual gains some awareness of self and so becomes aware that he is dreaming. Sleepwalking/talking and other NREM parasomnias represent a hybrid between NREM and waking. In these cases the individual remains in N2 or N3 sleep but can nevertheless engage in complex behavioral actions without awareness. Here the brain can coordinate complex behaviors without awareness because the waking state (presumably mediated by an activated dorsolateral prefrontal cortex) has intruded upon a brain not fully disengaged from slow wave activity. In REM behavior disorder the muscle atonia associated with REM is abolished due to disease. and thus the sleeping brain is not fully in REM and we get dream enactment behavior – once again complex actions and behaviors but this time under the control of the sleeping brain. The REM/wake and NREM/wake hybrid states suggest that consciousness requires participation of dorsolateral prefrontal cortex and its connections, as whenever that brain network is activated self-awareness and critical insight ensue.

We have discussed the hybrid states of REM plus waking and NREM plus waking. What about the hybrid of REM and NREM? Most sleep scientists believe that the REM/NREM hybrid just yields unconsciousness.

But it is possible that some parasomnias may involve the REM/NREM hybrid. Although nightmares typically arise out of REM, trauma-related nightmares can occur outside of REM. The phenomenon of sleep terrors suggests that the individual experiencing the NREM parasomnia is also experiencing an intense nightmare, as the individual typically screams in terror. Theoretically, I see no reason why some REM features like intense amygdala activity cannot temporarily occur with slow wave activity in many other parts of the brain. Such a state would produce a hellish nightmare.

Each brain state and their hybrids produce differing experiential worlds with the waking state being the state we choose to identify with. All other human cultures choose likewise, but some add the REM state as an additional state of being that, while not equal to the waking state, is nevertheless considered ontologically real and sometimes privileged vis-a-vis the waking state. These same cultures privilege some hybrid REM/wake states (e.g., waking dreams/visions). Apparently, no cultures privilege the NREM state, but many cultures produce religious, magical, and medical treatments to prevent hybrid NREM /wake states (e.g., sleep walking) and some REM/wake states (e.g., sleep paralysis). While the unusual states of consciousness associated with the parasomnias clearly interacts with culture, sleep science has yet to develop a clear evidence-based theory of these hybrid brain states, leaving it as a task for future sleep scientists.

Review Questions

- What might failures to transition from one brain state to another teach us about consciousness?
- What is the significance of abnormal N3 delta wave activity for NREM parasomnias?
- How does failure to transition out of REM explain sleep paralysis nightmares?
- What are the major causes and consequences of insomnia?

Further Reading

Lugaresi, E., Medori, R., Montagna, P., Baruzzi, A., Cortelli, P., Lugaresi, A., et al. (1986). Fatal familial insomnia and dysautonomia with selective degeneration of thalamic nuclei. *New England Journal of Medicine*, 315, 997–1003.

Mahowald, M. W., & Schenck, C. H. (2011). "REM sleep parasomnias." In M. Kryger, T. Roth, & W. C. Dement (eds.), *Principles and Practice of Sleep Medicine* (5th edn). Philadelphia: W. B. Saunders Co.

Mahowald, M. W., & Cramer Bornemann, M. A. (2011)."Non-REM arousal parasomnias." In M. Kryger, T. Roth, & W. C. Dement (eds.), *Principles and Practice of Sleep Medicine* (5th edn). Philadelphia: W. B. Saunders Co.

Matheson, E., & Hainer, B. L. (2017). Insomnia: Pharmacologic therapy. *American Family Physician*, 96(1), 29–35. Review. PMID: 28671376.

CHAPTER 6

Theories of REM and NREM Sleep

Learning Objectives

- Identify and evaluate the evidence for the claim that NREM promotes enhanced immune responses
- Evaluate strengths and weaknesses of the restorative theory of sleep
- Identify and evaluate the evidence for sleep-related memory consolidation processes
- Describe functional significance of REM-NREM physiologic interactions

6.1 Introduction

Although we know a lot about sleep, there is no scientific consensus on its function or functions. Its functions, however, must be extraordinarily significant given that it renders us vulnerable to predators each time it overcomes us. It is involuntary. Everyone must eventually succumb to sleep or die. We must have it as surely as we must have oxygen, food, and water. But we do not know why.

It is possible and even likely that sleep has more than one function. Indeed, NREM sleep may have separate functions from REM sleep and the two sleep states may have complementary or contrasting functions. The functions of sleep may have arisen in concert or separately during sleep's evolutionary history. If functions arose sequentially during evolutionary history, then later functions would likely utilize physiologic systems designed to meet earlier functional needs. For example, although lungs likely evolved for gas exchange, they now can also handle speech and language vocalization functions. Similarly, although mammalian sleep may have originally evolved for thermoregulatory purposes, it now is crucial for brain and cognitive functions as well.

Yet, we can find simple quiescent-activity patterns in even very simple organisms like the worm (*C. elegans*) which has only 302 neurons. If sleep can occur in these simple organisms without complex nervous systems, then the primordial form of sleep must be an emergent property of small neuronal assemblies.

6.2 NREM

As discussed in previous chapters, NREM is composed of three stages but there are no evidenced-based theories of the potential functions of N1 or N2 stage sleep. Therefore we will focus first on potential functions of stage N3 and specifically slow wave activity and then REM.

A tried-and-true method for discovery of function of a particular system in neurophysiology is to block or delete the system and then see what physiological functions are lost. In the 1980s, Allan Rechtschaffen and colleagues (Rechtschaffen et al., 1989) at the University of Chicago, studied the consequences of total sleep deprivation in rats. Using a variant of the platform method for sleep deprivation whenever the experimental rat fell asleep, it was woken up. Basically the platform method involved the rat sitting on a platform that dipped into water if the rat ever fell asleep. The water would then awaken the rat so the rat could never sleep. Control rats were given the same platform stimulation but allowed to sleep some of the time. Of course, this is an incredibly stressful procedure for rats so it is difficult to factor out the effects of stress from the effects of sleep deprivation per se. While the control rats were normal with no health consequences noted, the sleep-deprived rats died after sixteen to twenty-one days without sleep. The sleep-deprived rats lost weight even though they ate voraciously. Their fur became oily and matted, and they developed sores on their skin and feet. They could no longer regulate their metabolic and internal heat systems. Most died of septicemia, indicating immune system collapse.

6.2.1 NREM Sleep Promotes Optimal Immune System Responses

These results and others we will review suggest that sleep, and SWS in particular, very likely contributes to regulation of immune system response. In humans and other animals sleep loss leads to the increased production of pro-inflammatory cytokines. Chronic sleep loss leads to chronic inflammation. Sleep duration of laboratory animals increases after an infection when mounting an immune response. Presumably evolved increases in sleep duration allow animals to channel more metabolic resources into their immune system components, maintenance, and repair. Short-term increases in sleep duration appear to be triggered by immunomodulatory cytokines that are released by white blood cells during immune reactions (Opp and Krueger, 2015). For example, administration of interleukin I (IL1) is associated with immediate production of slow wave sleep. IL-1 stimulates the synthesis and/or release of the growth hormone-releasing hormone, prostaglandin D2, and adenosine. Each of these substances is implicated in regulating or modulating NREM sleep, and antagonizing these systems attenuates or blocks IL-1-induced increases in NREM sleep. Adenosine production, as reviewed in previous chapters, is known to be directly related to slow wave sleep homeostatic mechanisms. If larger numbers of white blood cells produce a greater immune response to antigenic challenge, and hence a greater release of sleep promoting cytokines, this could potentially drive evolutionary increases in sleep durations.

Preston et al. (2009) assessed the correlated evolution of sleep and the immune system. To do so they extracted data on sleeping times for different mammalian species from the published literature and matched these data where possible with white blood cell counts reported by the International Species Information System (ISIS). White blood cell counts were used as a proxy for immune system investment as they are central to all immune responses and are a validated measure of immunocompetence. White blood cells originate in bone marrow and are derived from the same hematopoietic stem cells that produce red blood cells and platelets. As these latter cells have no direct immunological function, the investigators used them as natural controls to test the specificity of any relationship between sleep and the immune system. If a key selective advantage of NREM sleep is that it allows greater investment in the immune system, then species that sleep for longer periods of time should have increased numbers of immune cells in circulation, but there should be no similar relationship with control cells. After matching species values from each database the authors were able to analyze data for twenty-six mammalian species while controlling for confounding factors (e.g., body size and activity period). As expected, species that engaged in more sleep had higher numbers of white blood cells circulating in peripheral blood. A fourteen-hour increase in sleeping times across species corresponded to an additional 30 million white blood cells in each milliliter of blood (a 615 percent increase). Crucially, no similar patterns were evident with either red blood cells or platelets. These relationships were also tested using phylogenetically independent contrast methods to account for the lack of statistical independence in species data. These analyses identify evolutionary change in relation to other variables (in this case change in sleep durations of different lineages in relation to immunity variables). Preston and colleagues found that when lineages evolved longer sleep durations, they also increased their white blood cell counts. Again, this relationship was specific to immune cells, leading to an increase in the ratio of immune cells to other blood cell types when species evolved longer sleeping durations. The lineages and species that developed longer sleep durations also turned out to be less parasitized. That is, those species' parasite loads were far lighter than species with shorter sleep durations even after accounting for potential confounds like body weight, size, ecologic niche, and activity schedules. These data strongly support the contention that one evolutionary function of NREM sleep is that it promotes immunocompetence.

6.2.2 Sleep Is for Rest/Replenishment: Sleep Restores Energy

The most common sense explanation for sleep is that it restores our energy level. These energy stores get depleted during wake and then replenished during sleep – or so the theory goes. Certainly, overall metabolic rates decline during sleep relative to the quiet resting state during wake. But the energy saving one gets during sleep-related declines in metabolic rates relative to wake-related rest periods turns out to be not that substantial. So the feeling of restoration after a good night's sleep must be related to more than just the energy saving one could get from quiet rest.

The brain accounts for about 20 percent of the entire body's energy expenditure, even though it is only about 2 percent of the total body mass. The brain's only energy source is the sugar glucose. Sugar in the brain is manifested as glycogen. Glycogen molecules are long, branched chains of glucose molecules. There are two major neural cell types in the brain – neurons and glial cells. Glia make up about 90 percent of brain tissue, and they synthesize and store glycogen. When the activity in a brain area suddenly and rapidly increases, and the glucose in the blood flowing through that area is not sufficient to fuel that activity, the glia rapidly break down their glycogen and supply fuel to the neurons.

Glia also forms a kind of lymphatic system for neurons. Just as the lymph nodes in your body remove toxic by-products of the metabolic machinery in your body so too does the glymphatic system help to remove toxic by-products of the neuronal metabolic machinery. During NREM N3 this glymphatic system steps up its activity ten- to twenty-fold relative to its daytime activity. During N3 the glial cells shrink to half their size during NREM, thus allowing CSF to bathe the neurons and flush out toxic by-products from the system. One of these toxic by-products of neuronal activity is amyloid proteins, which are known to entangle and kill neurons building up clumps of dead tissue in the brain that in turn can ultimately contribute to neurodegenerative disorders like Alzheimer's disease.

As mentioned glia also participate in the breakdown of glycogen in order to produce fuel for the brain. One potential major function of N3 SWS is to enable the restoration of the brain energy reserves in the form of glycogen. The brain and body's key metabolic machinery to produce energy is adenosine triphosphate (ATP). The accumulation of extracellular adenosine is a signal that cells or tissues are running out of energy. In the brain, adenosine opens potassium channels in the neuronal cell membrane. Opening those channels increases the movement of positively charged potassium ions out of the neurons. This movement of positive charges leaves behind negative charges, so the electrical potential across the membrane becomes more negative. We say that the neuron is hyperpolarized. When the calcium channels open, calcium rushes into the neuron, it becomes depolarized, and the neuron generates action potentials. It is these action potentials that are measured as slow waves in the EEG. Bennington and Heller (1995) demonstrated adenosine activity levels covaried with brain slow wave activity. When they injected a molecule that mimics the action of adenosine into the blood or brains of rats, they showed what appeared to be normal sleep for several hours with very high slow wave activity. During sleep, adenosine levels gradually fall in all brain areas, but during waking, adenosine levels gradually and significantly rise predominantly in two brain areas – the cerebral cortex and the basal forebrain. Adenosine acts in the basal forebrain to influence the switch from wake to sleep and to maintain this flip-flop switch in the sleep position; second, it acts in the cortex to produce and sustain the slow wave activity that seems to be the homeostatically regulated variable of sleep.

Glycogen breakdown (known as glycogenolysis) is accomplished through the actions of an enzyme called glycogen phosphorylase. Glycogen synthesis is accomplished through the actions of an enzyme called glycogen synthase. The neurochemicals that promote wake, such as norepinephrine, activate the glycogen breakdown enzyme and inhibit the glycogen synthesis enzyme. When those neurochemicals are withdrawn – less activity in the brain stem nuclei that promote wake – the glycogen breakdown enzyme is inhibited, and the glycogen synthesis enzyme is activated. In addition, ATP inhibits the glycogen breakdown enzyme. Thus, if the cell has plenty of energy and its ATP levels are high, it does not use its glycogen reserves. During wake, the glia are poised to give up their glycogen at a moment's notice if energy levels start to fall, and during sleep, the glia are put into the mode of replacing their glycogen stores.

Adenosine seems to have dual actions: working at the level of the basal forebrain to promote the transition to sleep and working at the level of the cortex to promote the intensity of sleep. It turns out that activity in different regions of the cortex – activity that could deplete the glycogen in those specific areas – result in regional sleep responses. Cortical regions that work harder, such as the ventromedial portions of the frontal lobes, have greater slow wave activity during subsequent sleep.

One of the strongest pieces of evidence that N3 sleep functions to restore energy is the phenomena of sleep rebound after sleep deprivation. Periods of enforced waking lead to increased NREM sleep drive or sleepiness. This sleep need can be relieved by subsequent sleep, thus supporting the restorative theory for NREM sleep. Interestingly, the recovery sleep typically occurs first for NREM and only after NREM is made up does REM follow suit. Sleep deprivation, in other words, produces compensatory increases in both NREM sleep time (specifically NREM delta activity) and REM sleep time during recovery sleep, but NREM is made up first. NREM delta activity has been shown to accumulate during normal periods of consolidated wakefulness and it discharges or declines during subsequent NREM sleep. Apparently mammals need a certain amount of slow wave sleep (SWS) in order to function properly.

Many theorists of sleep function have argued that NREM functions to restore physiological functioning. Certainly the subjective feeling of being refreshed after a good night's sleep supports these restorative theories as do the findings of sleep rebound after sleep deprivation. A potential problem for the restorative theory of N3 SWS is that there is a rebound of delta sleep (slow wave NREM sleep) after *hibernation* in hibernating animals. Hibernation, of course, is a low energy state and thus should not need a process to restore energy or to repair tissue since little or no energy was consumed and little or no tissue was damaged during the hibernation period. Indeed the standard explanation for hibernation is that it is a state designed to conserve energy! Yet animals undergoing hibernation or torpor generally have to arouse periodically in order to engage in slow wave activity.

6.2.3 NREM Restore Optimal Cognitive Performance for Frontal Lobes

Sleep deprivation leads to performance decrements on a variety of cognitive tasks – especially tasks that depend on integrity of the frontal lobes (Achermann et al., 2001; Anderson and Horne, 2003). The degree of impairment is wake-dependent and use-dependent. The greater the use of the frontal lobes for tasks that depend on the frontal lobes, the greater the degree of compensatory delta activity in the frontal lobes. Normal performance can be restored by sleep in a sleep dose-dependent manner – the more intense the delta activity the better the subsequent performance on the cognitive tasks. Clearly, sleep can function to restore cognitive performance, particularly for tasks depending on the frontal lobes.

6.2.4 NREM Promotes Optimal Neuronal Connectivity

Perhaps the most commonly proposed function for sleep put forward by neuroscientists is that sleep promotes neuronal connectivity (Benington and Frank, 2003; Huber et al., 2004). Synapses between neurons and via extracellular signaling regulatory molecules form functional networks that are the physiologic basis of the brain/mind. Synapses are formed on the basis of use; they are activity-dependent. The greater the activity, the greater and the stronger the synaptic connectivity. Use and reuse of synapses leads to strengthening of synaptic efficacy of active synapses and therefore reuse. But this strengthening of connections leads to problems for brain dynamics. The eventual consequence of use and reuse of synaptic circuits would be an overly connected set of rigid networks and ultimately a totally connected brain without any residual brain plasticity. Without plasticity, of course, learning would be impossible. Negative feedback mechanisms are needed to disturb rigidly connected networks and to continuously introduce plasticity. Sleep, in these connectivity theories, paradoxically does two things: It performs that function of introducing disruption of rigidly connected networks while also strengthening use-related synapses. It both strengthens some synapses and weakens others. How does sleep simultaneously strengthen synapses in a use-dependent fashion while also introducing mechanisms that avoid creation of rigid networks? We do not yet know the answer to this question.

6.3 REM

The case for a functional role for REM is more complicated than that of NREM. In the case of NREM we have seen that deprivation of NREM produces a clear compensatory rebound effect of recovery NREM sleep that apparently makes up for some of the lost NREM sleep. After decades of experimental work involving hundreds of REM sleep deprivation (RSD) experiments (mostly in rats, cats, and humans) there is still no consensus on whether the compensatory REM rebound represents a form of sleep that must be made up (i.e., obligate sleep; see Horne, 2000). Aside from a partial REM rebound effect, no significant psychologic or biologic effects are noted with REMD – at least for short-term REMD in humans. With prolonged (sixteen to fifty-four days) REM deprivation there appears to be a heavy price to pay; in rats prolonged REM deprivation leads to death (Rechtschaffen et al.,1989). But it is questionable whether death is due to selective REM deprivation since SWS deprivation results in death as well (in twenty-three to sixty-six days). In addition, it is difficult to separate out the aversive/stressful effects of REM deprivation from effects of REM deprivation per se. It is very difficult to selectively deprive an animal of a given sleep type over a long period of time. Death in the prolonged SWS/REMD studies is believed to be due to a significant decline in core body temperature (as much as 2C) with compensatory attempts to increase temperature through increased energy expenditure. Another potential cause of death in rats after REMD may be a systemic bacterial infection. On the other hand administration of antibiotics to REM-deprived rats did not prevent death.

REM probably does *not* function to restore energy. REM does not appear to replenish stores of metabolic energy – instead it dissipates significant amounts of energy. Neuroimaging studies of REM show that it reaches brain activation levels and brain glucose utilization levels exceeding those of the waking state. If the restorative theory is correct then the energetic gains that accrue from sleep must be greater than what can be achieved by simple daytime rest. Another problem with the energy replenishment or energy conservation theories is that body temperature does not decrease during REM and metabolic activity does not decrease during REM. Nor do metabolic rates correlate with REM times. If we recall that REM alternates with NREM throughout the night then energetic savings would have to accrue selectively during the NREM periods. The energy savings must somehow be maintained across REM periods to result in any significant net reduction in metabolic rates across the night, or else whatever savings accrued in a given NREM period would be immediately dissipated in a subsequent REM period, resulting in no net gain for the animal.

6.3.1 Memory Consolidation

A number of sleep researchers have proposed that REM functions to consolidate various types of memories (Stickgold, 2005; Smith, 1995).

REM times, for example, increase after intense learning episodes, particularly after procedural types of learning tasks. Consolidation of learning of Morris water maze tasks in rats can be blocked if the animal is deprived of REM during a critical time window, which typically occurs some time (on the order of hours) after the learning trials. By comparison Crick and Mitchison (1983) postulated a kind of reverse learning function of REM to rid relevant neural networks of unnecessary bits of information. Crick and Mitchison, however, did not consider the role of NREM.

Despite the focus on REM, sleep-associated consolidation of information gathered during the wake state appears to depend on hippocampal-cortical interactions that occur during both SWS and REM and involve some sort of replay of learned associations acquired while awake during REM sleep (Buzsaki, 1996; Plihal and Born, 1997; Smith, 1995; Wilson and McNaughton, 1994). Wilson and McNaughton (1994), for example, showed that hippocampal cells that are active when rats learn a new maze are also active during subsequent sleep. Using PET scanning techniques, similar effects (reactivation of brain sites activated during learning) have been reported in humans. Stickgold found that learning a visual discrimination task was disrupted by selective deprivation of both REM and NREM. Similarly, Plihal and Born (1997) have reported that learning of paired associates and mental rotation tasks but not procedural memory tasks, is dependent on subsequent NREM (early sleep) rather than REM (late morning sleep) periods for their consolidation. Thus, while both sleep states appear to participate in learning and memory, their roles in consolidation of memories are postulated to be quite different.

While both sleep states probably participate in formation and consolidation of memories, critics have pointed out that individuals with lesions to the brainstem and subsequent loss of REM can nevertheless learn. In addition, individuals with reductions in REM due to sleep apnea or to antidepressant medications can nevertheless learn. The properties of both REM and NREM appear to be less than optimal for learning.

There is a general consensus that NREM sleep, especially SWS, is essential for the consolidation of hippocampus-dependent episodic and spatial memories, whereas REM sleep is more important for procedural and emotional memory consolidation (Walker and Stickgold, 2004). While Carlyle Smith was an early pioneer in the study of sleep-related memory consolidation effects, Plihal and Born (1997) conducted a landmark study in the field by capitalizing on the unequal distribution of NREM (including SWS) and REM sleep in different parts of the night.

They assessed the recall of word pairs (an episodic memory task) as well as performance on a mirror-tracing task (which taps procedural memory) after retention intervals of early sleep (the first three to four hours of the sleep cycle) and late sleep (the last three to four hours of the sleep cycle).

Plihal and Born found that recall of word pairs – the episodic task – improved significantly more after a three-hour sleep period rich in SWS than after a three-hour sleep period rich in REM or a three-hour period of wakefulness. The procedural memory task, on the other hand, improved significantly more after a three-hour sleep period rich in REM than after three hours spent either in SWS or awake. In short, retention of episodic memories seemed to be more dependent on SWS than on REM, while procedural memory was more dependent on REM than SWS. While this experiment and many others like it demonstrated that each sleep state (NREM vs. REM) affected different types of memories, the intense activation of the limbic system, the amygdala, and ventral medial prefrontal cortex during REM (Maquet et al., 1996) sleep suggested that it would also be crucial for the consolidation of emotional memories.

Emotional memories, which rely critically on the amygdala for their consolidation, do indeed appear to benefit most from REM sleep. In a typical study of the role of sleep in emotional memory consolidation, Wagner et al. (2001) found that three hours of late night REM-rich sleep (but not three hours of early night slow wave-rich sleep or three hours of wakefulness) facilitated memory for narratives with intensely negative emotional content.

What about the role of REM dreams in memory processing? It may be that dreams do not affect memory consolidation processes at all. Thus there is nothing much to say about dreams and memory consolidation processes except that the two have nothing to do with one another. Another possibility is that dreams do not causally participate in the memory consolidation process but they do reflect it – they are by-products of the process in this view (e.g., Foulkes, 1985). So we can learn about memory consolidation by studying the ways in which dream content change over a single night of sleep and how it changes over time within a single person's life. A third school of thought asserts that dreams do not merely reflect memory consolidation processes but instead are causally implicated and may even be required for the consolidation of certain types of memories – especially emotional memories. Nielsen's (Nielsen et al., 2004) work on the dream lag effect is instructive. The dream lag effect refers to the empirical finding that items being encoded into long-term memory sometimes appear in one's dreams usually the night after the event was experienced and then subsequently five to seven days later. If dreams were mere reflections of ongoing memory consolidation processes, then one would expect dreams to reflect ongoing memory experiences each night, but instead we get this interesting lag effect, which suggests a more important role for dreams than previously expected. Another line of evidence that suggests an important role for dreams in memory consolidation processes comes from Hartmann's work (Hartmann, 1998) on central images in nightmares that apparently facilitate encoding of intense emotions into long-term memory.

6.3.2 Dialogue between the Hippocampus and Cortex during REM

It has been known for years that damage (via stroke or head injury or surgery, etc.) to the hippocampus impairs acquisition of new memories. Recent advances in neuroplasticity research has demonstrated that one of the areas of the brain that can generate new neurons (neurogenesis) is the hippocampus. Sleep deprivation can impede neurogenesis in the hippocampus.

Most models of how sleep facilitates memory processes involves communication between the hippocampus, amygdala, and the cerebral cortex, where long-term memories are stored and formatted for later use in cognitive processes. In these models, the hippocampus is considered a temporary repository for abstracting context from memories, the amygdala separates context from emotions, and the cortex is the site where context-free memories are stored over long periods. Both the hippocampus and the amygdala (along with critical subcortical sites such as the dopaminergic "salience system" centered in the ventral striatum) act as selectors or gatekeepers or sieves for what information ultimately gets encoded into long-term stores versus what information gets discarded. During sleep external input is reduced so memory consolidation processes can occur "offline," free of potentially interfering effects of ongoing incoming information from the external environment. Each of the two major sleep states are believed to play a specialized role in the preparation of (e.g., the encoding and formatting) and storing of long term memories with NREM playing a central role in stripping context from episodic and procedural memories and REM playing a central role in stripping context from emotional memories.

As the brain cycles between NREM SWS and REM across the night, there occurs a complex interaction between activity patterns in the amygdala/hippocampus subcortically and the cortex. The communication between the hippocampus and cortex involves an interesting choreography of different brain waves. The slow waves of non-REM sleep, the sleep spindles, which originate in the circuits involving the thalamus and the cortex and the brief sharp-wave ripple events that originate in the hippocampus, all appear to index key steps in the memory consolidation process. Sleep spindles index activation of the thalamus and cortex while the slow wave oscillations index synchronizing activity in the hippocampus so that hippocampal activity also occurs in frames synced up with the spindling activity in the thalamus/cortex. As a result, sleep spindles and sharp-wave ripple events in the hippocampus occur together. It is believed that these spindle-ripple events reflect communication of information between the hippocampus and the cortex. In short, during non-REM sleep, there is a dialogue between the hippocampus and the cortex that is coordinated by slow waves, sleep spindles, and sharp-wave ripples.

While information appears to flow from the hippocampus to the cortex during SWS and is indexed by sleep spindles and sharp-wave ripple activity, theta rhythms are thought to support the transfer of information in the opposite direction during REM sleep. Theta waves enhance hippocampal long-term potentiation (LTP), a candidate mechanism for memory formation. Interestingly, this synchronization with theta wave activity during REM sleep appears to shift from in-phase (i.e., correlating with the peak activity of the theta wave) to out-of-phase (correlated with the troughs of inactivity) over four to seven days of daily exposure to a new environment. Such a shift could produce a switch from LTP and memory consolidation to long-term depression (LTD) and memory erasure. The time course of this shift is similar to the dream-lag effect mentioned earlier and suggests that that is the time required for hippocampally dependent memories to be transferred to the neocortex for long-term storage.

Sejnowski and Destexhe (2000) provided a model of the sleep-related consolidation process that depends on spindle oscillations during early SWS and an alternating pattern between slow-wave complexes and brief episodes of fast oscillations as SWS deepens. Together, these considerations suggest a model of sleep-dependent sequential memory processing in which different types or aspects of memories, including emotional memories, are processed progressively over the course of the night. In this model, specific memories from the recent past could be identified at sleep onset for subsequent reprocessing, and then stabilized (via context stripping) and/or strengthened, possibly during NREM sleep and integrated into cortical networks during REM. The alternating REM and

---

Table 6.1 Targeted memory reactivation in sleep

Targeted memory activation refers to a new technique to get at memories during sleep. Researchers present cues or stimuli such as a smell that was associated with events or information or materials that the subject learned prior to sleep. Then when the subject is asleep the subject is re-exposed to the associated cues (e.g., a smell) and then later tested (after awakening) for memory of the original materials. When the cues are presented to the subject during sleep there is better retention of the original materials. For example, if you studied a foreign language in the presence of the smell of roses and then went to sleep. You would do better on a test of that foreign language after awakening if you had smelled roses during sleep. The smell facilitates consolidation of the memory during sleep.

TMR has been shown to result in a performance gain of around 20%, as compared to natural sleep. This gain in performance could make a huge difference for people who are experiencing memory loss. Essentially TMR is a kind of priming or activating of the memory system using specific sensory cues. Priming effects in social psychology are generally small effects and have proven difficult to replicate. Experimental data in TMR studies are not consistent across studies and extensive research is warranted to address many open questions before TMR can be considered as established, effective, and safe.

Schouten DI, Pereira SI, Tops M, Louzada FM. (2017). "State of the art on targeted memory reactivation: Sleep your way to enhanced cognition." Sleep Medicine Reviews; 32:123–131. doi: 10.1016/j.smrv.2016.04.002. Epub 2016 Apr 21. Review. PMID: 27296303.

NREM periods would then permit several cycles of stabilization and integration.

In summary, while REM clearly plays a crucial role in memory consolidation it does so in concert with NREM sleep states. Does REM exhibit any functions not also exhibited by NREM sleep states? The answer appears to be yes.

6.3.3 REM Functions to Promote Brain Development

We spoke of REM's role in brain development in an earlier chapter. Here we will discuss some of the potential functional implications of the relation between REM and brain development. Early (neonatal) suppression of REM results in later (adult) alterations in behavior or in neurotransmitter activity or in reductions in cell and tissue volumes in certain regions of the cerebral cortex. The large amount of REM that occurs during the juvenile period also suggests a specific role for REM in brain development.

But it is unclear how a physiologic process like REM would promote brain development. REM only selectively activates certain parts of the brain in both juveniles and adults. If whole brain development is desired (and it surely should be), and brain activation serves to retain functional synaptic circuits, then why not create a system that activates whole brain rather than only selected regions of the brain? In addition, the REM-related autonomic nervous system storms, the collapse in thermoregulatory reflexes during REM and the muscle atonia during REM argues against a simple effect on brain development. In addition, it is difficult to understand why, if REM's function is purely to promote brain development, it should persist into adulthood or have the properties it has both in the juvenile and in the adult. Some juvenile aquatic mammals may not have REM at all, yet their brain growth is normal.

Perhaps rapid eye movements are crucial for only a portion of the brain – in this case the brain centers (e.g., frontal eye fields and visual centers) dedicated to visual processing. The available data is consistent with this more focused brain development function for REM.

Jouvet (1999) has suggested yet another version of the brain development hypothesis for REM. He has suggested that REM is important for maintenance of synaptic circuits that mediate inherited behaviors. If the cells that mediate the muscle atonia associated with REM are destroyed in cats, you see them engage in instinctual predatory behaviors when they go into REM sleep. The penile erections associated with REM are another example of instinctual behaviors manifested in REM.

6.3.4 REM Regulates Expressions of Emotions and/or Emotional Balance

Many studies involving deprivation of REM have resulted in enhanced motivational states and changes in emotional state. Thus, some investigators have suggested that REM functions to inhibit or to modulate emotional arousal and motivational striving. Cartwright (2010) argued that daytime mood is associated with nighttime sleep amount and quality. Vogel demonstrated that REM deprivation improves depressive mood states in depressed patients (Vogel, 1999). REMD presumably alleviates depression by enhancing drives and other motivated behaviors (i.e., REMD removes REM's tonic inhibitory effects on drives and emotions). Hartmann (1998) has argued that REM values and REM dream content vary with a person's stress levels and emotional history and that REM dreaming functions to rebalance emotional responses. Neuroimaging studies are consistent with the emotional regulation view of REM as REM is associated with high activation levels in the limbic system and the amygdala. Van der Helm and Walker (2011) have produced experimental evidence that supports a role for REM in emotional memory consolidation and emotional regulation. Sleep periods rich in REM sleep as opposed to NREM sleep are associated with significantly greater amounts of emotional memory consolidation and recall. REM sleep is rich in acetylcholine activity (which is known to be crucial for memory encoding processes) and may act to decontextualize negative or fearful memories and thus make them easier to consolidate into long-term memory stores.

6.3.5 NREM-REM Interactions and Genetic Conflict

We have seen that REM and NREM may sometimes interact in an antagonistic fashion such that REM undoes something NREM does and vice versa. REM and NREM seem to express functionally antagonistic traits and processes across a spectrum of functional states (see Table 6.2). REM and NREM are in fact in mutual inhibitory balance – when values of NREM increase, values of REM decrease and vice versa. REM sleep is promoted by cholinergic neurons originating within the LDT/PPT and is inhibited by noradrenergic and serotonergic neurons in the locus coeruleus (LC) and dorsal raphe (DR), respectively. NREM sleep is promoted by turning off the cells that promote REM or wake. For example, inhibiting (via GABA-ergic-mediated processes) the firing of cells in the reticular activating system, LC, DR, and thalamus, results in synchronous bursts of thalamic and then cortical neurons, the loss of wake-related alpha waves, and gradual slowing of the forebrain EEG frequency. Removal of inhibition exerted by aminergic efferents on cholinergic cells in the LDT/PPT results in reentry into REM.

Why are there only two major sleep states and why do they interact in this antagonistic fashion? The simplest explanation for this state of affairs is that REM and NREM are regulated by separate sets of genes with opposing genetic or evolutionary interests (McNamara, 2004). Inbred mice strains C57BL and C57BR are associated with increased REM and short SWS episodes, while the BALB/c strain is associated with short REM and long NREM episodes, indicating separate genetic influences on REM and NREM sleep amounts.

Some neurodevelopmental sleep syndromes express strikingly opposite profiles in terms of sleep and related clinical characteristics and these

Table 6.2 REM-NREM characteristics suggesting opposing functional states

	REM	NREM
Mouse strains indicating separate genetic influences	C57BL and C57BR are associated with increased REM and short SWS episodes.	BALB/c is associated with short REM and long NREM episodes.
Prader-Willi syndrome (paternal deletions / maternal additions on C15)	Decreased	Increased
Excessive sleepiness		
Angelman syndrome (paternal additions/ maternal deletions on C15)	Increased	Decreased
sleeplessness		
Nursing (rat)	Neonate typically in REM during nursing and REM % increases during milk ingestion up to 4% of body weight.	Mother must be in NREM-SWS for milk ejection to occur.
Percent of total sleep time in adult	20–25%	75–80%
Distribution during sleep phase	Predominates in last third of night	Predominates in first third of night
Response to infection	Decreased	Increased
Sleep deprivation-related rebound (both REM and NREM)	Repaid after NREM debt paid	Repaid before REM
Cerebral blood flow	Increased; social brain network structures reconnected and activated	Decreased; social brain network structures taken off-line
Arousal thresholds	+	++
Eye movements	Rapid eye movements with occasional bursts or clusters of REMs	Slow rolling eye movements
EEG	"Desynchronized"	Synchronized
	Phasic events: REM bursts, muscle twitching, middle ear	

Table 6.2 (cont.)

	REM	NREM
	muscle activity, Hippocampal theta waves	
	Tonic events: muscle hypotonia or atonia, especially in the anti-gravity muscles, penile tumescence	
		Stage NI (light falling asleep), Vivid dream-like imagery
		Stage N2 (light sleep with K-complexes and spindles)
		Stage N3 slow wave sleep with delta waves
Muscle tone	Decreased	Intact
Metabolic rate under thermoneutral conditions	Increased	Decreased
Thermoregulatory reflexes	Decreased to absent	Present
ANS	Increased variability/ANS storms/increased HR and BP	No significant changes
Neurochemistry	Cholinergic REM-on cells 5-HT and NE REM-off cells	GABA important for NREM onset
Parasomnias/sleep disorders	Nightmares, narcolepsy; depression	Sleep terrors, sleep walking, i.e., confusional arousals
Mentation	Vivid dreams with narrative structure	N3 Ruminative; N2 less story-like dreams; N1 vivid imagery
Hormones	Somatostatin Prolactin	Growth hormone GHRH

data suggest the ultimate cause of these syndromes lies in a sets of genes that control expression of these contrasting clinical phenotypes. For example, Kleine-Levin syndrome affects mainly young males and, like Prader-Willi syndrome (PWS, described shortly), is characterized by bouts of hypersomnia, compulsive eating, cognitive changes ("dreamy" states and derealization), signs of dysautonomia, and, unlike Prader-Willi, episodes of hypersexuality. Anorexia nervosa on the other hand affects mainly young females and is characterized by bouts of sleeplessness, self-starvation, cognitive changes, and hyposexuality.

Like anorexia and Kleine-Levin, Angelman and Prader-Willi syndromes are neurodevelopmental syndromes that involve opposite and contrasting sleep state changes. Prader-Willi syndrome is associated with maternal additions/paternal deletions of alleles at chromosome 15q11–13 and is characterized by poor sucking response, temperature control abnormalities, and excessive sleepiness. Sleep architecture changes have also been noted in children and young adults with PWS, most specifically REM sleep abnormalities such as sleep onset REM periods, REM fragmentation, intrusion of REM into stage 2 sleep, and short latencies to REM. Conversely, Angelman syndrome is associated with paternal additions/maternal deletions on chromosome 15q11–13 and is characterized by prolonged sucking, severe mental retardation, and insomnia or reductions in sleep. These children may sleep as little as one to five hours a night, with frequent and prolonged night wakings.

These syndromes can be construed as disorders related to the phenomenon of genomic imprinting (Haig, 2002; Isles et al., 2006; Ubeda and Gardner, 2010). Imprinting involves the inactivation or silencing of one allele of a gene, depending on its parental origin. Expression of the associated allele likewise depends on whether it was inherited from the father or the mother. Haig's (2002) evolutionary conflict model of the way genomic imprinting works suggests that paternally derived alleles act to enhance growth of a developing fetus or child regardless of its effects on the mother or siblings of the child, and that maternally derived alleles act to restrain growth or transfer of resources to any given offspring. The mother wants to restrain growth as it becomes easier to care for that child while also caring for the other children (siblings) as well. It is in her genetic interests to raise as many offspring as possible so she has to divide up her investment across all her young. When the child is asleep the mother can turn her attention to other siblings or perhaps get some sleep herself. The father's genetic interest is in having the current child get all available resources without limit. So the father wants the child awake and demanding more resources from the mother at all times. The reason the father wants to invest without limits in the current child is because he is much more certain of paternity (that he is the real biological father) for the current child than he is of future possible children. Independent studies have shown that "extra-pair couplings" that cuckold the father occur at significantly high rates in most mammalian lineages and in many avian species as well. The father has to assume that the next child the mother has will not be his so he wants the mother to invest all she has in his current child and thus increase his fitness accordingly.

Tucci and colleagues (Tucci 2016) showed that loss of expression of paternal Snord116 results in enhanced REM sleep, implying that the normal function of this gene is to decrease REM sleep. Double expression of maternal Gnas (due to loss of imprinting) results in decreased REM sleep, which might imply that the normal role of imprinted single dose Gnas is also to decrease REM (assuming additive effects of expressed gene dosage of Gnas on REM).

Imprinted genes expressed in the brain can shape brain function and behavior. Garfield et al. (2011) studied the gene Grb10 which is expressed from the maternal allele during embryogenesis; Grb10 encodes an intracellular adaptor protein that can interact with several receptor tyrosine kinases and downstream signalling molecules. Tyrosine kinase is a rate-limiting enzyme important in the metabolism of several neuromodulators including dopamine – the central neuromodulator involved in reward and motivational behaviors. Garfield et al. demonstrated that loss of the peripherally expressed maternal allele leads to significant fetal and placental overgrowth and that in the adult, all grooming and social dominance behaviors increase in paternal Grb10-deficient animals. Thus, Grb10 influences both fetal growth and adult behavior, owing to actions of the two parental alleles in different tissues at different times in the lifecycle.

We have seen in a previous chapter that REM sleep may involve relatively selective activation of the brain network known as the "social brain network." The social brain network includes subcortical hypothalamic, amygdalar, and limbic sites as well as ventromedial prefrontal sites. All of these sites may be differentially influenced by paternal line genes. Maternal line genes, conversely, may influence the parietal-prefrontal network centered on the dorsal striatum and caudate nuclei and projecting to dorsolateral prefrontal lobes. Keverne and colleagues (Keverne and Curley, 2008) showed that functionally distinct regions of the brain may reflect the distinct contributions of the maternal and paternal genomes with paternal line genes influencing a circuit centered on the hypothalamus and limbic regions and maternal line genes expressed more often in the neocortex.

If during the course of the night NREM involves the gradual deactivation or the taking off-line of key structures of the social brain network and REM gradually reactivates these structures, and if imprinted genes control these deactivation and reactivation sequences during each sleep cycle, then sleep may be construed as a theater of evolutionary genetic conflict with maternal line genes battling paternal line genes each night over control of the organism's brain structures in the social brain network, and daytime social (ultimately reproductive) behaviors.

6.4 Conclusions

In all of the foregoing theories of REM and NREM functions we have been assuming that the sleep state is doing something for the wake state; i.e., that NREM SWS restores energy for waking consciousness or that REM supports emotional memory consolidation for waking consciousness. But it is also possible that the functions of REM and NREM have more to do with the sleep states themselves rather than with waking consciousness. REM may be undoing something that NREM is doing since REM typically follows NREM in the sleep cycle. Or conversely, NREM SWS may be doing something important for the organism (e.g., immune system repair) but that function is costly, so REM functions to complete, complement, repair, or undo something that NREM had to do to accomplish its primary functions. In this scenario, SWS sleep repairs the immune system each night, but that is so onerous a job that NREM then requires REM to restore NREM's functional capacity so that it can do its immune system repair again the following night.

These sorts of scenarios raise fundamental questions about REM and NREM: How are these two forms of sleep related? Are they mutually inhibitory? Do they support or oppose one another's effects? Are they antagonistic or complementary? Let us take the scenario just mentioned where REM undoes something or repairs something with NREM that NREM needs to accomplish its primary function (immune system repair). In this scenario the wake state creates a need for non-REM sleep, and the expression of non-REM sleep (not something during wake) creates the need for REM sleep. In other words, the longer you are awake the greater the intensity and duration of NREM and likewise, the longer or more intense the NREM, the more intense the subsequent REM episodes will be. Delta waves index the intensity dimension for SWS and eye movement density index the intensity dimension for REM. If REM indices are in reaction to or oppose those of SWS indices then the need for REM sleep might be due to or related to the delta waves occurring in SWS during NREM. Benington and Heller (1994) noted that percentage REM (of total twenty-four-hour period) was significantly associated with percentage NREM, not to percentage of time spent awake.

If NREM sleep is homeostatically regulated but REM need depends on NREM need, then the relationship between the two sleep phases should be partially but not entirely opposing. REM need should build up during NREM sleep, and NREM need should build up during waking. As the REM need accumulates during NREM sleep, it is more likely to intrude into waking state or to interrupt the NREM episode. The drive to enter REM sleep – in other words, the magnitude of the need for REM sleep, would then be another indicator of homeostatic regulatory process at work in the relation between the two sleep states. NREM sleep undoes something that occurs during waking life and REM undoes something that occurs during NREM in this theoretical approach to the two sleep states. In this scenario, however, REM is in service to NREM while NREM is in service to waking consciousness.

Yet another theoretical possibility is that while NREM may be in service to the waking state (e.g., immune system repair), REM is not in service to NREM but actually opposes NREM physiology. This sort of scenario could happen if sleep states are influenced by evolutionary genetic conflict as discussed earlier (see also McNamara, 2004). In this case one set of genes would shape characteristics and functions of NREM and a separate set of genes with opposing interests would shape characteristics and functions of REM (see Table 6.2). Tucci et al.'s (2016) work on the association of imprinted genes with REM partially supports this scenario.

REM sleep was discovered in 1953 and its association with dreams was discovered soon thereafter. We will see shortly that its role in production of dreams has yet to be considered one of its primary functions.

Review Questions

- What is the theoretical significance of REM-NREM interactions?
- What are the strengths and weaknesses of the evidence that REM undoes something that occurs in NREM?
- Why are there only two major sleep states?
- Compare and contrast sleep and biobehavioral characteristics of Prader-Willi syndrome and Angelman syndrome.

Further Reading

Benington, J. H., & Heller, H. C. (1994). Does the function of REM sleep concern non-REM sleep or waking? *Progress in Neurobiology*, 44, 433–449.

Haig, D. (2014). Troubled sleep: Night waking, breastfeeding and parent-offspring conflict. *Evolution, Medicine, and Public Health*, (1), 32–39. doi: 10.1093/emph/eou005. Epub 2014 Mar 7. PMID: 24610432.

Halász, P., Bódizs, R., Parrino, L., Terzano, M. (2014). Two features of sleep slow waves: Homeostatic and reactive aspects – from long term to instant sleep homeostasis. *Sleep Medicine*, 15(10), 1184–1195. doi: 10.1016/j.sleep.2014.06.006. Epub 2014 Jul 8. Review. PMID:25192672.

McNamara, P. (2004). *An Evolutionary Psychology of Sleep and Dreams*. Westport, CT: Praeger/Greenwood Press.

Dreams

CHAPTER 7

What Are Dreams?

Learning Objectives

- Evaluate the strengths and weaknesses of the definition of dreams as sleep-dependent cognitions
- Identify formal properties of dream phenomenology and distinguish these formal properties from content of dreams
- Evaluate the significance of the role of emotion in shaping dream narrative form and content
- Evaluate story or narrative structure in creation of dream properties and phenomenology

7.1 Introduction

The most common definition of dreams among scientists appears to be that dreams are sleep-dependent cognitions (Table 7.1). They are thoughts and mental images that occur during sleep. If, however, dreams are sleep-dependent cognitions, then they require sleep if they are to occur. If REM sleep can erupt or invade daytime consciousness and REM-related mentation can occur with that daytime eruption, then we can get dreams or dreamy thoughts and images while awake. Indeed, that is what we call day dreams. Even if we cannot strictly claim that dreams are always sleep-dependent, they nevertheless typically occur in association (even when daydreaming) with a brain state (REM) that is normally activated during sleep.

Since dreams typically occur during sleep and since we claimed in Chapter 1 that sleep is *a restorative process that is brain state-regulated, reversible, homeostatic, embedded in both a circadian and social-physiologic organization, and involving a species-specific quiescent posture, some amount of perceptual disengagement, and elevated arousal thresholds,* then dreaming refers to the cognitions that take place within that biologic framework, i.e., within a *restorative process that is brain state-regulated, reversible, homeostatic, embedded in both a circadian and social-physiologic organization, and involving a species-specific quiescent*

Table 7.1 Dreams are sleep-dependent cognitions

- Vivid images and increased emotion in dreams
- Increase memory access, so hypermnesia and decrease memory for dream when awakening (amnesia)
- Mind reading
- Visual sense predominates
  –decreased taste
  –decreased smell
  –decreased pain, despite painful scenes
- Narrative structure with:
  –thematic discontinuities
  –quick changes in plot
  –occasional improbabilities (defy laws of physics)
  –incongruities (plot elements don't fit together)
  –characters can be real or fantastic
  –lapse in self-reflectiveness
  –hypercreativity (mental simulation)
  –scene is hyperreal
  –effortlessly created and combined
  –some problem solving
- Automaticity
- Perceptual disengagement
- Metaphor
- Dreamwork (Freud)/Literary tropes (White)
  –Condensation: two figures resolved into one *(metaphor)*
  –Displacement: affect appropriate for one character is directed onto more neutral characters *(metonomy)*
  –Symbolization: *(metaphors* are used to express meanings)
  –Secondary revision *(irony)*
  –Presentation *(synecdoche)*

This dream phenomenology is realized most completely in REM dreams and in N2 dreams when N2 occurs in early morning hours. It is realized partially in N2 dreams when N2 occurs in first part of the sleep cycle. N3 dreams realize only a few of these characteristics such as presentation of thoughts and images.

posture, some amount of perceptual disengagement, and elevated arousal thresholds. That definition of sleep then tells us something about the cognitions that occur during sleep: They will occur within a brain state that is homeostatically regulated, reversible, constrained by circadian and social physiologic variables, and characterized by some amount of perceptual disengagement. In short, dreams will be products of the sleeping brain, will be sensitive to social factors, and will not be constrained by some forms of external perceptual stimuli.

We do not know if dreams themselves are homeostatically regulated, though they appear to be so. Individuals who are on medications that suppress REM sleep for long periods of time report less dreaming during that time and abundant dreaming when the medications are discontinued. We do not know if dream rebound occurs with NREM rebound, but dream rebound does appear to occur with REM rebound. Similarly, when we experience sleep deprivation over a period of a few days we normally experience very vivid and abundant dreams when we are allowed to sleep again.

So, dreams are cognitions that depend on sleep and occur in sleep and presumably would not occur without sleep, but what do we mean by cognitions? As a first pass, definition of the term cognitions includes everything that is part of mental life: thoughts, mentations, affects, images, emotions, visual simulations, memories, etc. But we will immediately need to qualify this claim because not all forms of mental activity occur regularly in dreams. Dream researchers have shown, for example, that instances of reading, writing, arithmetic, and reflective thought are relatively infrequent occurrences in dreams as compared to their frequency in waking life. And conversely, some forms of mental experience occur in dreams more frequently than they occur in waking consciousness. For example, Freud pointed out that some dreams allow us to engage in vivid hallucinatory wish fulfillment. If the child is hungry he will dream of some delicious foods. In addition, a long line of experimental research demonstrates that dreams allow us to more easily make disparate connections between otherwise unconnected concepts. That ability to make connections where the waking mind sees no connections underlies the ability of dreams to promote creativity. Similarly, dreams allow us, or better, force us to interact with supernatural beings, from monsters and demons to angels and gods, thus demonstrating that dreams involve a unique form of cognition that is probably related to spiritual and religious ideas. These are only a few examples of how dreams differ from the waking mind in terms of the cognitions they exemplify.

The philosopher Jennifer Windt (Windt, 2015) has argued that the phenomenal core and distinctive experiential properties of dreams can be captured by her *immersive spatiotemporal hallucination* or ISTH model of dreams. Dreams for Windt are essentially immersive spatiotemporal hallucinations. In her view dreams involve a shift in the spatiotemporal location of the self from a veridical perception-based reference frame to a non-veridical hallucinatory reference frame. Windt's term "immersive" refers to the ways in which the experience of self are always indexical: The self inhabits a specific place and time relative to other selves or objects in the same reference frame. Dreams are immersive in that they involve the experience of spatiotemporal situatedness of the self. As in waking experience, there is a self as well as a world in dreams, and the boundary between the two is felt or taken for granted in dreams. In waking experience, according to Windt, the situated self is related to a real word whereas in the dream, the situated self is related to a hallucinated world. The immersive self need not be composed of history, emotions, or memories for ISTH. It is simply a point in space and time relative to other such points. Windt is even willing to entertain the idea that the self in dreams can involve nothing more than an un-extended point of awareness or a disembodied point or entity. She points to reports of lucid dreamers who claim to have experienced dreams without images or emotions. She also cites the experiences of Buddhist meditators who report the experience of no-self and the experience of dreamers who cannot recount details of dreams but report "just knowing" that they dreamed, etc. For Windt then, this minimal self, this point in an imagined space and time, relates to a fully hallucinated world but this self might not form any beliefs about the hallucinated world it finds itself in. Doxastic belief formation is a problem for the dream self according to Windt. It is unclear whether Windt believes that the self itself forms the hallucinated world or if some other structure in the dream forms the hallucinated world. She speaks in terms of the dream or the dreaming brain forming the hallucinated world. Dreams (not the self, apparently) integrate distal memory sources and internally generated imagery into a hallucinated world for the self to relate to. But the self in dreams does not form a fully fledged first-person perspective according to Windt, and therefore the self has difficulty forming beliefs or opinions about the dream world it inhabits. In fact, according to Windt, a cogitative self is prevented in dreams. Windt claims we need this account of the dream as an experience of a minimal self in a hallucinated world that does not construct and does not evaluate anything, in order to capture the core phenomenology of dreams that involve an unstable, unreflective, and disoriented self as well as those rare accounts of dreams without images, emotions, or events.

Nir and Tonini (2010) are also impressed with how labile the sense of self is in dreams. For these authors the self changes, mostly in negative ways, during the dream. For them, dreams are characterized by a sense of self that has reduced voluntary control during the dream (we supposedly cannot pursue goals in dreams), reduced self-awareness (we uncritically accept bizarre occurrences in dreams), reduced reflective thought (we typically do not know we are dreaming), heightened emotionality, and altered (mostly increased) access to memories during the dream despite being largely amnestic for the dream after awakening. But as both Nir and Tononi (2010) and Windt (2015) note there are many exceptions to their rule of the impaired self in dreams. We can have dreams where we vigorously pursue and attain goals; where we have self-awareness and self-reflection (we deliberate about options and puzzle over bizarre encounters in dreams); where we are appropriately emotional and are not particularly amnestic about the dream upon awakening.

In fact, dreams are not mere chaotic assemblages of bizarre images that occur in the presence of a minimal and impaired self. Rather dreams mostly involve perceptually and thematically organized material in the form of narratives containing appropriate images, themes, and simulations of the dreamer's life-world. Nevertheless, dreams are not like waking cognitions in all respects. The following are the key phenomenological features of dreams (see Table 7.1)

7.2 Increased Emotions in Dreams

Emotions occur in virtually all dreams (Merritt et al., 1994). When using the Hall/Van de Castle scoring rules, negative emotions appear in about 80 percent of dreams for both men and women. Strauch and Meier (1996) noted that the emotions reported in dreams are appropriate to the action occurring in dreams. If sadness is reported then the dream scene contains a sad event and when fear is reported the dream scene contains some scary events, etc. It is a remarkable fact that almost all dreams contain emotions as not all waking states contain emotion, and certainly not all emotional states are as intense as they typically are in dreams.

7.3 Hypermnesia within the Dream and Amnesia for the Dream

Hobson (1988) pointed out that when we dream we sometimes have access to memories that our waking mind does not have access to, yet we are often amnestic for dream content when we wake up. Foulkes (Foulkes, 1962) reported that non-contemporaneous images (images dating back to the person's more distant past) were more likely to occur in REM than in NREM dreams. Offenkrantz and Rechtschaffen (1963) and Verdone (Verdone, 1965) reported a relation between date of memory images in dreams and time spent in sleep such that as the night progressed the dreamer was more likely to report older personal memories. So although the dreaming mind/brain is digging through older memories as the night progresses, upon awakening the waking brain/mind often forgets that the dreaming mind/brain was doing all that memory rummaging during the night.

7.4 The Visual Sense Predominates in Dreams

Dreams are composed mostly of vivid visual images. Within a dream the dreamer feels as if he or she is seeing a scene or a life-world. Touching, smelling, and tasting things in the dream-world do not occur as often as they do in waking life. Auditory experiences occur fairly frequently in dreams but the visual sense predominates. Waking perception includes full color and three-dimensional views of a relatively stable world. In waking life visual clarity varies with attentional focus of the individual and this is true also of dreams. Dreams exhibit greater clarity in the foreground of the dreamer's attention while background details are vaguely represented. Unlike the full color world of waking consciousness, up to 20–30 percent of dreams are achromatic. Dreams also contain a greater number of visual distortions and transformations than waking vision. For example, we may see the facial features of a character in a dream change several times while we focus on those features in the dream.

7.5 Automaticity

Dreams come to us or happen to us whether we want them to or not. We cannot stop them and we cannot bid them to come anytime we like. They happen to us independently of our will. We can increase the chances of having a dream via certain ritual practices like dream incubation (discussed in the next section) but in general dreams happen to us regardless of our wishes. We have dreams whether we want to or not. Dreams, as Foulkes suggested, can therefore be construed as involuntary cognitive and symbolic events that occur during sleep and utilize perceptual and memory fragments to construct new narratives that more or less successfully simulate features of the dreamer's life-world.

7.6 Perceptual Disengagement

Virtually every scientist and scholar who has studied dreams has claimed that the key distinguishing mark of the dream is its lack of access to current perceptual information about the external world. That is why the philosopher Jennifer Windt and the neuroscientists Nir and Tononi believe that dreams are basically hallucinations and that the self in dreams is unreflective, minimal, and impaired. The self cannot check or correct its perceptions via use of incoming sensory information and so it naively accepts what it sees as reality. In short, the common view is that the dreaming brain is totally cut off from the environment.

But it may be that the brain in REM is not simply dormant and fully disconnected from the environment (Hennevin et al., 2007). Thalamo-cortical gating of incoming sensory information is not complete during REM. During REM, evoked responses of thalamic neurons are only slightly attenuated compared with waking. Cortical neurons are still responsive to incoming auditory stimuli during REM sleep. Evidence gathered from event-related potentials (ERP) studies demonstrates that auditory discrimination, recognition of an intrinsically meaningful stimulus (e.g., the dreamer's own name), and categorization of stimuli are intact during REM. In addition, convergent evidence from behavioral and neu-roimaging studies suggest that the neuronal patterns prevailing in thala-mocortical systems, a burst-silence mode during SWS versus a sustained single-spike activity during waking and REM, are strongly modulated not just by subcortical sites in the brainstem, the hypothalamus, and the basal forebrain, but in addition by widespread cortical networks, for example, the default mode network, but including secondary sensory areas that process semantic and abstract attributes of sensory stimuli.

Although it is now clear that auditory information is processed during REM it is also clear that the ways in which the dreaming brain processes this information is different from the ways in which the waking brain processes the information. The processing of auditory information is slower and takes longer during REM as compared to the waking state. Brain responses to deviant tones are significantly larger during REM.

Auditory information is not the only external sensory information that maintains access to the sleeping brain during REM. Chemical, smell, somato-sensory, and kinesthetic senses all continue to be processed during REM. Indeed, the only modality that is dramatically attenuated during REM is the visual modality but even here visual information is not completely abolished during REM. Ambient light energy is pro-cessed despite closed eyes for example.

7.7 Hyper Creativity

It is not true that dreams only utilize existing memory fragments to construct simulations and narratives. Inventories of the images and events in dreams reveal that dreams are composed mostly of images that have never before been encountered by the dreamer. Dreams in short are creative, productive, generative, and fecund. They are not mere reflections of waking consciousness, nor are they mere catalogs of floating memory fragments. They take specialized input (e.g., including that produced by selective brain activation associated with REM, memory fragments, day residues, fleeting visceral sensations, and other sources of content not yet characterized), subject that input to specialized processing algorithms using selective neural processes to do so, and then take the transformed imagery into the dream machinery system to output a unique cognitive product that we call the dream.

7.8 Self-Reflectiveness in Dreams

Most dream researchers believe that self-reflectiveness is impaired in dreams. That means that the dreamer often accepts bizarre or incongruous dream events uncritically as if they were normal or not bizarre. The view that self-reflectiveness is impaired in dreams is supported by findings from neuroimaging studies that demonstrate downregulation of the dorsal prefrontal cortex during REM sleep. On the other hand, some investigators have pointed out that these same neuroimaging studies show clear activation of other structures known to participate in high-level evaluative and reflective processing such as the ventromedial prefrontal cortex (especially area 10). In addition, the P300-evoked potential wave is intact during REM. The P300 is elicited in the waking state whenever high-level attentional and evaluative processes are activated in response to unexpected events in the environment. It may be that levels of self-reflectiveness fluctuate considerably in the dream state just as they do in waking consciousness, but dreaming per se does not require impaired self-reflectiveness.

7.9 Mind-Reading in Dreams

Can the dream-self read the "minds" of other dream characters – characters the dreamer himself has putatively created? You would think that since the dreamer conjured the other dream characters out of his or her own mind that the mental states of these characters would be transparent to him. It appears, however, that while the dreamer makes frequent theory of mind attributions to other dream characters, not all of their mental states are clear to the dreamer. McNamara et al. (2007) tabulated all clear references of the dreamer attributing mental states to other dream characters and found that theory of mind attributions were ubiquitous in dreams – especially REM dreams. Nevertheless, there were plenty of dreams wherein the dreamer behaved as if he did not know what other characters intended toward him.

7.10 Basic Ontology of the Dreamworld

The scientific gold standard taxonomy/ontology for dream content studies has been (for decades) the categories of the Hall/Van de Castle coding system (see review in Domhoff, 1996). Decades of research has established that its basic categories capture the essentials of dream content across cultures and demographic groups. Its coding rules and system have been validated in dozens of studies. The Hall/Van de Castle basic categories are as follows (canonical instances and definitions given in parentheses):

Characters (people, animals, mythical figures)
↓ engage in
Social interactions (aggression, friendliness, sex)
And engage in
↓
Activities (walking, talking, seeing, thinking, etc.)
And experience in those activities/interactions:
↓
Success and Failure (dreamer engages in and perseveres toward a goal and succeeds or fails in that pursuit)
And these characters can also experience /undergo
↓
Misfortune or Good fortune (adverse or happy events happen to dreamer)
↓
Emotions (anger, apprehension, sadness, confusion, happiness) associated with those experiences.
And all these events and interactions occur within:
↓
Settings (Location, familiarity)
That also contain objects that a character notices or handles or interacts with
↓
Objects (architecture, household, implements, etc.)

Built on this basic taxonomy, Hall and van de Castle derive these social interaction ratios:

Table 7.2 Hall/Van de Castle social interaction content ratios

Aggression/ Friendliness percent	Dreamer involved aggression/(dreamer-involved aggression + dreamer-involved friendliness).
Befriender percent	The percentage of all dreamer involved friendly interactions in which the dreamer befriends some other character. Dreamer as befriender (dreamer as befriender + dreamer as befriended).
Aggressor percent	The percentage of all dreamer-involved aggressions in which the dreamer is the aggressor. Dreamer as aggressor (dreamer as aggressor + dreamer as victim).
Physical aggression percent	The percentage of all aggressions appearing in reports whether witnessed or dreamer involved that are physical in nature. Physical aggressions/all aggressions.
Aggression (A/C) index	Frequencies of aggressions per character (all aggressions/all characters).
Friendliness (F/C) index	Frequencies of friendly interactions per character (all friendliness/all characters).
Sexuality (S/C) index	Frequencies of all sexual encounters per character (sexual encounters/all characters).

A major limitation of the Hall/Van de Castle system is that it is labor-intensive, requiring hundreds of hours of manual coding of lots of dream reports. In order to circumvent this limitation, Bulkeley (2014) used word search techniques to develop a word count method that yields similar findings as the Hall/Van de Castle manual coding system for the following categories:

Perception
Emotion
Characters
Social Interactions
Movement
Cognition
Culture
Natural Elements

In addition, to Hall/Van de Castle and Bulkeley taxonomies of the dream-world, some sleep/dream scientists would include two further categories for a complete dream ontology: cognitive processing and story structure.

On cognitive processing, McNamara et al., (2016) have used the text word count program Linguistic Inquiry and Word Count to tally instance of words denoting cognitive processing. This cognitive processes category picks up words indicating insight, causation, discrepancy, tentativeness, certainty, inhibition, inclusion, exclusion, etc. To supplement the main cognitive processing variable we added the function word category, which is made of words that function as grammatical markers (and, or, etc.). We thought that as narratives contain increased numbers of syntactical markers, so too would cognitive processing increase. Similarly, the verb category refers to "common" verbs such as walk, went, see, and includes verbs in all tenses, i.e., past tense (went, ran, had), present tense (is, does, hear), future tense (will, gonna). Not included under the verb category is auxiliary verbs (am, will, have). The verb analysis would capture additional evidence of grammatical processing, thus adding to confidence that cognitive processing was being accurately captured with these analyses. Using these word count categories to capture indications that cognitive processing was occurring in dreams, the authors found that virtually all dreams contained an abundance of cognitive processing. Dreams appear to be doing significant cognitive work.

The last major category to characterize the typical dream world is story or narrative structure.

7.11 Narrative Structure

Dreams unfurl like story plots or narratives. There is a beginning, middle, and end. The dreamer is typically at the center of the story. He or she is attempting to do something but faces obstacles or conflicts. Stories, including dream stories, tell us "who did what to whom and in what order." Remarkably, the dreaming brain creates narratives effortlessly so it may be no exaggeration to claim that the dream's natural cognitive product may be a narrative.

REM dreams are better at creating narratives than NREM dreams. Using a very detailed story grammar to score story-like structure in dream reports, Kuiken et al. (1983) reported that REM dreams exhibited more story-like structure than NREM reports did. Nielsen et al. (2001) reported that more stage REM than stage N2 reports contained at least one story element and a greater proportion of instances of episodic progression, but only for late night reports of high frequency dream recallers. So both REM and NREM generate dreams as narratives but REM does so more fluently. Nevertheless, the narratives that are generated often involve thematic discontinuities or disruptions in the story line and incongruous twists and juxtapositions. Some may feel that this makes for a better story while others might deem these quirks as yielding the bizarre elements we all find in our dreams.

The dreaming mind/brain generates stories. Stories are not imposed on dream images after awakening. To construct those stories the dreaming mind/brain very likely uses cognitive operations that can be described via Freud's "dreamwork" or by the four standard literary tropes that literary scholars claim are the engines that construct stories. For example, Hayden White (White 1999) has argued that people utilize the four major literary stylistic tropes – metaphor, metonymy, synecdoche, and irony – when cognizing their worlds, including their histories. To oversimplify White's rich tropological narrative philosophy of history, metaphor involves a comparison of materials with something familiar. Metonymy involves breaking up those materials into parts; synecdoche involves reorganizing those materials into a new whole, and irony involves reflection on that new whole. White showed that these four tropes are effectively equivalent to Freud's dreamwork operations such as displacement (metonymy), condensation (metaphor), presentation (synecdoche), and secondary revision (irony). "The four operations identified by Freud function in the same way that the tropes do in allegory to mediate between the literal and the figurative levels of meanings of the text." (White, 1999, page 103). A perusal of any corpus of dreams would yield an abundance of instances of each of these four literary tropes, functioning to perform the dreamwork that results in dream narrative plots and structure.

Many dreams instantiate the common story lines or plots that literary theorists have identified to be ubiquitous in texts of all kinds. For example, Christopher Booker's *The Seven Basic Plots: Why We Tell Stories* (Booker, 2006) identified seven basic story types as follows:

"Overcoming the monster" (e.g., *Beowulf*)
"Rags to riches" (e.g., *Cinderella*)
"The quest" (e.g., *King Solomon's Mines*)
"Voyage and return" (e.g., *The Time Machine*)
"Comedy" (e.g., A *Midsummer Night's Dream*)
"Tragedy" (e.g., *Anna Karenina*)
"Rebirth" (e.g., *Beauty and the Beast*)

Most dreamers and scholars who study dreams would agree that people experience these story lines in dreams. "Overcoming the monster" involves the hero confronting a monster and escaping or destroying that monster. That story line is common in scary dreams. "The quest" is common in so-called epic dreams wherein the hero travels a long way, faces obstacles, encounters fantastic scenes and obstacles, and overcomes those obstacles. "Voyage and return" is also a very common dream theme wherein the hero leaves home, gets lost for a while, and then attempts to get back home. The *Cinderella* "rags to riches" theme is also very common, wherein the hero is given honors that he thinks he deserves but was denied for some period of time. All of the common story tropes are found in dreams. But so are their contraries. The contrary to the *Cinderella* theme is when a poseur is exposed as a phony. The contrary to the "man in the hole" theme involves the hero failing to rise after a fall, and so forth.

The frequent appearance in dreams of all of these common story types (and their contraries) argues against a view of narrative dreaming as confabulatory or ad hoc creations of an impaired dreaming mind. It is currently unknown whether the narratives constructed during the dream experience are essentially confabulatory tales created "on the fly" by the dream itself, in order to "explain" the strong emotions occurring in the dream. According to this view dream narratives contain no inherent purpose or logic. They are constructed on the fly and after the fact, a chaotic assemblage of random images loosely strung together by an impaired cognitive system operating without the benefit of reflective thought. They are, to paraphrase Shakespeare, "tales told by an idiot and signifying nothing." If, however, the dream was a mere, after the fact, confabulation or rationalization for a series of decontextualized memory images or emotions, there would be no reason to expect consistent content across dreams. But decades of carefully conducted dream content studies have demonstrated beyond reasonable doubt that dreams contain consistent content across groups and within individual dream series. Longitudinal analyses of dream series demonstrate clearly that dreams display intricate, thematically connected, consistent storylines, characters, events, emotions, and narratives across time.

7.12 Conclusions

Dreams are cognitions that are typically dependent on sleep. However, not all forms of cognition occur during sleep. In spontaneously recalled dreams the visual sense predominates. It is rare to remember a smell or a taste from the dream. Reading and computations (arithmetic) do not frequently occur in dreams. Many dreams contain unusual amounts of emotion, and may provide greater access to older memories – especially during late morning REM dreams. While impairment in critical self-reflective capacities may occur in dreams, it is not clear if all dreams are characterized by impairment in self-reflectiveness. The dreaming mind/brain spontaneously and automatically produces dreams in the form of narratives and likely uses cognitive operations like Freud's dreamwork to do so.

Theoretical models of the dream must be consistent with formal cognitive properties of the dream including narrative structure, creativity, "mind-reading," hypermnesia within the dream, partial amnesia for the dream upon awakening, enhanced emotional levels for many dreams, enhanced visual (and to some extent auditory) impressions with diminished impressions from the other senses, and finally the involuntary nature of dreaming: We dream whether we want to or not.

These formal properties of dreams also make it clear that dreams are a different species of cognition than that which occurs in the waking state. While off-line simulations do occur in the waking state, they are not obligatory and they do not typically involve intense emotion and are not narratively structured. Daydreams are instead focused on wishes, goals, and plans. They are also more often episodic and fleeting impressions rather than organized narratives. We should entertain the possibility that dreams are specialized products of the sleeping mind/brain. Dreams are one of the things that the sleeping brain is designed to produce: vivid, visually based, narrative simulations of our social worlds with the dream self-interacting with other characters along a storyline involving conflict and resolution.

Review Questions

- How is the sense of self (of the dreamer) typically experienced in dreams?
- How is mind-reading (one dream character discerning the thoughts and intentions of a different dream character) possible in dreams given that there is only one dreamer?
- What are the strengths and weaknesses of Windt's immersive spatio-temporal hallucination (ISTH) model of dreaming?
- What is the significance of the dream property "perceptual disengagement" for dream phenomenology?

Further Reading

Hobson, J. A. (1988). *The Dreaming Mind*. New York: Basic Books.
Hobson, J. A., Pace-Schott, E. F., & Stickgold, R. (2000). Dreaming and the brain: Toward a cognitive neuroscience of conscious states. *Behavioral Brain Sciences*, 23, 793–842.

McNamara, P. McLaren, D., Kowalczyk, S., & Pace-Schott, E. (2007). "Theory of mind" in REM and NREM dreams. In D. Barrett & P. McNamara (eds.), *The New Science of Dreaming: Volume I: Biological Aspects* (pp. 201–220). Westport, CT: Praeger Perspectives.

Windt, J. M. (2015). *Dreaming: A Conceptual Framework for Philosophy of Mind and Empirical Research*. Cambridge, MA: MIT Press.

CHAPTER 8

Dreams across the Human Lifespan

Learning Objectives

- Describe how dreams of children differ from dreams of adults
- Evaluate the significance of the social content of dreams
- Evaluate the significance of the overlap in the neuroanatomy of REM with the neuroanatomy of the "social brain" network
- Describe basic dream content themes derived from the standardized Hall/Van de Castle scoring system

8.1 Introduction

Dreaming both reflects the stage of life in which we find ourselves and influences the character of that stage of life. For example, adolescence would not be adolescence without the wild, melodramatic, passionate, and swirling epic dreams teens have that center around those existential questions of "Who am I" and "Why am I here?" etc. We will see in this chapter that dreaming appears to reflect and perhaps promote waking social interactions of the dreamer and this is true across the entire lifespan of the dreamer, from toddlerhood right through to death. Of course, that is not the whole story. Dream content across the lifespan involves far more than social interactions but it is a striking and consistent fact that simulations of social interactions are a constant feature of dream life throughout the lifecycle. If we want to understand the development of dreams and dream content across an average human lifespan we will need to first summarize the key milestones or periods of the human lifecycle from the cradle to the grave. Table 8.1 displays key characteristics of each of the major human lifecycle stages and sketches corresponding dream findings.

8.2 Dreaming and the Social Brain

Why are dreams so filled with social content even in childhood? The human infant is immature neurologically at birth and thus utterly

Table 8.1 Stage characteristics of the human life cycle

Stage	Period	Key characteristics	Dream life
Fetal life/ gestation	Nine-month pregnancy	Neurogenesis; fetal growth; fetal/ placental conflict	Signs of active sleep (AS) begin by second trimester and vary in response to placental changes/ maternal activities. AS predominates throughout rest of pregnancy
Neonatal and infancy	Birth to end of lactation (typically two- to three-years old)	Most rapid rate of growth in body, brain, and behavior; language acquisition; attachment orientation established	First reported dreams in toddlers are static scenes of family members or animal characters; child believes dreams come from outside of self
Childhood	Three to seven years	Moderate growth rates; second order "theory of mind" and other social cognition skills	Frequent dreaming; clear representation of self in interactions with familiar others; occasional nightmares
Juvenile	Seven to twelve years	Moderate growth rates; further development of social cognitive skills; peer group social interactions become important.	Dreams become more elaborate; involve friends and unfamiliar characters in addition to family members; occasional nightmares
Puberty	Twelve to sixteen years	Rapid growth rates; activation of sex hormones and secondary sexual characteristics; continued development of social cognitive skills	Elaborate vivid dreams; frequency of animals in dreams drops off; "wet" dreams (orgasm during dreaming); dreams of attachment or romantic objects

Table 8.1 (cont.)

Stage	Period	Key characteristics	Dream life
Adolescence	Fourteen to nineteen years	Rapid growth rates; growth spurt in height and weight; sociosexual maturation; social cognitive skills now directed at self ("Who am I?")	Elaborate dreaming; full panoply of characters (self; family; friends; strangers; romantic targets, etc.); Increased physical aggression levels in male's dreams and verbal aggression in female's dreams
Adulthood	For women from end of adolescence to end of menopause; for men from end of adolescence to senescence	Stable growth rates; sexual and reproductive activities; child-rearing	Elaborate dreaming around current concerns as well as counterfactual simulations of everyday social interactions; male/female differences in dream content
Senescence	Post-reproductive and child-rearing period	Gradual bodily and mental decline; generative social activities; grandparenting	Generative and reflective dreaming; scenes of loved ones living and dead
Death	End of senescence	Dissolution of bodily and mental activities	Spiritual, epic, and reflective dreaming; interactions with loved ones who have died

dependent on caretakers for at least the first few years of life. That is one reason why securing "attachment" with caretakers is so crucial an aim for human children. I discussed the role of REM sleep in attachment in previous chapters. Bodily and brain growth is rapid during infancy and is followed by steady growth rates in childhood and dramatically increased growth rates again in adolescence. The major proportion of effort in growth goes to development and maintenance of brain function. Upwards of 85 percent of the infant's, 50 percent of the five-year-old's, and 20 percent of the adult's resting metabolic rate supports brain processes and development. Why is all of this effort expended on brain development? While human culture and technologies have undoubtedly contributed to the need for greater resources being funneled into brain development among humans, it also appears that large brains and prolonged development are required to succeed in complex societies.

Dunbar (1998; 2012) has articulated the "social brain hypothesis," which states that primates have larger than expected neocortical volumes (given body size) because they need to deal with the complexities of group or social life. Given neocortical volume in humans, Dunbar theorized that the average human social network should be about 150 individuals. Ethnographic and social evidence support this prediction. For example, it is the typical size of a hunter-gatherer group; of a company in a military organization, of a personal network (number of individuals a person knows directly); of a church congregation; of a small business company, and so on. Within this large personal network there are hierarchically organized subgroups, alliances, coalitions, and cliques, etc. that reflect differing degrees of familiarity with the individual at the center of the network. These coalitional alliances need to be maintained, updated, and renegotiated on a semi-constant basis by members of the alliance, all of which require substantial cognitive resources.

Consider the cognitive demands that such a hierarchically organized network involving constantly shifting social alliances places on individuals. Human societies succeed to the extent that problems can be solved cooperatively. Cooperation is based on trust, and trust can only be earned over time after many social interactions have taken place between the parties involved. Those social interactions have to be remembered, archived, and recalled repeatedly when evaluating current trustworthiness of one's potential partner in an enterprise. Maintaining the stability of relationships over time requires constant renegotiation of the terms of the cooperative agreement. People are capable of deception and thus that capacity needs to be taken into account when weighing evidence of trustworthiness. It requires that individuals learn how to read the intentions or minds of others in the group so as to manage conflict, anticipate strategic moves of the other, and repair strained relationships and so on.

The capacity to appreciate that another individual has a mind like one's own, capable of cooperation but also of deception, etc. is called the "theory of mind" or ToM capacity. Dunbar points out that this capacity involves several layers of cognitive complexity. First order ToM involves having knowledge of one's own mental states ("I believe that ..."). Second order intentionality or ToM involves knowledge of another person's mental states ("I believe that you understand that ..."). Third order intentionality involves individual A thinking about what individual B is thinking about A's thinking ("I intend that you think that I think that we are going to ..."), etc. Most scholars working in the area of social cognition think that human beings are capable of perhaps five orders of intentionality but no more. The computational demands on the brain for this kind of social cognition are considerable.

8.3 Overlap of the Social Brain with the REM Dreaming Brain

As discussed in previous chapters, the areas of the brain that handle these computational demands around social cognition have been identified as the "social brain network." They are listed in Table 8.2. The amygdala is important for evaluation of the emotions of self and others. In addition, the amygdala helps to modulate hormonal levels important in social interactions such as oxytocin and vasopressin. Oxytocin has been called the trust molecule as it enhances level of trust and emotional closeness

Table 8.2 Overlap of social brain with default mode network

Key Nodes that Occur in Both Networks	Known Waking Functions
Amygdala	Emotion; salience Evaluation
Fusiform gyrus	Face processing
Ventro and dorsalmedial prefrontal cortex	Self and other processing; theory of mind
Fronto-polar Brodmann Area 10	Multitasking
Superior temporal sulcus	Mirror neurons
Temporal-parietal junction	Theory of mind
Insula	Empathy; moral evaluation
Posterior cingulate and precuneus	Self awareness; mental simulation; time traveling
Hippocampus	Memory processing

between people. Vasopressin appears to be crucial for social memories – especially in males. Its activity levels fluctuate in relation to testosterone activity. The fusiform gyrus supports rapid recognition and processing of faces. The face, of course, is crucial for social interactions as it emits all kinds of signals concerning the intentions and emotions of the individual. The ventromedial and dorsomedial prefrontal regions are known to support processing of self-related information as well as understanding the mental states of others (i.e., ToM tasks). The frontopolar region (BA 10) evidences a uniquely complex structure in humans and is one of the evolutionarily most recent regions of the brain in primates. It is involved in multitasking, working memory, and cognitive branching, and therefore may support processing of third and fourth, etc. orders of intentionality. The superior temporal sulcus contains mirror neurons that support social imitation behaviors and possibly emotional empathy. The temporal-parietal junction supports ToM tasks and language processing. The insula supports empathetic responses as well as moral emotions and the precuneus is involved in a range of activities from mental simulation to self-awareness. Finally the hippocampus is involved in memory functions.

Many neuroscientists (e.g., Mars et al., 2012) have noted that this network of structures called the social brain overlaps to a significant extent with the so-called default mode network (DMN) discussed in a previous chapter as being activated and functionally reconnected during REM sleep. Dream investigators (see review in Pace-Schott and Picchioni, 2017) have noted that the dreaming brain during REM sleep is essentially composed of the reactivation of all of the key nodes in the DMN. It therefore appears that the dreaming brain is also the social brain. The DMN activates in a resting state when the mind is free to wander. It appears that what most people daydream about are social interactions. It should not be surprising then that nightdreams, including dreams right across the lifecycle, are concerned primarily with social interactions.

The theme of social concerns occurring in dreams begins right at the birth of dreaming in toddlerhood. In a previous chapter we noted that human developmental schedules were prolonged relative to other apes in order to enhance brain growth. The need to prolong developmental schedules and brain growth was fueled by the increasing complexities of human social life. The child needs to form stable attachment bonds with caretakers in order to survive and thrive during the long developmental phase of childhood. Dreams in children facilitate this process of attachment formation in multiple ways. Current cognitive models of the attachment formation process postulate "internal working models" of self (child) and the attachment target (e.g., mother) as key regulators of attachment formation and maintenance. Internal working models are constructed unconsciously and in dreams. In addition, children dream often of those people most important to them like family members and close friends. They try out all kinds of alternate scenarios of interaction with these people in their dreams.

In their review of methodologies used in research on children's dreams, Sandor et al. (2014) suggest that results from studies conducted in the child's familiar home environment or school setting are richer in terms of representations of social interactions between the child and significant others when compared to dreams obtained from children in a sleep lab with EEG equipment and measurements. This is not surprising given that children are uncomfortable away from home and in a lab. Thus, we will focus on dreams collected in the familiar home or school environment in our review of children's dreams. There is reason to trust that children honestly share their dreams rather than make them up to please parents, etc. Children as young as three years old know what dreams are and can differentiate them from waking fantasy, events, and stories. When working with children in dream studies there are established criteria that can increase confidence that the narrative the child produces in response to a request for a dream are credible (see Table 8.3). We can therefore obtain reliable dream reports from children just as we can from adults.

Table 8.3 Establishing the credibility of children's dreams

How do we know when a child is sharing a true dream versus some waking fantasy made up on the spot? Colace (2010) and Sandor et al. (2014) suggest the following guidelines:

(1) The child starts the report without hesitation.
(2) The child reports the dream quickly in one go (although fulfilling these criteria could be difficult even for an adult when it comes to the recollection of possibly fragmented or bizarre dream content).
(3) The child's self-definition of the story as a dream.
(4) The placement of the experience itself during sleep period.
(5) The coherence between the dream report and certain daytime experiences of the child in connection with the dream.
(6) Good comprehension of the dream experience.
(7) Consistency between specific dream report and the general concept of dream.
(8) The last point introduces a new channel of storytelling through drawing, which should be consistent with the verbal channel even after a certain time lapse.

8.4 Children's Dreams and Nightmares

There have been remarkably few well-controlled studies of children's dreams. From sporadic published reports on children's dreams, it appears that children can report dreams as soon as they start to speak. When studied in the lab, most kid's dreams are said to be relatively static with simple plot lines, some interactions with family members, and lots of animals in them up to about middle childhood. When, however, parents collect the dreams of their children in the home, we get a different picture: Children's dreams seem to be just as dynamic and rich as adult dreams (but there are indeed more animal characters in children's dreams).

While Foulkes (1982) launched the longitudinal study of children's dreams in the 1970s he collected most of these dreams in the sleep lab and therefore his results and analyses of the content of these dreams were colored by the lab setting. Foulkes found that young children recall very few dreams and when they are recalled they are static and may not contain representation of the self, and that not much happens in the dreams. Home-collected dreams, however, told a different story. Resnick and colleagues (1994) found no difference in dream recall frequency between the four- to five- and eight- to ten-year-old age groups (56 percent and 57 percent, respectively). Nor did they find significant differences in active self-representation between four- to five- and eight- to ten-year-olds (89 percent) age groups. The child was an active presence in up to 85 percent of their dreams and self-character was virtually always depicted in interaction with others in the dream story. Oberst (2005) found that boys tend to dream more about male charac-ters (other boys his age), whereas girls dream equally often of boys and girls. Boys' dreams involve greater levels of physical aggression and aggressive interactions with other characters (aggression/character index: 61 percent for boys and 24 percent for girls). Younger children express higher victimizations (where dreamer was target of an aggres-sion in the dream) than older children.

Strauch (2005) found a gradual appearance of active self in late child-hood dreams, and a dramatic increase in social interactions. Overall aggression/friendliness percentage declined for boys (70 percent at nine to eleven years old) and increased for girls (36 percent at nine to eleven years old), until the two plateaued at around 50 percent aggression/friend-liness percentage during the teenage years. Colace (2010), found that 68 percent of the dreams of young children (three to seven years) con-tained an active self in an overall sample of home and school-obtained dreams. Resnick et al. also found that the most frequent characters in young children's dreams were family members (29 percent of all characters) and other known children (28 percent).

Children's dreams whether collected in the lab or at home contain a lot of negative emotions and are often described as scary for tor the children. Children are more likely to experience nightmares than adults. Up to 50 percent of children between three and six years of age, and 20 percent between six and twelve years, experience "frequent" nightmares. Persistence of nightmares during the preschool and school years (two and a half to nine years of age) is associated prospectively with psychotic experiences at twelve years of age. This association holds regardless of family adversity, emotional or behavioral problems, IQ, and potential neurological problems. Questionnaire-based nightmare and bad dream studies typically show that nightmare frequency is highest between the ages of five to ten and is related to other sleep disorders, trait anxiety, emotional problems, and behavior problems.

8.5 Adulthood: Male vs. Female Dreams

Dream of adults are also intensely social in terms of their content. Adult men and women dream about their family members and close friends. They engage in a huge variety of social interactions with these close familiars. When strangers (unknown characters) appear in the dreams of children or adults they typically indicate threat to either the dreamer or one of his close family members. Threat and aggression levels vary according to gender with males evidencing greater levels of aggression and females evidencing greater feelings of threat (coming from strangers) in their dreams. Cross-sectional studies have documented gender differences in adult dream content. In the 1960s Hall and Van de Castle studied content of five dreams of each of 100 male and 100 female college students (N = 1,000) which had been collected in the years 1948 to 1952 (reviewed in Domhoff, 1996). They found that unfamiliar, outdoor settings were present more often in men's vs. women's dreams and that there was a higher proportion of male dream characters, unknown characters, more physical aggression, weapons, and sexuality in men's vs. women's dreams. These basic cross-sectional content differences between the dreams of men and women have largely been confirmed in more recent studies.

Longitudinal studies of dream content changes in adults are rare. In examining the longitudinal effects of a cognitive processing variable on other dream content variables in dream series collected from

Table 8.4 Hall/Van de Castle norms on male and female dreams

	Male Norms (%)	Female Norms (%)	Effect Size	p
Characters				
Male/female percent	67	48	+.39	.000**
Familiarity percent	45	58	−.26	.000**
Friends percent	31	37	−.12	.004**
Family percent	12	19	−.21	.000**
Animal percent	6	4	+.08	.037*
Social interaction percents				
Aggression/friendliness percent	59	51	+.15	.014*
Befriender percent	40	47	+.06	.517
Aggressor percent	40	33	+.14	.129
Victimization percent	60	67	−.14	.129
Physical aggression percent	50	34	+.33	.000**
Social interaction ratios				
Aggression/character index	.34	.24	+.24	.000**
Friendliness/character index	.21	.22	−.01	.852
Sexuality/character index	.06	.01	+.11	.000**
Self-concept percents				
Self-negativity percent	65	66	−.02	.617
Bodily misfortunes percent	29	35	−.12	.217
Negative emotions percent	80	80	+.00	.995
Dreamer-involved success percent	51	42	+.18	.213
Torso/anatomy percent	31	20	+.26	.002**
Other indicators				
Physical activities percent	60	52	−.38	.000**
Indoor setting percent	48	26	−.26	.000**
Familiar setting percent	62	79	−.38	.000**

Table 8.4 (cont.)

	Male Norms (%)	Female Norms (%)	Effect Size	p
Percent of dreams with at least one				
Aggression	47	44	+.05	.409
Friendliness	38	42	−.08	.197
Sexuality	12	4	+.31	.000**
Misfortune	36	33	+.06	.353
Good fortune	6	6	+.02	.787
Success	15	8	+.24	.000**
Failure	15	10	+.17	.007**
Striving	27	15	+.31	.000**

Note: The p values are based on the formula for the significance of differences between two proportions. The effect size derives form Cohen's h. The h statistic is determined by the following formula: $h = \cos^{-1}(1-2P_1) - \cos^{-1}(1-2P_2)$ P_1 and P_2 are proportions between 0 and 1, the $\cos^{-1}$ operation returns a value in radians. * significant at the .05 level **significant at the .01 level; Table 8.4 originally published as Table 3.2 on page 73 of Domhoff, G. W. *The Scientific Study of Dreams* (Washington, DC: American Psychological Association, 2003). Reprinted with permission from the American Psychological Association.

thirty-seven men and forty-six women, McNamara et al. (2016) found that on a month-by-month basis cognitive processing is significantly associated with markers of grammatical complexity (verbs and function words), the personal pronoun I, social processes, perceptual processes, health, and emotion (both negative and positive). All of this indicates that dreams are being used by adults to cognitively process information related to social interactions. The rate of change on a monthly basis for cognitive processes differed significantly for men vs. women. Men exhibited a significantly positive rate of change in cognitive processing on a monthly basis, while women did not show a significant rate of change over time. Moreover, the difference in the rate of change in words denoting cognitive processing differed significantly in men compared to women. Pulling these results together suggests that people do in fact use dreams to "work through" or cognitively process selected types of social emotional information and the rate at which they do so appears to increase, at least for men. The topics subject to or associated with cognitive processing in dreams appears to be concerned primarily with social processes rather than health or perceptual processes. Why might men evidence increasing rates of cognitive processing around social information over time while women's rate of cognitive processing remained relatively constant over time? It cannot be due to differences in frequencies of baseline content variables, as we adjusted for baseline frequencies of words denoting cognitive processing in our analyses. Nor can it be due to age differences among males vs. females as we also adjusted for age in our analyses.

The continuity hypothesis on dream content states that dream content largely reflects waking life. The continuity hypothesis is broadly supported by empirical evidence. It may be that women find it easier during waking lives to process emotional content, while men prefer to process socio-emotional content "off-line."

Results from our analyses provide partial support for continuity but also raise significantly new issues regarding the way men and women use dreams to process emotional concerns, as men appear to engage in increasing amounts of cognitive processing around socio-emotional information over time compared to women.

8.6 Attachment Dreams

Both dream recall and dream content varies significantly in both children and adults as a function of attachment status or attachment security/insecurity (see for example McNamara et al. 2014 and review therein). People who self-report an insecure attachment orientation tend to recall dreams that reflect their attachment orientations either in a compensatory manner (where people with anxious orientation recall more dreams focused on romantic targets) or in a reactive manner (where people with an avoidant orientation tend to not recall dreams or report dreams without affective or romantic content). Selterman and his associates (Selterman, Apetroaia, and Waters, 2012) examined partner-specific attachment representations/cognitive working models in dreams that contained significant others. Attachment orientation was measured using the "Secure Base Script Narrative Assessment" technique. This assessment takes participant responses to word cues as well as free narrative responses and then codes them for elements/scenes where the romantic target or secure base figure supports the participant's exploration or comes to the aid of the participant or comforts the participant, etc. Selterman and colleagues assessed their participants on this secure base script and then coded participant dreams for secure base script elements. They assessed sixty-one undergraduate students all of whom were in committed dating relationships of six months duration or longer. Selterman and colleagues then collected two weeks of dreams from all these participants and coded all those dreams that contained a romantic partner for secure base script elements.

Results revealed a significant association between relationship-specific attachment security and the degree to which dreams about romantic partners followed the secure base script. Secure base content was identified in a significantly large proportion of dreams that contained current romantic partners. In addition, daytime attachment security as measured by the objective secure base script narrative task was significantly associated with "scriptedness" or the degree to which dreams were judged to reflect the secure base script.

These studies of dreams and attachment orientations suggest that one thing that dreams support is construction, maintenance, and adjustment of cognitive working models of attachment. As discussed in earlier chapters those working models include representations of the self in relation to the attachment object such that if both self and other (attachment object) are cognitively evaluated and represented in a positive manner then we get secure attachment. If on the other hand the other is valued above the self and the self is seen as too dependent and needy vis-a-vis the other, then an insecure and anxious preoccupation attachment orientation is formed. If the self is overly valued vis-a-vis the other, then we get an insecure avoidant orientation and so forth. McNamara et al. (2001) showed that dream recall rates varied significantly with these attachment orientations. In addition, McNamara et al. (2001) found associations between attachment orientation, dream recall rates, and image intensity in dreams. McNamara, Pace-Schott, Johnson, Harris, and Auerbach (2011) found that people classified as anxiously attached evidenced reduced REM latencies and were more likely to have dreams containing themes of aggression and self-denigration compared to people with other attachment styles. Mikulincer, Shaver, and Avihou-Kanza (2011) reported similar findings regarding associations between insecure attachment and negative self-concept in dreams. Mikulincer, Shaver, Sapir-Lavid, and Avihou-Kanza (2009) found that both attachment-related avoidance and anxiety correlated with less dream content denoting secure attachment such as less support seeking, less support availability, and less distress relief in dreams. As mentioned, Selterman and Drigotas (2009) found associations between attachment insecurity (avoidance and anxiety) and conflict in dreams that contained romantic partners. Selterman et al. (2012) later reported that participants classified as secure in their current relationships tended to report dreams that contained more secure base content. Selterman, Apetroaia, Riela, and Aron (2014) later demonstrated that attachment-related dream content influenced daytime attachment behaviors. Specifically they found that the frequency with which participants reported dreams about their romantic partners was positively associated with the extent to which they interacted with their partners and felt more love/closeness on days subsequent to dreaming about them. When people high in attachment avoidance had greater negative affect in dreams of their partners, they reported interacting less with their partners on subsequent days. For those high in interdependence, having a dream containing sexual behavior with one's partner was associated with increased love/closeness on subsequent days. In a rare EEG study of dream content across the night, McNamara et al. (2014) found that a variable capturing comfort with and actual "emotional intimacy" content increased over the course of the night as REM amount increased. While REM-dependent intimacy content tended to increase for all three attachment orientations, the rate of increase (slope) was slower for the avoidant group (0.31) relative to both the secure (0.52) or the preoccupied (0.44) groups.

8.7 Changes in Dream Content with Age

Dreams of elderly individuals have not received as much attention as dreams of children or young adults but they are just as important for the science of dreams as those of children or young adults. That is because as we age, slow wave sleep starts to drop out of the sleep cycle and we are left only with N2 light sleep and some REM. Thus, REM dreams no longer need to respond to or be constrained by the need for slow wave sleep. Dream simulations should therefore be longer, more free, and wide ranging. The dreams of the elderly do appear to include a wider range of themes than dreams of younger people, though the central theme of social interactions remain a constant – even in dreams of the elderly.

Dale et al. (2017) reported that in a group of 231 males aged twelve to eighty-five aggressive social interactions between the dreamer and other characters in dreams tended to decline with age while friendly interactions, total number of characters, and gender representation among the characters tend to remain stable over the lifespan. However, one caveat with these overall trends was the total absence of sexual content in the dreams of the last two age groups (forty to sixty-four and sixty-five to eighty-five). This same research group reported similar findings (Dale et al., 2015) with respect to dreams of women across the lifespan. There were no significant trends for either total characters or male characters in the dreams of women across the lifespan, but female and familiar characters decreased across the lifespan. There was a slight decrease (linear trend) with age for both total aggressive interactions and dreamer as victim interactions, as well as a decline for total friendly interactions and the F/C index in the dreams of women from adolescence to old age.

Domhoff (2003) was given access to the dream journals of "Barb Sanders," a woman in her late fifties. Sanders had kept records of her dreams covering the years from 1970s to the late 1990s. In addition to being able to interview Barb Sanders herself, Domhoff was also able to interview four of Sanders close female friends who had known her for many years. Thus, Domhoff was able to score the content of Sanders' dreams, to study how that content changes over time, and the extent to which that content reflects themes in Sander's own life. Results showed that Sander's dreams pretty faithfully simulated her current and past social interactions as well as desired social interactions, including those with her ex-husband, her ambiguous feelings toward her mother, her strong love for her favorite brother and her friends and children, a momentary romantic infatuation with a younger man, etc. Levels of aggressiveness versus friendliness in social interactions were remarkably stable in Sanders' dreams across decades while the quality of social interactions with the significant people in her life changed over the years with depictions of some relationships becoming more friendly and others more distant. We will see that dreams of loved ones remain a constant feature of dream life even into old age.

8.8 Death and Dreams

Dreams have been collected from individuals who are about to die. Early studies found that themes of dreams of the dying contained greater numbers of supernatural agents, otherworldly settings, and images that seemed to "announce" the approach of death, such as uncanny tunnels, wilting plants, and natural disasters. Some dreams seemed to ease the transition from this world into whatever awaits us after we die. Dreams of pregnancies, babies, and children appear frequently in those who are aware that they are dying. Scenes of trees bearing fruit, doors opening onto a light-filled path, and meetings with angelic and benevolent beings have been reported in dreams of the dying. Dreams of reunions with a loved one who has died are common in all parts of the world.

8.9 Conclusions

Most dreams are filled with social interactions between the dreamer and familiar people in the dreamer's life. Dream content changes significantly according to the stage in life of the dreamer but social interactions remain a constant in dream content across the lifespan. Much of the social interactions that occur in dreams can be characterized as attachment interactions; that is, interactions that reflect and help shape daytime attachment orientations (e.g., romantic attachments or familial attachments, etc.) of the dreamer. In old age and in death dreams continue to simulate social interactions, but new unfamiliar characters enter the dreams of the old and dying. These are supernatural beings but also include images of loved ones who have previously passed away. And so dreams that carry the child into the social world of his caretakers during early life gently escort the dreamer into the arms of his loved ones when the dreamer's time to leave this life arrives. Dreams accompany us and our loved ones literally from the cradle to the grave.

Review Questions

- What is the significance of the experimental findings concerning associations between attachment orientations and sleep/dream measures in both children and adults?
- What kinds of evidence will increase confidence that children are really sharing their dreams rather than simply making up stories?
- Why do you suppose women dream equally often of both sexes while males dream more often of other males?
- What kind of experimental evidence would demonstrate that dream content influences daytime behavior rather than the other way round (daytime events influence dream content)?

Further Reading

Colace, C. (2010). *Children's Dreams: From Freud's Observations to Modern Dream Research* (1st edn). London: Karnac Books Ltd.

Domhoff, G. W. (2003). *The Scientific Study of Dreams: Neural Networks, Cognitive Development, and Content Analysis*. Washington, DC: American Psychological Association.

Pace-Schott, E. F., & Picchioni, D. (2017). Neurobiology of dreaming. In M. Kryger, T. Roth, & W. C. Dement (eds.), *Principles and Practice of Sleep Medicine* (6th edn., pp. 529–538). Philadelphia: Elsevier.

Sándor, P., Szakadát, S, & Bódizs, R. (2014). Ontogeny of dreaming: A review of empirical studies. *Sleep Medicine Review*, 18(5), 435–449. doi: 10.1016/j.smrv.2014.02.001. Epub 2014 Feb 12. Review. PMID: 24629827.

Selterman, D. F., Apetroaia, A. I., Riela, S., & Aron, A. (2014). Dreaming of you: Behavior and emotion in dreams of significant others predict subsequent relational behavior. *Social Psychological and Personality Science*, 5(1), 111–118. doi: 10.1177/1948550613486678.

Simard, V., Chevalier, V., & Bédard, M. M. (2017). Sleep and attachment in early childhood: A series of meta-analyses. *Attachment and Human Development*, 19(3), 298–321. doi: 10.1080/14616734.2017.1293703. Epub 2017 Feb 20. PMID: 28277095.

CHAPTER 9

Characteristics of REM and NREM Dreams

Learning Objectives

- Describe typical content of dreams associated with awakenings from NREM
- Describe typical content of dreams associated with awakenings from REM
- Describe interaction of REM-NREM dreams across a single night of sleep
- Describe the role of dream content in emotional regulation

9.1 Introduction

While REM sleep is the phase of sleep from which dream reports are most reliably elicited, dream reports can also be elicited from any other stage of sleep including sleep onset and N3 SWS. Reports after awakenings from NREM stages of sleep tend to be shorter, less emotional, and less visually vivid than reports obtained from REM – but we do get reports of "dreams" from NREM sleep states. Indeed, you can get dream reports without REM when REM is chemically suppressed via antidepressant medications. Just as dreams can occur without REM, REM sleep can occur without dream reports. About 20 percent of awakenings after a REM episode results in no dream report. Activation of REM, therefore, does not necessarily eventuate in a dream or at least a dream report. In addition, children who have abundant REM do not consistently report dreams until visuo-spatial and cognitive skills have matured enough to support reporting of visual narratives (Foulkes, 1982). Similarly, patients with lesions in the orbitofrontal cortex, basal forebrain, and near the occipitotemporoparietal junction sometimes report complete cessation of dreaming (Solms, 1997). In addition, Solms emphasized that disconnection of the ascending meso-limbic-cortical dopaminergic tracts from their termination sites in ventromedial frontal lobes could also lead to the loss of dreaming. Given that this tract is associated with instinctual appetitive drive and motivational states it seems reasonable to conclude that this dopaminergic system may participate in the generation of some dreams. The loss of dreaming in these patients is not due simply to the inability to recall dreams, as their basic memory and recall abilities are largely intact. REM physiology as measured by sleep EEG is normal in these individuals, thus REM is still operating.

You can have activation of REM and no dreams and you can have dreams without activation of REM (as in the case of NREM dreams). On the other hand, REM is the brain state that most reliably produces what human beings have for centuries called dreams. And REM dreams are somewhat different from the "dreams" obtained after awakenings from NREM sleep states.

If you awaken someone at any point in the nightly sleep cycle and ask them "Were you experiencing anything just now while asleep?" they will often (though not invariably) report some sort of mentation. At the transition between wake and sleep when persons enter the N1 stage they will likely (60–90 percent of awakenings) report vivid, bizarre images, some emotion, and vivid characters but they will not likely report dramatic scenes or story lines involving these characters. At N2 early in the night, people generally report (about 40 percent of awakenings) vivid characters who interact with other characters and the dreamer, some emotion, and some plot, though the emotional intensity and story lines are not as intense or well-defined as reports derived from REM sleep awakenings. N2 awakenings later in the morning hours when REM sleep predominates are associated with longer mentation reports with more intense emotions and more clearly defined story lines. When subjects are awoken from stage N3 or slow wave sleep they often report no mentation at all but occasionally (20–50 percent of awakenings) will report static scenes or thought-like mentation, disconnected memory fragments, and the like. However, when people are awoken from REM, at least 80 percent of the time they will report vivid "dreams" with intense emotions, vivid imagery, long well-defined story lines, dramatic social interactions, and occasional bizarre imagery. In short, early night mentation reports mostly from NREM stages are shorter, less vivid, less bizarre, and less story-like with differing social interactions than mentation reports obtained from sleep states occurring later in the sleep cycle (mostly from REM but also some N2).

What might account for the qualitative differences in sleep mentation that occurs across the sleep cycle? Some scholars suggest that the two mentation types are generated by two different brain regions. This is called the two-generator model (Hobson et al., 2000). Alternatively, others (e.g., Antrobus, 1991) argue for a one-generator model with one brain network continuously generating mentation throughout the night with differing physiologic and cerebral activation levels determining how much of that mentation can be recalled at each point in the sleep cycle. A third model, dubbed the "covert REM sleep" model suggests that while sleep mentation is tightly coupled to REM sleep processes, periods of NREM sleep can generate "dreams" or mentations to the extent that those periods borrow from REM sleep brain networks. For Nielsen, covert REM sleep processes at sleep onset (N1) and during NREM sleep in the early morning hours that occur near REM sleep episodes produce the mentation associated with these sleep stages. In his review of REM vs. NREM awakenings studies, Nielsen (2000) showed that if the NREM awakenings occurred towards the morning (when REM sleep predominates) then the NREM reports become harder to distinguish from REM reports. Another model of dream generation is Solm's motivational reward theory wherein dream generation is tied to mesolimbic prefrontal dopaminergic activity. This is a reward circuit so Solm's hypothesizes that this mesolimbic-prefrontal dopaminergic activity supports the simulation of hallucinations (mediated by posterior cortical sites) of wish fulfillment during the dream.

Thus, in one-generator, theories of dream generation and in Nielsen's covert REM theory of dream generation, REM activation levels are crucial for dream generation. Dreaming depends on REM according to one-generator models. But what happens to dreaming if you eliminate REM? People on antidepressants report reduced levels of dreaming but not a complete elimination of dreaming. Oudiette et al., (2012) found that long, complex, and bizarre dreams persist even after pharmacologically suppressing REM sleep either partially or totally. Indeed while NREM "dreams" are indeed less bizarre, complex, and story-like than REM dreams, they nevertheless contain abundant social interactions, dramatic scenes, and intense emotions.

McNamara et al. (2005) investigated potential REM vs. NREM content differences by studying 100 REM, 100 NREM, and 100 wake reports that had been collected in the home from eight men and seven women using the "Nightcap" sleep/wake mentation monitoring system. The nightcap system reliably identifies episodes of REM and of N2 NREM. We scored these reports for number and variety of social interactions. We found that (1) social interactions were more likely to be depicted in dream than in wake reports (Table 9.1); (2) aggressive social interactions were more characteristic of REM than NREM or wake reports (Table 9.2); but (3) dreamer-initiated friendliness was more characteristic of NREM than REM (Tables 9.1–9.2 and Figure 9.1). It is important to note that *dreamer-initiated* aggressive interactions were *reduced to zero* in NREM dreams, while dreamer-initiated friendly interactions

Table 9.1 Frequency of social interactions by state

	REM	NREM	Wake	REM vs. NREM	REM vs. Wake	NREM vs. Wake
Total social interactions	56	34	26	.002**	.0001**	.21
Social interactions/ social reports	1.4	1.55	1.13	.18	.015*	.001**
Reports with at least one social interaction (of any type)	40	22	23	.005**	.009**	.86
Reports with at least one aggressive interaction	24	12	8	.025*	.001**	.34
Reports with at least one friendly interaction	17	15	17	.70	1.00	.70
Reports with at least one sexual interaction	2%	0%	0	.045*	.045*	1.00

* = < .05; ** = < .01

were twice as common in NREM as in REM. It is therefore apparent that the lack of aggression in NREM was not due simply to fewer social interactions occurring in NREM relative to REM as friendly interactions in NREM were more likely to be dreamer-initiated than in REM (90 percent vs. 54 percent respectively, p < .05). This fact, along with the total absence of dreamer-initiated aggression in NREM, suggests that an active process is operative in NREM that inhibits unpleasant and aggressive social impulses while promoting the emergence of pleasant and cooperative social impulses. Conversely, REM appears to facilitate the emergence of unpleasant aggressive impulses. We replicated these results in a 2010 study (McNamara et al., 2010) using EEG-verified REM and NREM awakenings instead of the nightcap method.

Table 9.2 Hall/Van de Castle social interaction percentages

	REM	NREM	Wake	REM vs. NREM	REM vs. Wake	NREM vs. Wake
Aggression/ Friendliness %	65%	33%	23%	.026*	.001**	.456
Befriender %	54%	90%	76%	.043*	.192	.354
Aggressor %	52%	0%	100%	.0001**	.014*	.0001**
Physical Aggression %	25%	18%	0%	.540	.007**	.043*

Note: Aggression/friendliness % = Dreamer-involved aggression/(Dreamer-involved aggression + Dreamer-involved friendliness); Befriender % = Dreamer as befriender/Dreamer as befriender + Dreamer as befriended); Aggressor % = Dreamer as Aggressor / (Dreamer as Aggressor + Dreamer as victim); Physical aggression % = Physical aggressions/All aggressions; *$p = < .05$; **$p = < .01$

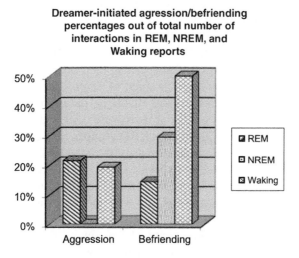

Dreamer-initiated agression/befriending
percentages out of total number of
interactions in REM, NREM, and
Waking reports

Figure 9.1 Dreamer-initiated aggression/befriending percentages out of total number of social interactions in REM, NREM, and waking reports.

Note: Aggression p-values: REM vs. NREM $< .0001$; REM vs. Waking $< .1$; NREM vs. Waking $< .0001$; Befriending p-values: REM vs. NREM $< .09$; REM vs. Waking $< .001$; NREM vs. Waking $< .15$. Roughly equal numbers of subjects (either six or seven) contributed to results depicted in each of the six columns (except of course the NREM aggression column)

9.1.1 NREM-REM Content Differences: Evidence from Dream Enactment Studies

Uguccioni et al. (2013) report some hard-to-get, unique data on enacted dreams, or dreams that patients appear to enact while asleep. The patient may start to vocalize while asleep as if talking to someone and then thrash around as if fighting some opponent, etc. The patient may actually get out of bed and run around the room as if trying to escape from a threat and so on. These types of dreams typically occur as part of the symptom complex associated with REM behavior disorder (RBD) or with sleepwalking or sleep terrors. Enacted dreams are uniquely important for a science of dreams as they give us a very unusual glimpse into dream content. Here we can see dreams being enacted as if on a stage while the patient is asleep and dreaming. We do not have to rely only on the patient's verbal report of a dream after he awakes.

In this study of enacted dreams, the investigators were interested in, among other things, the question of whether the content of REM dreams differed from the content of dreams that occurred in other stages of sleep – NREM dreams. The investigators could get at REM dreams via analysis of enacted dreams reported by the RBD patients and at NREM dreams via analysis of the enacted dreams reported by the sleepwalkers/ sleep terror patients who typically enact their dreams in NREM stages of sleep. Thirty-two patients with sleepwalking/sleep terrors (SW/ST) and twenty-four patients with REM behavior disorder (RBD) were consecutively recruited and interviewed concerning their enacted dreams. These were dreams experienced during a night of sleep videosomnography as well as recent and lifetime dreams involving parasomniac events and enacted dreams. A total of 121 dreams were analyzed in both groups (sleepwalking group, n = 74 dreams; RBD group, n = 47 dreams). Dream content was then scored using primarily the standardized Hall vs. de Castle criteria and Revonsuo's threats scale. There was a significantly higher level of aggression in the RBD than in SW/ST subjects but these aggression levels were not correlated with daytime waking behaviors. Sleepwalkers had more frequent misfortunes in their enacted dreams than patients with RBD (28 percent vs. 8 percent, p = 0.01) and tended to exhibit less frequent aggression (17 percent vs. 33 percent, p = 0.06) during the enacted dreams. In dreams with aggression both RBD and sleepwalkers/sleep terrors (SW/ST) patients were more often victims than aggressors. In dreams with misfortunes the sleepwalkers mostly fled from a threat/disaster while patients with RBD counterattacked when assaulted. The settings for SW/ST enacted dreams tended to be familiar/

domestic, while the settings in RBD dreams were less familiar. In summary, aggression (such as counterattacks) is rare (8 percent) in SW/ST enacted dreams, but common (reported by at least 33 percent of dreamers) in RBD. Given that SW/ST sleep parasomnias are associated with a dissociated state between N3 sleep and arousal, and RBD is associated with REM sleep, it is reasonable to suggest that the enacted dreams reflect brain state differences in these two sleep states. As the authors point out in their discussion, content analyses of thousands of dreams from healthy participants reveal strikingly similar content differences for REM vs. N2/N3 sleep dreams. It is a remarkable and now a fairly well-established fact that REM dreams appear to specialize in simulation of aggressive interactions while N2/N3 dreams specialize in simulation of non-aggressive and friendly interactions.

The authors suggest that their data is at least partially consistent with Revonsuo's threat simulation theory of dream content (Revonsuo, 2000) that states that dreams simulate daytime threats and thus make us better able to handle those daytime threats, because both SW/ST and RBD dreams appeared to have simulated threats to the dreamer with the RBD patients reacting with aggression and the SW/ST reacting with flight or awakenings. But note that the threat simulation hypothesis cannot explain the key question as to why the REM dreamers responded with aggression and the SW/ST with flight. In REM sleep there is some diminution of prefrontal inhibition on limbic brain sites. While this physiologic fact can account for the mechanics of the aggressive responses in REM dreams, it does not explain the question as to why such responses should occur while we are asleep in the first place. Why are limbic circuits disinhibited in REM in the first place? The dream content data suggests the reason is that Mother Nature wants the organism to simulate aggression-related behaviors while asleep. But again, why only for REM dreams? If activating aggression circuits while asleep is adaptive, why not do so in NREM states as well?

9.1.2 The Interaction of REM and NREM Dreams

NREM dreams very likely interact with REM dreams over the course of a single night. After the discovery of REM sleep, several authors (e.g., Trosman, Rechtschaffen, Offenkrantz, and Wolpert, 1960; French and Fromme, 1964) suggested that dreams at the beginning of the night would announce an emotional wish or emotional conflict that dreams later in the night would then pick up and work with in an attempt to contain or resolve the emotional conflict. Offenkrantz and Rechtschaffen

(1963) studied the sequential sleep patterns and dreams of a patient in psychotherapy for fifteen consecutive nights. They noted that scenes from childhood memories never occurred early in the night but did occur on eight of the fifteen nights in dreams late in the night, after 4:30 A.M. They also noted that all the dreams of a night tended to be concerned with the same emotional conflict or a small number of such conflicts. They also claimed that they found evidence that the organization of a particular dream depended on the results of the dream work of the preceding dream, such that dream wishes required less and less disguise as the night progressed. Rechtschaffen et al. (1963) studied sequential NREM-REM dreams within a single night in three subjects who had previously demonstrated good dream recall from NREM sleep. They found repeated instances of dream elements recurring throughout the dream sequence. For example, the image of a street corner appeared in the first NREM dream of the night. It later appeared as the place where the dreamer met a girl. Cartwright (1999; 2010) later discussed similar findings for emotional dream content continuity across a single night of sleep.

9.2 Characteristics of REM Dreams

9.2.1 Introduction

Dream recall after awakening from the REM state is associated with theta oscillations immediately preceding awakening (NREM recall is associated with alpha oscillations). Since theta activity in the hippocampus is associated with memory encoding more generally, it is not surprising that we have better and more detailed recall of dreams after REM awakenings than we do for dreams after NREM awakenings. Most REM dreams are of ordinary social interactions occurring in familiar settings with the dreamer and other characters talking about something of personal concern to the dreamer. Nevertheless, dreams obtained from subjects after awakenings from REM are longer in word length; evidence a greater character density; more social interactions with higher levels of aggression; more emotions, emotional intensity, and emotional memory consolidation; greater and more cohesive narrative structure (though with significant thematic discontinuities and occasional bizarre elements); and a reduced level of self-reflectiveness than dreams obtained from any other sleep state. In a previous chapter we discussed how REM dreaming involves activation and re-connectivity of the key nodes in the default mode network (DMN) or the set of structures of the social brain that are active during daytime mind wandering. We noted how DMN structures and the so-called "social brain" network overlap to a considerable extent. Those overlapping set of brain regions, the DMN and social brain, are essentially the set of structures most consistently activated in REM dreaming.

9.2.2 REM Dreams Are Associated with Reduced Self-Reflectiveness

Virtually all REM dreams involve the self or the dreamer interacting with other characters, and this self is usually at the center of the action. Although there is debate as to whether the dream self should be described as a full-fledged agent, it is clear that the dreamer not only intends certain actions in dreams but that in many dreams this intention is actually a striving toward a goal and this striving helps to create the narrative structure dreams typically employ. Although dreamers should be considered agents in the full sense of possessing intentional states and deploying plans to achieve those goals, the dreamer is nevertheless unable to critically reflect on the actions and interactions he or she undergoes in the dream. Most "damming" in this respect is the dreamer's inability to know that he is dreaming and the related non-critical acceptance of bizarre dream events as "normal." This reduction in self-reflectiveness is associated with reduction in activity levels of the dorsolateral prefrontal cortex during REM.

9.2.3 REM Dreams Have an Unusually Large Number of Familiar and Unfamiliar Characters

In REM dreams women dream equally often of men and women but men dream more of other men than of women, and usually these other men are in physically aggressive interactions with the dreamer. This latter sex difference (women dream equally often of males and females while men dream about aggressive encounters with other men) is consistent with theories of sexual selection and mating strategies in humans: Males compete among themselves for access to females.

In a study of 320 dream reports from thirty-three adults, Kahn et al. (2000) reported that 48 percent of characters in dreams were known to the dreamer. The average report length was 237 words and contained an average of 3.7 characters. According to the Hall/Van de Castle norms, only about half of the characters in dreams are familiar to the dreamer. In the background of most REM dreams some unidentified characters lurk, people that the dreamer cannot identify. Nevertheless the dreamer could often tell that the strangers or unidentified people in the dream were males. In some dream series up to 80 percent of characters are unknown males that are vaguely threatening to the dreamer. In an early study of over 1,000 dreams, Hall (1963) reported (1) that strangers in dreams were most often male, (2) that aggressive encounters were more likely to occur in an interaction with an unknown male than with an unknown female or with a familiar male or female, and (3) that unknown males appeared more frequently in the dreams of males than of females. Domhoff (2003) has shown that when male strangers appear in the dream, the likelihood that physical aggression will occur in that dream far exceeds what would be expected on the basis of chance. Strauch and Meir (1996) reported that in about every third dream the dreamer encountered only strangers!

9.2.4 REM Dreams Have Greater Numbers of Social Interactions and Higher Levels of Aggression

The results just summarized concerning the greater number of unfamiliar characters who turn out to be male strangers in REM dreams as well as the statistical association between the appearance of male strangers and physical aggression against the dreamer predicts that aggression levels will be higher in REM dreams as compared to NREM dreams. While overall aggression levels may not differ between REM and NREM dreams, when the dreamer is the initiator of an aggression then aggressive interactions are far more commonplace in REM dreams as compared to NREM dreams – even when the length of dream report is held constant. In 2010 McNamara et al. (2010) replicated the finding of higher aggression levels in REM vs. NREM with a convenience sample of sixty-four healthy participants (twenty-eight males, thirty-six females; mean age = 20.89, SD 2.56 years). The authors studied their sleep EEG in the sleep lab and conducted REM vs. NREM sleep awakenings. Key results are depicted in Figure 9.2.

This figure represents the dreamer's role in all dreamer-involved social interactions. There were thirty-eight REM dreams with dreamer involved social interactions and thirty-seven NREM dreams. This means that in 71 percent of the dreamers' social interactions in NREM dreams, the dreamer was a befriender.

Figure 9.2 shows that when we look only at those dreams where the dreamer was directly involved in (e.g., initiating) a social interaction, then clear REM–NREM differences emerge. As in our previous study

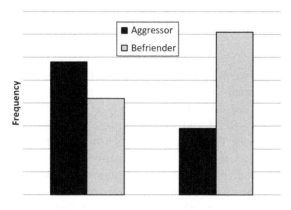

Figure 9.2 Frequency of dreamer's role in social interactions for REM and NREM dreams

with the nightcap technology, we find (with standard EEG methods) that in dreamer-involved friendly interactions, the dreamer was the befriender in only 42 percent of REM sleep dreams (N = 24) but was the befriender in 71 percent of NREM sleep dreams (n = 14; p = .070). In dreamer-involved aggressive interactions, the dreamer was the aggressor in 58 percent of REM sleep dreams (N = 12) and only 29 percent of NREM sleep dreams (N = 17).

It is important to note that these REM-NREM differences emerge only when you look at *dreamer-involved* social interactions. One has to take the point of view of the dream ego to understand what is happening in dreams. When we analyzed the entire REM/NREM dream set using the standard Hall/Van de Castle categories mentioned, we found that among the social interaction scales, REM sleep dreams were *less aggressive* and more friendly than NREM sleep dreams. Of aggressive and friendly social interactions in REM sleep dreams, only 37 percent (N = 38) were aggressive compared to 57 percent of interactions in NREM sleep dreams (N = 37; p = .082). Fifty percent of aggressive interactions in REM sleep dreams (N = 24) were physically aggressive (as opposed to verbal aggression or other types) as opposed to 43 percent of aggressive interactions in NREM sleep dreams (N = 23; p = .654). We believe that most of the N2 aggressions were verbal in nature and were from our female participants. *However*, as depicted in Figure 9.2, looking at just dreamer-involved social interactions, the dreamer tended to be the aggressor in REM sleep dream interactions and the befriender in NREM sleep dream interactions.

9.2.5 REM Dreams Engage in Greater Amounts of Emotional Processing

Strauch and Meier (1996, page 138) comment that in their dream series, "barely every second NREM dream featured the dream self emotionally related to the dream situation, whereas four out of every five REM dreams involved the dreamer emotionally in its events." Smith et al. (2004) scored both REM and NREM reports for emotion content from twenty-five dreamers. They identified eight emotions and found that most of them were rated as more intensely expressed in REM vs. NREM dreams. They then divided these eight emotions into positive and negative categories. The positive emotion category consisted of joy/elation and love, while the negative emotion category consisted of anger, anxiety/fear, sadness, and shame. They found that negative emotions were significantly more intense in REM than NREM, whereas positive emotions were not.

Van der Helm et al. (2011b) presented evidence consistent with the claim that REM sleep functions in part to facilitate emotional regulation. The authors point out that REM sleep is associated with a massive reduction in noradrenergic tone in forebrain centers including the amygdala. (The amygdala is known to be involved in the processing of emotions – especially negative emotions like fear.) In addition, processing of emotional memories via amygdalar-hippocampal interactions takes place during REM. Thus, two events take place in REM that are crucial to daytime emotional regulation: (1) reactivity of the amygdala is down-regulated due to suppression of central noradrengic tone and (2) emotional memories are reactivated in amygdalar-hippocampal networks during REM. The latter process involves the processing of memories in absence of norepinephrine such that they are stripped of their stress-related arousing capacities before being stored in long-term networks. In short, REM is hypothesized to de-potentiate amygdalar reactivity and reprocess emotional memories in a state where noradrenergic activity is suppressed, thereby decreasing the overall intensity of negative emotional memories.

In the study, van der Helm et al. performed two repeat fMRI tests on thirty-four volunteers (test 1, test 2), separated by twelve-hour intervals containing either a night of EEG-recorded sleep or a waking day. During each test, participants viewed and rated the subjective emotional intensity of 150 standardized emotional pictures. Importantly, participants viewed the same stimuli at both test sessions, affording a measure of change in emotional reactivity to previously experienced affective stimuli (test 2 – test 1) following wake or sleep.

Results showed that those who slept between the image viewings reported a significant decrease in their ratings of the intensity of the emotional images as well as a decrease in amygdala reactivity, while the participants who were awake between viewings/ratings demonstrated increases in both ratings and amygdala reactivity. Interestingly the extent of overnight decrease in both amygdala reactivity and ratings was significantly correlated with the extent of reduced prefrontal EEG gamma activity (a biomarker of arousal and possibly central noradrenergic activity) during REM such that those with the lowest levels of REM-gamma expressed the largest overnight decrease in emotion reactivity. Thus, the authors have shown that amygdalar activity is decreased in REM and that this is associated with both a reduction in behavioral ratings of intensity of emotional pictures and a reduction in EEG gamma power in PFC. The reduction in emotional reactivity associated with sleep may be a by-product of other processes occurring in REM. For example, the authors also reported a significant group (wake, sleep) by test (test 1, test 2) amygdala connectivity interaction with the ventral-medial prefrontal cortex (vmPFC), that indicated an overnight increase in functional connectivity in the sleep group and a corresponding decrease in functional connectivity across the day in the wake group. These data suggest that the overnight reduction in amygdala activity was due to or related to an increase in vmPFC connectivity. PFC functioning is crucial for a huge array of higher cognitive functions including of course dreaming. If so then the facilitation of emotional memory consolidation during REM likely also requires cognitive products of REM, including of course REM dreams. During REM sleep, memories are being reactivated, decontextualized, and then integrated into long-term memory. These findings are consistent with Nielsen and Levin's (2007) proposal that dreaming normally functions to extinguish fear memories.

9.2.6 REM Dreams May Be More Story-Like than NREM Dreams

Nielsen et al. (2001) reported greater story-like complexity in REM vs. NREM dreams and greater evidence for episodic progression in REM vs. NREM dreams. More recently, however, Montangero and Cavallero (2015) reported that none of fourteen dream reports elicited from N2 or REM was structured like a canonical story; nor did the REM and NREM reports differ in terms of their sequential regulation of events in the narratives.

So what account is correct? Do REM dreams exhibit greater story-like qualities than NREM dreams? Certainly, on the face of it, REM dreams are far more story-like than NREM dreams. If you wake someone up from REM you are far more likely to obtain a story of who did what to whom and why than if you woke that same person up from an NREM episode. But to date all studies attempting to capture the story-like structure of REM dreams have been inadequate. Nielsen and colleagues (2001) attempted to capture story content focused on the concept of episodic progression, defined as a three-step causal chain of events. An event causes a character to react, and this reaction entails another event. But stories are made of more than cause and effect sequences. They build to a climax and often involve dramatic tension and resolution. Episodic progressions go somewhere, they do not just continue indefinitely and aimlessly. As Montangero and Cavallero (2015) point out, about half of the dreams in Nielsen and colleagues' sample did not include a single, well-defined episode. Similarly, Montangero and Cavallero (2015)'s attempted to capture story qualities of dream reports using microanalysis of the linguistic connections between successive temporal units. But stories are far more than sequential ordering of elements in a discourse. In addition, Montangero and Cavallero studied only about seven dreams from each sleep state. Finally, while Cipolli and Poli (1992) used a more sophisticated measure of story structure they still confined their analysis to episodes and hierarchical event structures, but again, stories are more than episodes and embedding one episode within another does not necessarily capture dramatic tension and progression within a true story.

In summary, while it is safe to say that the phenomenological appearance of REM dreams manifestly reveals them to be well-formed stories, researchers have not yet been able to adequately measure just what makes REM dreams story-like.

Pace-Schott (2013) has suggested that the story-like quality of REM dreams is similar in some respects to confabulation seen after damage to the frontal lobes. Confabulation after prefrontal damage involves patients using whatever cues or suggestions are at hand to construct a fabrication to explain some puzzling behavior. They do this effortlessly and automatically when they find themselves needing to explain something to themselves or others. They are unaware that the explanation they just concocted is largely made-up and false. Just as in the case of REM dreams there is a fictive narrative produced effortlessly and without insight that it is not reality. Pace-Schott also pointed out that the brain regions implicated in REM dreaming shares some of the same brain regions implicated in confabulation. Spontaneous confabulation, for example, results from lesions of the anterior limbic system including posterior medial orbitofrontal cortex (pmOPFC, part of vmPFC) and its subcortical connections. REM dreams, Pace-Schott concludes "may represent a potent, naturally occurring form of confabulation in which imaginary events are not only created and believed but are vividly experienced as organized, multimodal hallucinations" (Pace-Schott, 2013, page 2).

But the comparison of REM dreams with confabulation may be problematic in some respects. REM dreams are more story-like than confabulations – at least the confabulations I have seen and heard produced by many patients at Neurology and Aphasia rounds at the Boston VA hospital through the years. Most confabulations do not rise to the level of stories. They are after the fact ad hoc explanations. They are more like rationalizations or explanations than dramas with a hero, plot, climax, and resolution. In addition, as Pace-Schott himself notes, vmPFC/pmOPFC *damage* leads to confabulation, whereas its *activation* accompanies dreaming. Nevertheless, dorsolateral prefrontal cortex down regulation in REM sleep does occur and this may lead to the inability of dreamers to monitor and correct their ongoing self-understanding of their behaviors.

9.2.7 Conclusions

While it is now clear that REM dreams and NREM dreams differ in terms of content and phenomenologies, these two dream types do not exhaust dream phenomenology. Relative to REM dreams, NREM dreams tend to be less story-like, bizarre, and contain fewer aggressive social interactions and greater numbers of friendly interactions, at least where the dreamer-initiated interactions are concerned. In the next chapter we will present some unusual dream types so as to demonstrate the amazing variety of dream experiences people undergo each and every night of every year.

Review Questions

- Some antidepressants depress aspects of REM sleep. What might happen to dreams and their role in emotional regulation when REM is chemically suppressed?
- Evaluate the strengths and weaknesses of the evidence for greater aggression levels in REM vs. NREM dreams and discuss the significance of this finding.

- What role do dreams play in consolidation of memories?
- What is the dream-lag effect and what is its significance for a theory of dream function?

Further Reading

Nielsen, T. A. (2000). A review of mentation in REM and NREM sleep: "Covert" REM sleep as a possible reconciliation of two opposing models. *Behavioral and Brain Sciences*, 23(6), 851–866; discussion 904–1121.

Nielsen, T. A., Kuiken, D., Alain, G., Stenstrom, P., & Powell, R. A. (2004). Immediate and delayed incorporations of events into dreams: Further replication and implications for dream function. *Journal of Sleep Research*, 13(4), 327–336.

Stickgold, R. (2013). Parsing the role of sleep in memory processing. *Current Opinion in Neurobiology*, 23(5), 847–853.

Van der Helm, E., & Walker, M. P. (2011). Sleep and emotional memory processing. *Sleep Medicine Clinics*, 6(1), 31–43. PMID:25285060.

Wichniak, A., Wierzbicka, A., Walęcka, M., & Jernajczyk, W. (2017). Effects of antidepressants on sleep. *Current Psychiatry Reports*, 19(9), 63. doi: 10.1007/s11920–017–0816–4. Review. PMID: 28791566.

CHAPTER 10

Dream Varieties

Learning Objectives

- Evaluate the significance of the huge variety of dreaming experiences reported by people
- Evaluate the mechanisms and signficance of dream recall in dream phenomenology
- Distinguish properties and content of unusual dream types like lucid dreaming, sleep paralysis dreams, and nightmares
- Identify the impact of the big data revolution on documenting dream variety and experiences

10.1 Introduction

It is not possible to understand dreams unless we become familiar with the whole terrain of dreams. We have discussed ordinary run-of-the-mill dreams that are associated with both REM and NREM sleep states. But there is a very large variety of dream types reported by people. To build an adequate understanding of dreams and a testable theory of dreams we therefore need to marshal all of the salient facts concerning dreams, and those facts must include the chracteristics of the wide variety of dream types. Scientists who study dreams agree that dreams vary substantially in terms of their content and their formal phenomenologic features. For example, children's dreams are very different from adult's dreams and men's dreams differ substantially from women's dreams. There are nightmares, "big" or emotionally significant dreams, lucid dreams, shared or mutual dreams, twin dreams (dreams reported by twins), "spiritual" dreams, precognitive or prophetic dreams, visitation dreams (where dead loved one appear in a dream), and many other types. Dreams also vary by historical period: Dreams of the ancient Greeks and Romans are different than dreams of people in the Renaissance period of European history. Dreams also vary by culture: Dreams of people living in traditional societies are very different from dreams of modernized peoples. Similarly, dreams of people living in Islamic cultures differ from dreams of people living in cultures where other religions predominate and so on. All of this should be pretty obvious but dream variation is an understudied topic in the field of sleep and dream studies. While the variation in dream content and types has been documented there is little discussion of the theoretical importance of that variation. I will argue that the fundamental theoretical importance of dream variation is that it suggests that dream function is probably multiple. Dreams do not have only one function. No one theory can account for this huge variation in dream content. The evident fact that there are multiple dream types is also consistent with the idea that dreams are products of the social brain, and function, at least in part, to shape, alter, influence, or manipulate social relationships. Now that is NOT all that dreams do. It is likely that dreams transcend mundane social functions in multiple ways, but we simply do not know enough about these suprarational functions of dreams to comment upon them intelligently. I urge further research on so-called anomalous phenomena and dreams but I focus here on available empirical data we currently have on hand.

I will survey a number of dream types in order to give the reader a feel for the large terrain of dream phenomena any dream theory must account for. I have discussed typcial dreams of men, women, and children in previous chapters. I will now discuss a variety of dream types as well as atypcial dream phenomena as it is often in the study of atypcial cases that we can gain insight on basic functional design chracteristics of the phenomenon under study. But first we need to consider the fundamental act of recalling a dream in the first place, as dream recall is the primary biologic constraint on dream variety.

10.2 Dream Recall

Why is it that some people seem to be able to recall dreams frequently while others claim they never dream at all? Although spontaneously or experimentally induced awakenings from REM sleep result in 80 to 90 percent dream recall rates and everyone has REM sleep, we still get people claiming not to dream at all. Survey studies show that most people recall one to two dreams per week at home (Stepansky, Holzinger, Schmeiser-Rieder, Saletu, Kunze, and Zeitlnofer, 1998). About 31 percent of the population recall dreams about ten times per month or more, 37 percent report dreaming one to nine times per month, and 32 percent report dreaming less than once per month. That break down of dream recall rates suggests that there is a normal distribution of dream recall in the general population with about a third of the population being high dream recallers and a third being relatively low dream recallers. A small percentage of people in the low recall wing of the dream recall distribution claim to never dream. What is going on with these people? Do they actually dream and just not recall their dreams or do they really not dream at all?

In a recent ingenious study by Herlin and colleagues (2015), the study authors were able to show that people who claim not to have ever dreamed actually do dream because the authors witnessed the non-dreamers actually acting out their dreams! The authors capitalized on the fact that these individuals had Parkinson's disease, which is frequently (though not invariably) accompanied by REM behavior disorder or RBD. RBD patients act out their dreams whenever they go into REM sleep because the cells associated with the motor paralysis that normally inhibits overt behaviors during REM are destroyed by the disease process associated with PD. The authors studied patients who reported no dream recall for at least ten years, and "never-ever" recallers who claimed never to have dreamed. These non-dreamers were compared to ordinary dream recallers. All of the individuals in these distinctive dream recall groups had RBD. Of the 289 patients with rapid eye movement sleep behavior disorder, eight (2.8 percent) patients had no dream recall, including four (1.4 percent) patients who had never ever recalled dreams, and four patients reported no dream recall for ten to fifty-six years.

Thus, Herlin et al. really did find some individuals who would have been classified as non-dreamers in other studies. These were people who claimed to have virtually never had a dream. Then the authors watched these individuals overnight, using videosomnography or other techniques to verify they were in REM sleep. "All non-recallers exhibited, daily or almost nightly, several complex, scenic and dreamlike behaviors and speeches, which were also observed during rapid eye movement sleep on video-polysomnography (arguing, fighting and speaking)." In short, like every other person with RBD, these individuals exhibited the classical dream enactment behaviors of RBD. In typical cases of RBD when we query these patients as to whether they recall any dreams they had during the night, they will often describe dreams that match up to varying degrees with the behaviors they exhibited during their dream enactment behaviors while asleep. In the case of Herlin et al.'s poor dream recallers, however, they denied recalling any dreams when they were asked about dreams in the morning after they exhibited classic dream enactment behaviors! Neither did they recall a dream following sudden awakenings from rapid eye movement sleep. Why can't these individuals, these poor dream recallers, recall the dreams that their own dream enactment behaviors suggest they had during the night? The eight non-recallers with rapid eye movement sleep behavior disorder did not differ in terms of cognition, clinical, or sleep measures from seventeen "control" dreamers studied by the authors. So it can't be that the poor recallers could not recall their dreams simply because they have poor memory or particularly severe disease and so on.

So what prevents poor dream recallers from remembering their dreams? As this and other studies have shown there is a small percentage of the population (up to 3 percent) who swear that they never dream. But this study suggests that they simply cannot recall their dreams. Why?

10.3 Neural Correlates of Dream Recall

The probable answer is that the brains of poor dream recallers differ slightly from the brains or ordinary recallers. The neural correlates of dream recall has been studied using quantitative scalp electroencephalographic or EEG measures. Dream recall from stage N2 is associated with a lower level of alpha oscillatory activity in the right temporal area. On awakening from REM, dream recall is associated with a higher level of frontal theta activity. Theta and alpha oscillations are correlated with successful dream recall with involvement of temporoparietal (TPO) and ventromedial prefrontal (vmPFC) areas. Interestingly, lesions in the white matter tracts to and from ventromedial prefrontal cortex or lesions disconnecting temporal parietal junction from other regions in the circuit that make up the social brain can result in cessation of dream recall. Regional cerebral blood flow to TPO and vmPFC is higher in frequent dream recallers compared to low frequency recallers. Thus, people who claim never to dream very likely have reduced (relative to the rest of the population) brain activity levels in the TPO and vmPFC.

Siclari et al. (2017) reported a very interesting set of findings on the neural correlates of dreaming/dream recall. Since the 1950s we have known that if we awakened people during REM we would reliably get reports of dreams. About 70 percent of the time if we awakened people during the N2 light stage of sleep we would also get reports of dreams. Even if we awoke people during deep slow wave sleep states (N3) we could still get reports of dreams, though certainly not as reliably as when we awoke them from REM or N2. In short, even though REM, N2, and N3 were defined by dramatically different EEG signatures we could still get reports of dreams in each of these sleep states. Clearly, the standard

EEG sleep montage was too gross an instrument to isolate those brain states most reliably associated with dream reports.

Siclari et al. used high density EEG recordings to isolate neural correlates of dreaming regardless of standardly identified sleep state. The authors contrasted the presence and absence of dreaming in both NREM and REM sleep. When a posterior "hot zone" showed a decrease in low-frequency EEG activity – traditionally known as "EEG activation" – subjects reported upon awakening that they did have dream experiences. By contrast, when low-frequency EEG activity increased in the same area, subjects reported that they had no dreams. Thus, those neural sites that were consistently activated whenever participants reported dreams and consistently inactivated whenever participants reported the absence of dreaming – regardless of standardly defined sleep states – included sites within the "hot zone" that comprised the occipital cortex, precuneus, and posterior cingulate gyrus. By monitoring neural activity in this posterior "hot zone" the authors could predict when a subject would recall dreaming.

Use of high density EEG is extremely technically challenging. That is why so few sleep studies use this technique. It is subject to all kinds of artifacts and so researchers have to use extraordinary precautions (e.g., specially built soundproof rooms, etc.) to control noise when using these huge EEG montages. The authors not only used high density EEG during sleep; they were apparently able to avoid artifactual contaminants even when repeatedly awakening subjects for dream reports!

The neural correlates for dream experience was localized to the so-called hot zone for dream experience in the posterior cortical region in this study. That region included occipital cortex (visual center) and the precuneus and the posterior cingulate. This site seems reasonable to me to be a hot zone for dream experience. Precuneus activation, for example, has been associated with self-awareness and is part of the social brain circuit. It has been known for some time that damage to the temporal-occipital-parietal (TPO) junction can result in cessation of dream recall. The hot zone described in this chapterlikely overlaps to some extent with the TPO.

When the authors looked at the hot zone during REM, cortical activation patterns extended far beyond the posterior cortical hot zone into the frontal lobes. Lesions to the ventromedial frontal lobes, also results in cessation of dream recall. In summary, Siclari's results are consistent with previous research on neural correlates of dream recall but adds to it the precuneus. Thus, we have the precuneus, the TPO, and the vmPFC as key nodes in a circuit responsible for generation of dreaming and subsequent recall of dreams. These nodes are also the key nodes in the social brain circuit.

10.4 Lucid Dreamers Are Especially High Dream Recallers

People who report that they frequently have lucid dreams are also evidence of the highest dream recall rates. This is not surprising given that you need to frequently dream and recall your dreams if you are going to have any hope of becoming aware or lucid in one of them. What is it about these high dream recallers that makes them the world champions in dream recall? Studies show that they differ from ordinary dream recallers in terms of their ability to solve puzzles, to achieve sudden insight in solving a puzzle, and in control of their attentional skills. Presumably their brain activity levels in the social brain circuit are also high.

What can be done to boost dream recall rates for people who wish to recall more of their dreams? Until we can directly boost brain activity levels in the social brain circuit, all you need to do to boost dream recall is to set the intention to recall dreams and then use a journaling technique to record the dreams you remember. Here is where the new apps associated with smartphone devices can help.

A sleep and dream journaling app can be downloaded in two minutes on literally millions of phones. Consider for example if you had an app that could reliably detect REM sleep (via an accelerometer). When the movement data detected a REM profile the phone would then emit a wake-up alarm and turn on a recording function so that you can speak your dream directly into the phone before you forget it. This can be done via auto-dialing right into the phone's recorder or an app designed for recording audio files, etc. Most dream apps can transmit the dream audio files directly into a website where it is automatically content analyzed and aggregated into a huge database with other dreams sent by people from all over the world!

DreamON is a smart phone app launched by a group in Scotland. You activate the app, choose a soundscape (such as peaceful ocean waves) to work with for the night, and then place the phone on your bed. The phone uses its accelerometer to detect movements or the lack thereof to identify when a person enters REM. Once the individual is likely to be in REM the soundscape is triggered and played on the phone's speaker. The idea is to test the hypothesis that the soundscapes will reliably alter dream content in positive ways. Upon awakening the individual is asked to record their dream, which is then sent to a central database.

Harvard PhD student Daniel Nadler developed an iPhone app similar to DreamON called Sigmund. Instead of soundscapes Sigmund uses a list of 1,000 keywords that can be played while you are in REM sleep. After you select one to five words from the list, a female voice reads the words you select during your REM cycles. I have worked with the creators of the Dreamboard smartphone app (www.dreamboard.com). Dreamboard collects reports of your dreams over time and identifies themes and information sequences that appear from dream to dream. The Dreamboard tool can prompt users to remember details from their dreams and over time I expect the dreamboard tool will be able to select cue words from your own personal archive of dreams, thus dramatically enhancing the power to remember details of YOUR dreams as well as the links between past and current dreams.

10.5 Dreams in Traditional Societies

Nothing illustrates the social function of dreams better than examining the role of dreams in small scale traditional societies. By traditional societies I mean tribally based groups of perhaps a few hundred to a few thousand individuals living the way our hunter gatherer or horticultural ancestors lived 20,000 or more years ago. There is no straightforward concordance between traditional societies and early human groups. Traditional societies are not mere replicas of early human groups. They are not "primitive" or backward. Rather they are living the ways that early human groups likely lived and therefore we can learn something about our ancestors from studying these traditional societies. Small scale traditional societies are the closest thing we have to a picture of what ancestral human societies were like. Therefore they can tell us something about the ways in which dreams were regarded and used by our ancestors.

We now have excellent studies of the role and status of dreams in traditional societies from several ethnographers and anthropologists, such as Steward Lincoln (1935), Eggan (1949), Devereux (1951), Kilborne (1981), Kracke (1979), and Irwin (1994). In addition, the role that dreams play in the generation of social relationships and cultural artifacts such as rituals, sub-societies, religious myths, group alliances, medical practices, and much else has been reviewed several times in the anthropological literature (see, e.g., Barnouw, 1963; Bourguignon, 1972; D'Andrade, 1961; Eggan, 1961; Grunebaum and Callois, 1966; Irwin, 1994; Lohmann, 2003; Laughlin, 2011; Tedlock, 1987, 1992;). The work of these anthropologists and ethnographers has made it clear, for all who are willing to study their carefully documented ethnographies on aboriginal peoples all across the planet, that dreams were almost universally considered to be central sources for rules governing social relationships as well as sources of all kinds of cultural innovations – most especially religious innovations. In his study of the Plains Indian cultures of North America, Irwin (1994) noted that "Dreaming is a creative basis for what might be called higher knowledge in the Native American context . . . Dreams and visions constantly revealed new applications of many types such as: inventive technologies, hunting methods, warfare strategies, healing practices and herbal formulations, along with other innovations in culture. For example, the origin of fire making was attributed to visionary experience by the Lakota" (Irwin, 1994, page 191).

In many traditional societies certain members of the population underwent initiation rites to become specialists in dream sharing and interpretation. For example, the "daykeepers" among the Quiche Maya of Guatemala not only interpret dreams, they actively encourage tribal children to remember their activities in dreams and to consider these dream activities of equal importance to daytime waking activities. Many traditional societies (e.g., Huichol Indians of Mexico, Yansi of Zaire, many tribal groups of the Yoruba nation in central Africa, Mapuche Indians of Chile, Ojibay of North America, Lokota of North Dakota, and many others) practice daily dream sharing rituals where groups gather in the morning to share dreams and to occasionally enact them. For example, if a dream is considered to carry significance for the dreamer's life vocation or for the tribe's welfare, the scenes in the dream will be translated into dance and ceremony and then performed. The tribe may even set aside valuable time and resources to create new garments, masks, ornaments, and other cultural artifacts to fully bring to life the scenes, characters, and drama in the dream.

Dreams in traditional societies could confer on a person tremendously important social status – yet there are no accounts of attempts to fake significant dreams in all of the ethnographies I have studied. The best studied example of this status-inducing dreaming experience is the case of the shamans of traditional societies. Shamans were the expert practitioners of the spiritual and magical arts of the traditional world. They were a mix of medicine man and sorcerer. They often did not choose to be a shaman. Instead they had a dream one night, shared it with the group, and then was designated shaman. They then had to apprentice themselves to an existing shaman, learn the medical and religious lore of the tribe, conduct medical interventions, direct ceremonies, chant myths, and occasionally direct hunting parties to optimal hunting grounds. Initiatory dreams of a Siberian shaman almost always contain visions of dismemberment of the body, followed by a renewal of the internal organs and viscera, ascent to the sky and dialog with the gods or spirits, descent to the underworld, and conversations with spirits and souls of the dead shamans. These intense visceral experiences then lead to various revelations in a dream state.

The North American Ojibwa Algonguin-speaking Indians of Canada see the characters and events of dreams as carrying a significance almost equal to that of daytime vents but they do not confuse dream events with waking events. *Pawaganeak* or "dream visitors" are other than human characters (what we might call supernatural beings) that come to Ojibwa dreamers in their dreams to deliver information and gifts or demands. These exchanges with the visitors establish reciprocal relations between the visitors and the dreamer. These reciprocal obligations become public once the dream is shared and must be observed to the letter. If they are not, the tribe takes note and stigmatizes the individual as engaging in bad conduct. The bad conduct accrues to the individual's reputation and follows him until the obligations are discharged appropriately or some other ritual intervention is accomplished. The *Pawaganak* are highly sought after in Ojibwa culture not only because these relationships that alter a person's social standing in the tribe can be established but also because the gifts often create special powers in the individual – powers to see the future, cure the ill, or obtain the best hunt or best resources. Occasionally the dreamer obtains the power of sorcery so that he or she can inflict harm on an enemy by performing some ritual or incantation discovered in the dream. Death songs, curative songs, songs for the hunt, and other powerful songs can also come to the dreamer in dreams with the visitors. These songs then remain with the individual for the rest of his life.

Just as the Siberian shamans underwent their initiation into the shaman's life via initiatory dreams so too did Ojibwa boys find their special gifts via a dream initiation ritual. A boy about to enter puberty and become a man would undergo the dream fast. Once entered into the ritual he would be called a *kigusamo*. Before he could receive his initiatory dream he had to become pure or *pekize* via fasting, cleansing rituals, and avoidance of women. Then a group of male relatives would take him out into the wilderness and build a platform for him to sleep in, often naked to the elements. He was not allowed food until the initiatory dream came. His male relatives might perform a song they received in dreams to strengthen the boy but often the boy would be left entirely alone. Then the dreams would come and the supernatural beings would appear in his dreams. He would have been admonished to accept gifts from the first beings to appear to him as they were often evil or trickster spirits. The boy had to be patient and wait for a genuine dream visitor. He then had to prove to the spirit being that he was worthy to establish a personal relationship and reciprocal obligations with the being. Having passed these tests the dream visitor would then bestow gifts or exceptional powers or *pimadaziwin* on the boy in the form of incantations, songs, dances, or cures, etc. The boy would feel himself transformed into the form of his now titular spirit being and then leave the site to return to the village and share his dream. The tribe may then enact the dream in full ceremonial style thus making the boy into a man – a man with special powers to serve the tribe.

This all too brief summary of the role and power of dreams in traditional societies underlines the importance of dreams in these cultures to significantly alter social relationships for the dreamer. It should not be surprising therefore that dreaming taps the social brain circuits just discussed.

10.6 Physical Symptom Dreams

Because sleep is associated with reduced visual input it is commonly believed that the brain becomes more attuned to picking up internal somatic signals and then turning these signals into images that appear in dreams. But it is entirely possible that the the brain/mind can pick up faint or prominent internal somesthetic signals whether or not external sensory input is reduced. However, the evaluation criteria concerning these internally generated bodily signals changes as a function of whether the waking or the dreaming mind first evaluates them. There may be benefits to having the dreaming mind first evaluate a bodily pain or a developing infection. Sometimes images capture more information than do words or discursive accounts. In addition, dreams have a tendency to amplify sensation such that a barely audible tone in the bedroom becomes a rising siren in the dream and so on. For example,

Feeling feverish and light-headed shortly after a flu shot and aware of an exhaustion in my limbs associated with a rapid involuntary tremor, I lay on the floor, fell asleep and found myself in my study facing a rattlesnake. Its uplifted head was oscillating rapidly (at what I realized on awakening was the same rate and quality of my shaking leg muscles). Sinking to the floor, overcome by terror I crept backwards before its steady advance. Finally, I pushed a chair against it. To my surprize the rattlesnake stopped its advance and I awoke with the brief fever gone. (Hunt, 1989, page 80)

There are many documented cases in the literature on dreams capturing signals related to bodily dysfunction and illness often far before the illness was detectable by conventional means. This is an area of dream research that needs to be more rigorously examined as it could be of immense clinical significance.

10.7 Dreams of Patients with Multiple Personality Disorder/ Dissociative Identity Disorder (MPD/DID)

Dreaming in dissociative identity disorder is associated with many under-studied but fasinating phenomena. Therapists of patients with MPD/DID report that alter personalities can appear in dreams as characters in the dream. Often a new alter will first appear in a dream and then later take over control of the behavioral repertoire of the individuala and become a daytime alter. The dreamer will often experience a switch from her primary identity to an alter during a dream. Because there is amnesia for the actions of an alter during waking experience, the primary identity will occassionally experience the alter's daytime experience as a dream. Barrett presents the case where a woman with MPD/DID had recurring nightmares of catching evil cats and stuffing them in garbage bags but then awoke to find herself covered in cat hairs. She then worried that an alter had atually been capturing cats and stuffing them into garbage bags. Sometimes several alters will be in the same dreams. Alter number one will describe the dream in detail from her position as onlooker while alter number two will describe the same scene as experienced from her perspective rather than as onlooker and so forth. The host personality will sometimes gain memories in dreams that belong to one of the alters who experienced the events in question during a waking experience.

10.8 Sexual Dreams

While Freud made us all think that dreams were about sex, quantitative studies of dream content have revealed that only 12 percent of reported dreams contain explicit sexual content. Most dreams are about mundane daily social interactions with familiars and a couple of strangers. But of course, most people do not like to share content that they find embarassing so these numbers are probably underestimates of the number of dreams that contain explicit sexual content. "Wet" dreams or dream-induced orgasms peak for men in their twenties and for women in their forties. It may be that many people experience their first orgasm in a dream, though I could find no confirmatory data on this speculation. Most people experience the sexual content of their dreams as pleasurable. As discussed in previous chapters REM sleep is associated with genital arousal for both men and women, though this arousal is not always associated with sexual content in the dreams. Nor do sexual dreams typically reflect the sexual fantasies of the individual. We do not always dream our most common sexual fantasies – though of course, some dreams do involve the dreamer's sexual fantasies. Some sexual dreams are classic wish fulfillment dreams such as when we dream of making love with someone we desire but with whom we have no relationship. Virtually all types and kinds of sexual acts have been depicted in sexual dreams – even sexual acts not performed by the individual in waking life. There are many unanswered questions concernining sexuality and dreams. The dreams of homosexual, lesbian, and trangendered individuals have not been extensively studied. The correlations between daytime sexual activities and nightly dreams has not been studied either. If compensatory theories of dreams were correct we would for example expect an inverse correlation between the two series of activities but we do not yet have such data.

10.9 Incubated Dreams

Ritual invoking of a dream for healing or medical purposes was practiced for thousands of years in the ancient world. The best studied case is the Asclepian rituals wherein a person with an illness would travel to a temple of the God Asclepius and sleep in that temple until he or she had a dream that spoke to the issue of the illness. The evidence for the effectiveness of the ritual comes in the hard form of inscriptions incised on stone by grateful patients who were apprently cured or at least left improved after performing the incubation rituals, obtaining a dream, and then getting well. Sometimes the temple priests interpreted the dreams and then administered treatments prompted by the dream content. Perhaps it was these treaments that cured the patients rather than anything associated with the incubated dreams. But it must be remembered that priestly administration of treatments would often include items (potions, bleedings, administration of poinsons, scarifications, etc.) that would almost certainly make any patient worse, so these treatments are not likely the causes of the cures obtained in these temples. Suppliants to an Asclepian temple had to report an invitational dream from the god wherein the god invited the suppliant to the temple for a cure. Fasting, ritual bathing in cold water, and animal sacrfice had to precede admittance into the ritual area of the temple. The suppliant once entered into the temple would be shown a couch or abaton or adytum upon which to sleep. The suppliant would sleep there until an appropropriate dream came. Most propitious dreams involved the apperance of the god himself who touched the patient on the afflicted body part or delivered some information or an image or a kind of gift the patient could use to relive the suffering associated with the affliction.

There are many contemporary accounts of persons attempting to use incubated dreams for various purposes with varying degress of success. There is no question that dreams can be incubated to come to the dreamer. But there is no consensus on methods to promote incubation as we cannot reproduce the religious context that supported the Asclepian rituals in the ancient world.

10.10 Lucid Dreams

Lucid dreaming has long been a topic of interest in dream research. The term lucid dreaming was coined by Frederick van Eeden in 1911. He reported on lucid nightmares among other lucidity phenomena. In a lucid nightmare the dreamer is aware that he is dreaming and that the dream is a nightmare. The nightmare themes often involve demonic figures out to inflict terrible harm on the dreamer who struggles to wake up but can't.

But the more common lucid dream is a typical dream where the dreamer is aware of the dream and has no strong desire to wake up and end the dream.

Consider the fact that the dreamer quite clearly has awareness and self-consciousness. He can discriminate the real from the unreal within the dream. What about the reality sense in lucid dreams? Here we have a paradox. On the one hand the dreamer is aware he is dreaming. On the other hand the utter reality of what he is experiencing remains. Traditional peoples cultivated lucid dreams. They too could distinguish within the dreams what was real and what was unreal and yet they still considered spirit beings real. There can be no recourse to the credulity of the dreamer in this case. The dreamer's reason is intact and yet he still believes in the reality of what he is experiencing. The ability to reason and to engage in logical thought is intact. Access to the dreamer's autobiographical memories is intact. The ability to take on third person perspective is intact so the dreamer can consider, entertain, and imagine what another character in the dream is thinking or feeling as well. Indeed whole interactions and dialogues between the dreamer and dream characters can take place just as in waking life. The dream characters furthermore cannot be considered mere creations of the lucid dreamer as they act as if they had full mental capacity and autonomy and in many lucid dreams and certainly in lucid nightmares, they clearly act contrary to the wishes of the dreamer. In short, all of the constituents of the mind that we take for granted in waking life exist in the lucid dream state for both the dreamer and the dream characters.

In addition to the normal elements of the mind present in the lucid state, the lucid dreamer and other dream characters have added mental capacities. The lucid dreamer can very often make things happen in the dream that would be considered miraculous if they occurred in waking life. The lucid dreamer may be convinced he has supernatural mental powers in the lucid state. The lucid dreamer furthermore can sometimes control the unfolding of the dream plot so he stands in relation to the dream characters just as a novelist does to his fictional characters; yet at the same time the dream characters confront the dreamer as real beings, even hyper-real beings as in the case of lucid nightmares. Here the dream characters can make things happen in the dream that are contrary to the will of the dream. Actions initiated by dream characters can cause everything from orgasms in the dreamer to near-death experiences in the dreamer. There are testimonies on record for example, of a dream character shooting a dreamer in the heart and the dreamer waking up with a heart attack. Is this a case of the dreamer confabulating a story line in order to explain the pain of a heart attack? We will never know. In all likelihood dream characters have "caused" death to dreamers as well but we will never be able to document such an event.

Most interestingly of course is the fact that the lucid dreamer is essentially a fully awake human person who cannot be said to be hallucinating (because he knows what is real and unreal) and yet who observes a fully realized visual world replete with settings, environments, characters, supernatural beings, unusual movements, actions, story line, plot, and "atmosphere." Indeed this dream world and the characters in it are so real that they can intensely affect the dreamer's physiologic reactions even unto death.

While the lucid dream does in fact emerge very often from the REM state (and that is why it is legitimate to call it a dream), it functions in some sort of hybrid REM-NREM transitional state or rather a REM-partial awakening state. Thus, it is not strictly speaking a sleep state – even though it most often arises within a sleep state.

Lucid dreaming is not a waking state either, however. Unlike relaxed wakefulness with eyes closed, lucid dreaming shows no evidence of alpha band activity on EEG and instead is characterized by sleep-related low-frequency theta and delta activity. On the other hand lucid dreaming consistently demonstrates heightened power at the 40-Hz frequency band, especially at frontal sites on the EEG.

We now have confirmation that lucid dreaming is indeed associated with reactivation of prefrontal networks during the lucid state. Dresler et al. (2012) managed to collect functional neuroimaging data on at least one out of four lucid dreamers they studied. While the dreamer was in the lucid state bilateral precuneus, cuneus, parietal lobules, and prefrontal and occipito-temporal cortices displayed significantly greater activation as compared with the non-lucid REM state. As the authors themselves pointed out, these areas of activation (e.g., the parietal and dorsal, not ventral) prefrontal lobes overlap considerably with areas that are known to undergo deactivation during REM sleep. Thus, the neuroimaging data seem to confirm the idea that lucid dreaming is not an exclusively REM phenomenon even though it may begin in REM, and some elements of REM (e.g., muscle paralysis) remain while in the lucid state. The prefrontal and parietal cortical networks are reactivated in lucid dreams, thus explaining access to logical thought and awareness while in the lucid state. The lucid dream's most fascinating mysteries remain unexplained.

10.11 Twin Dreams

With twin dreams we have multiple case collections of twins who have dreamed the same dreams or have had precognitive dreams about the other twin. If identical twins have similar brain structures due to similar genetic endowments then they should have similar REM sleep capacities and therefore similar dream content; similar *but not* identical content. Occasionally two people claim that they had exactly the same dream. We have to take these reports seriously as we have two different people verifying that they in fact shared a dream. Twins commonly report that they share dreams. If we assume that twins do not lie about these experiences, then we have two choices: (1) the twins unconsciously and covertly, in some unknown manner, shared the information about dream content; (2) identical (or nearly identical) dreams can occur in two different (but very similar) brains.

Perhaps they had the same dreams because their brains are so similar? Yes, possibly, but then why have the same dreams on the same night? If structural brain similarities are producing the sameness of content you would not expect that sameness of content to happen on the same night unless your view of structural similarity was so deterministic as to be laughable. We know twins' brains are not structurally identical in any case. Brain plasticity makes that an impossibility. Runyan (2010), reported the following dream sharing accounts from twins:

One twin set reported nightmares with a similar threat, tornadoes, in recent dreams. One twin set reported the same occurrence from two points of view while sleeping side by side; one twin dreamt that she came to tell the other twin that she was not getting married, and the other twin dreamt that her twin came to tell her that she was not getting married. (Runyan, page 141)

In addition to these shared dreams Runyan reported apparent precognitive dreams where one twin foresaw in his dreams a calamity that was going to befall the other twin:

For a few weeks, I had a recurring dream (nightmare) where I was driving my car after dark. During this period of driving, I would be involved in an automobile accident where the car I was driving would flip over and over again causing my death. I was almost to the point of not driving any more after dark when my identical twin died in an auto accident where he flipped his car over with it landing on the top directly over him. This caused him to have a massive brain injury resulting in his death. (Runyan, page 140)

Runyan used the standardized Hall/Van de Castle rating scales to quantitatively compare the dream content of twins with the dream content of singletons. Some 44 percent of twin dreams contain the other twin as a character in their dreams. Singletons do not dream that frequently of their siblings. Indeed only 19 percent of characters in singleton dreams are family members (parents, siblings, etc.). Given that dreams of twins are often about their twin, it is not surprizing that social interactions in twin dreams are more friendly than what you see in singleton dreams. Friendliness appeared in 66 percent of the twin dreams but in only 42 percent of singleton dreams. Most interesting perhaps was the finding that 76 percent of the twin dreams took place in unfamiliar settings while only 38 percent of the singleton dreams did so. Why is this the case? Why should twins dream of unfamiliar surroundings far more than singletons? We do not know. Twin dreams represent a relatively unexplored realm of the human mind and dreams. It represents a very rich area for science as it will reveal clues as to the nature of dreaming, as well as the nature of the brain and mind relation itself.

10.12 Big Dreams

"Big dreams" are impactful, transformative dreams that typically involve direct encounters of the dreamer and a supernatural agent that mark turning points in the lives of the dreamers. They have been important in the history of religions and are certainly important in the religious and spiritual lives of the individuals who have them.

Scholarly interest in Big dreams has been increasing in recent decades. For example, Kuiken and his associates (see Kuiken and Sikora, 1993) studied impactful and spiritually transformative dreams in ordinary volunteers. They identified three major types of impactful dreams, which they dubbed existential, transcendent, or nightmare dreams. All three types of dreams are experienced as very intense, memorable, and absolutely veridical/real. Each of the three types exerts differing types of after effects. Existential dreams are followed by increased self-reflection about feelings that the dreamer was previously reluctant to accept, nightmares are followed by increased vigilance and sensitivity to threats, and transcendent dreams are followed by consideration of previously ignored spiritual possibilities.

10.13 Nightmares

The DSM-5 defines nightmare disorder (DSM-5 307.47 (F51.5)) as a parasomnia involving repeated awakenings from extremely frightening dreams that do not occur in the context of some other mental disorder. Upon awakening the individual is oriented and alert and has clear recall of the content of the dream, which in turn is associated with clinically significant distress and impairment in daytime functioning. Epidemiological studies indicate that 2–6 percent of the adult American population (about 6.4 to 15 million people) experience nightmares at least once a week. Between one-half and two-thirds of children experience recurrent nightmares. I have discussed nightmares in previous chapters but suffice to say, here they are distinguished from more run-of-the-mill scary dreams by the presence of monstrous supernatural agents. These supernatural agents evoke within the dreamer dread, terror, awe, and uncanny fear.

10.14 Meeting One's Double in a Dream/Nightmare

The experience of meeting one's own double (the doppelgänger) in a dream has been reported throughout recorded history and has most often been described by the people who experience it and in literature as a profound and dangerous encounter with one's own soul. Although doppelgänger dreams are rare they are memorable and most people, if pressed, will report at least one such dream in their lifetime. In most doppelgänger dreams the dreamer sees him or herself in the dream, though the double usually does not perform many actions. It is as if looking at oneself in a mirror. When the doppelgänger appears in a dream the dreamer almost always describes it as frightening and of special spiritual significance. One cognitive explanation of the doppelgänger is that it represents a memory of seeing oneself in a mirror or even a kind of doubling of autobiographical memory.

10.15 Visitation Dreams

In visitation dreams a loved one or an acquaintance who has died appears in a dream and looks alive and healthy and generally carries a message for the dreamer. Common themes in visitation dreams involve the deceased appearing in the dream as they did in life rather than as they did when they fell ill. In fact the deceased often appear much younger or more healthy than when they died. The deceased conveyed reassurance to the dreamer. "I am OK and still with you." This message tended to be conveyed telepathically or mentally rather than via spoken word. The dream structure is NOT disorganized or bizarre. Instead they are typically clear, vivid, intense, and are experienced as real visits when the dreamer awakens. The dreamer is always changed by the experience. There is resolution of the grieving process and a wider spiritual perspective. Often these visitation dreams can be quite emotional. See some examples of visitation dreams posted by people at my *Psychology Today* dreamcatcher blog: www.psychologytoday.com/blog/dream-catcher.

10.16 False Awakenings and Sleep Paralysis Dreams

A false awakening is a type of dream that involves the subjective experience of waking up while remaining in the dream state. The dreamer feels as if he has woken up and he then goes about his daily routine such as getting dressed or brushing his teeth. While performing these routine tasks the dreamer then really wakes up! Other false awakenings contain fantastic or unrealistic elements not associated with the dreamer's waking circumstances. The dreamer may wake up in the same environment as the dream that occurred prior to the false awakening. As in the movie *Inception*, the dreamer may have to undergo several false awakenings before he is really able to wake up. Occasionally the dreamer may awaken into a dream containing aspects of the dreamer's past. For example, a false awakening may entail waking up in the dreamer's childhood bedroom.

In the early twentieth century, the French zoologist Yves Deluge described a dream of being awakened by a friend knocking at his door, asking for his help. Alarmed, he got dressed and began to wash his face when he realized he was dreaming but then he would find himself asleep again, hearing the knock on the door, hurriedly getting dressed to help his friend, and then wiping a damp cloth across his face and realizing he was dreaming. This cycle occurred several times before he finally really woke up.

Sometimes false awakenings are accompanied by an inability to move one's body. This type of experience is likely a variant of the dreams associated with isolated sleep paralysis (discussed in a previous chapter and shortly). False awakenings and sleep paralysis both occur during transitional periods between waking and sleeping, and combine characteristics of both states in unusual ways. There are also significant overlaps between descriptions of false awakenings and reports of out-of-body experiences, apparition sightings, and alien abductions.

10.17 Sleep Paralysis Dreams

Isolated sleep paralysis (ISP) is a relatively common experience typically characterized by an inability to move or speak after waking up as well by the eerie sense that someone or something is in the room with you or is somehow evil or malignant and threatening you. (Cheyne and Girard, 2007) It is legitimately categorized as a dream because the individual often experiences both auditory and visual hallucinations as well as the muscle atonia or paralysis that normally accompanies REM.

The author Louis Proud (2009) provides this example:

I wake up but not completely. I can feel something touching my forehead; it is this that has drawn me kicking and screaming into a semi-conscious state. But in truth I cannot kick or scream; in fact, I can't move a single muscle in my body, even though my mind is awake. For God's sake I can't even open my eyes. All I can do is lie there while this thing attends to my forehead with delicate loving strokes. Whatever it is I can smell the stench of its presence. I can taste its mind just as it can taste mine. But its love, its child-like affection is sickening me and all I want is for it to leave me in peace. I continue to lie there, engulfed by the darkness as the shadow strokes my forehead. It then moves away to the left of my body and proceeds to lie down beside me. It writhes around annoyingly until it finds a comfortable position. Then once it's finished messing around it puts its arms around me. Its grip is so tight that my chest is aching. I want to scream out in fear and disgust but there is nothing I can do. (Proud 2009, pages 26–27)

Proud had this experience when he was seventeen and reports in his book that the experiences returned frequently, often with other more menacing demonic figures. But almost always the experiences involved some or most of the events described in his original experience. His mind is awake but he is paralyzed. He senses a demonic evil presence near him which then attempts to interact with him in some way. Most often the intent of the demon is to possess him or destroy him. Often he hears voices or senses more than one presence. The presence is evaluated as something of immense evil that wants to destroy Proud. The dominant emotion he experiences is virtually always fear or terror. The experience is caused by fragmentation of the brain state associated with REM such that one does not move entirely out of REM when one transitions from REM to wake.

10.18 Musical Dreams

While very few of us regularly recall dreams with music in them, most of us have had at least one dream that could be called a musical dream – a dream where music was the main ingredient. Why do we not have more musical dreams? After all, music is a very big part of daily life for a lot of people. If the content of dreams generally reflects our everyday activities one would expect "heard" music to show up in quite a few dreams but this is simply not the case. While Kern et al. (2014) recently reported an association between time spent in daytime musical activities and percentage of dreams reflecting some amount of musical activity, the frequency with which musical phrases occur in dreams still appears to be quite low. Why is music so rare in dreams?

Perhaps dreams treat musical phrases and other non-self-generated thoughts as "foreign" and therefore attempts to protect us against these sorts of "parasitic" ideas. This idea goes back to the novel hypothesis concerning the function of dreams advanced by Crick and Mitchison (1986). They suggested that the REM sleep/dreams system functions as a kind of reverse learning mechanism that isolates nonessential, and potentially parasitic informational elements and then eliminates them from the brain/mind. For most of us the dreaming mind treats musical phrases as nonessential and parasitic and it therefore prevents musical phrases from catching hold and entering long-term memory. This is not the case for musicians. For these people music is essential and non-parasitic so their dreaming systems allow processing of musical phrases.

10.19 Dreams of the Sensorially Limited

Blind people have a lot of dreams just like normally sighted individuals but their dream content varies in terms of visual imagery vividness. If individuals were blind from birth they typically do not report visual images in their dreams. Instead they will report verbal interactions and events and perhaps touch and sound images. Those individuals who became blind after around age seven still have dreams with visual images in them but over time those images become less vivid.

When amputees dream, they dream themselves intact. They do not experience loss of the limb in dreams even years after the amputation and even when the physical handicap was congenital.

Similarly, dreams of the congenitally deaf-mute or those of the congenitally paraplegic cannot not be distinguished from those of non-handicapped subjects. This was true for most aspects of both form and content. Dream reports from deaf-mute individuals involve them talking and hearing normally. Patients with varying degrees of paraplegia report themselves flying, running, walking, and swimming.

10.20 Recurrent Dreams

Recurrent dreams are dreams that reoccur over time while maintaining the same content over time. They are relatively common, with 60 to 75 percent of adults reporting having had one at some point in their lives. That is a remarkable fact. We can have the same dream multiple times. Given that brain structure and activity changes constantly how does it manage to produce the same content repeatedly? Most people who have recurrent dreams insist that the content is identical across repetitions. This means that not merely images are repeated but whole scenes and dramatic action events like being chased by a monster or being threatened by an animal and so forth. Note also that some recurrent dreams are not negative or scary dreams. Some recurrent dreams just repeat mundane scenes or locations or events. Nevertheless, scholars who study recurrent dreams insist that they are related to unresolved emotional difficulties in the dreamer's life. Retrospective accounts of recurrent dreams experienced during childhood suggest that almost 90 percent are described as being unpleasant or of a threatening nature. But as people grow older, fewer recurrent dreams are reported as having threatening contents. Up to 40 percent of adult recurring dreams were composed of non-threatening contents (e.g., descriptions of places, mundane activities, or acquaintances) while non-threatening contents occurred in only 10–15 percent of childhood recurrent dreams.

10.21 Conclusions

All of these atypical dream types must be taken into account when developing a complete account of dreams. A theory of dreams must be able to explain why people think they have mutual dreams, precognitive dreams, and visitations of loved ones from beyond the grave. Simple dismissive explanations that these people are gullible won't do as the gullibility account does not explain the similar phenomenologies and content features of these extraordinary dreams. The fact that sensorially limited individuals such as people with blindness, deaf-mute, and paraplegic conditions nevertheless have dreams where none of these impairments exist must also be explained in any decent theory of dreams. Freud would claim that these dreams confirm his theory of the dream as wish fulfillment, but the wish fulfillment explanation cannot account for content of these dreams. The dream stories do not involve dreamers doing things they wish they could do. They involve instead everyday mundane activities. Continuity theories of dreaming also cannot explain these dreams of the sensorially impaired as dream content is clearly not continuous with the everyday lives of these individuals. They engage in walking, hearing, seeing, etc. in their dreams but they obviously do not do any of these things in everyday life. Nor can the prediction-error theories of dreaming explain these kinds of dreams. The prediction-error account says that perception is a Bayesian process of constructing models of the world that are then corrected by sensory impressions. The model of the world is the prediction or expectation of how the world will be. Dreaming is a construction of model worlds or predictions but without normal sensory input since the visual modality is partially blocked during REM dreaming. There is always error in the model world or prediction, so sensory impressions are used to reduce the error variance around the prediction. Gradually over time the error variance is reduced and the models predict the world pretty accurately. The same is the case with dreams except the model is constructed without nighttime corrections from the visual modality. But these individuals cannot use incoming sensory impressions either in the day or night to build or construct predictive models, including dreams, and yet they still dream.

In the next chapter we will discuss some of the major theories of dreaming and gauge the extent to which they can account for all of the facts concerning dreams.

Review Questions

- How do the dreams of people living in traditional societies differ from dreams of people living in modern societies?

- Why might dreams contain indicators or early warning signals of imminent physical illness?
- How might visitation dreams or sleep paralysis dreams have influenced premodern cultural ideas of the supernatural realm?
- What is the significance, if any, of false awakening dreams for theories of consciousness?

Further Reading

Grunebaum, G., & Callois, R. (1966). *The Dream and Human Societies.* Berkeley: University of California Press.

Hobson, J. A., Pace-Schott, E. F., & Stickgold, R. (2000b). Dreaming and the brain: Toward a cognitive neuroscience of conscious states. *Behavioral and Brain Sciences*, 23, 793–842; discussion 904–1121.

Hunt, H. T. (1989) *The Multiplicity of Dreams: Memory, Imagination and Consciousness.* New Haven, CT: Yale University Press.

McNamara, P., Pae, V., Teed, B., Tripodis, Y., & Sebastian, A. (2016) Longitudinal studies of gender differences in cognitional process in dream content. *Journal of Dream Research*, 9(1). doi: http://dx.doi.org/10.11.588/ijord.2016.

CHAPTER 11

Theories of Dreaming

Learning Objectives

- Become acquainted with current evidence-based theories of dreaming
- Evaluate strengths and weaknesses of the social simulation theory of dreaming
- Evaluate strengths and weaknesses of neuroscience evidence in building theories of dreaming
- Evaluate the significance of the fear extinction and affective network dysfunction model of nightmares and dreaming

11.1 Introduction

At the dawn of the twentieth century Freud presented his theory of dreams in his landmark work *The Interpretation of Dreams*. Freud's basic claim was that the dream was a hallucinated wish fulfillment. Recent memories, and imagistic fragments called day residues provide raw material for dream images that then activate motivated content and affects or wishes, and these wishes conflict with the waking ego and so must be disguised by the dream censorship mechanisms. The dreamwork mechanisms (condensation, representation, displacement, etc.) take the basic content carrying the desire or motivational wish and construct elaborate disguises around it (via secondary revision) while still attempting a hallucinated fulfillment of the wish. Up until the discovery of REM sleep in 1953 most scholars and scientists studying dreams operated within this Freudian framework. Carl Jung broke with the framework and presented his own theory of dreams as simulations that compensate for some aspect of the personality or psychic structure of the individual. Jung also postulated the appearance of mythic archetype in dreams, consistent with Freud's claims concerning reenactments of the Oedipal tragedy and transgression in dreams.

Right after World War II Calvin Hall began to develop techniques to reliably tabulate the basic contents of dreams. He argued that to test Freud and Jung's dream theories we needed to establish some reliable numbers around basic content indicators such as number and identity of characters, background settings, social interactions, objects, emotions, and so on. He collected thousands of dream reports and basically counted each instance of all of these sorts of dream categories. He summarized two decades of work in his *The Meaning of Dreams* (Hall 1966). He argued that his results basically confirmed Freud's theory regarding the dream as a text or story that encodes and symbolizes some psychic conflict generated by unfulfilled wishes. Robert Van de Castle later finalized the development of the scales hall invented and so today we call the gold standard dream content scoring system the Hall/Van de Castle system.

After the discovery of REM sleep at the half century mark (1953) theories of dreaming began to incorporate provisional explanations of REM biology as well. Early on, investigators proposed that REM provided an arousal or preparatory phase to a brief awakening during the night that served a kind of sentinel or vigilance function for the animal who otherwise was vulnerable to predation while it slept. Hallucinated simulations of threat while the animal slept would also help prepare the animal for defense in case of attack. Jouvet (1980; 1999) proposed that REM supplied the endogenous stimulation necessary for a resculpting or reprograming of synaptic circuits that support epigenetic behavioral rules/strategies. Jouvet had placed lesions in the brainstems of cats that abolished the atonia usually associated with REM. When the cats' motor systems were no longer inhibited they appeared to act out "dreams" when electrophysiologic signs of REM appeared. These acting out episodes typically involved primary instinctual behaviors such as fear and rage postures as well as orienting reflexes and the like.

11.2 AIM Theory and Hobson

In the 1960s and 1970s Allan Hobson and his associates began to map out the neuronal networks that support REM initiation and cessations. They explicitly argued that you could derive the formal properties of REM dreams from the underlying neurological machinery of REM sleep. The activation-synthesis theory updated in 2000 by Hobson et al. (Hobson et al., 2000b) as the Activation-Input Source-Neuromodulation Model or AIM model of dreaming, summarizes decades of empirical work on the neuroscience of REM sleep and dreams. The activation-synthesis and AIM models begin with the fact that REM sleep is characterized by burst-like, random brainstem, and basal forebrain cholinergic activity while noradrenergic and serotoninergic modulation basically

ceases during REM sleep. High levels of cholinergic activation accompanied by monoaminergic demodulation were hypothesized to result in
bizarre and vivid hallucinatory activity that we call dreams. The
activation-synthesis name came when limbic and sensorimotor sites of
the forebrain engaged in a kind of reactive attempt to produce a coher-
ent experience from the barrage of otherwise chaotic impulses arising
from brainstem REM-on cellular activation. The forebrain attempt to
synthesize some sort of story out of the impulses generated by brainstem
REM-on networks resulted in confabulatory generation of dream scenarios. As in the activation-synthesis model, the AIM model rests on an
activation component, again centered in the brainstem, but now including thalamic and forebrain sites as well. Aminergic and cholinergic
interactions in the brainstem LDT/PPT are retained as one factor in
the regulation of REM expression. Unlike the original model, GABAergic, adenosinergic, and histaminergic influences are allowed to influence
REM-on and REM-off networks. Now cortical activation ("A" in the
AIM title) in addition to brainstem activation is given great weight in the
AIM model. Cortical activation allows for efficient access to significant
amounts of stored information during dream synthesis. Dream construction depends on access to internal ("I") or intra-psychic sources of
information. As in the older activation-synthesis model, the shift of the
brain from aminergic to cholinergic neuromodulation ("M") reduces
stability of cortical circuits in dream construction, thus increasing the
likelihood that dreams will contain bizarre elements. The three AIM
brain states can be thought of as inhabiting points in the space of a three-
dimensional cube defined by these three axes with REM situated at the
high end of the activation axis, the low (internal) end of the input source,
and the high end of the modulatory cholinergic (low end of the aminergic) axis. Waking consciousness shares REM's high activation level but
switches to an external input source and to high aminergic modulation.
Finally, NREM lies midway in the cube space with intermediate values
along all three axes.

One drawback of the AIM model is that the activation component of
the model has to somehow produce selective activation patterns in the
forebrain and cortex rather than global activation levels. REM, after all,
involves selective activation of limbic, amygdalar, and parietal networks
and relative deactivation of dorsolateral prefrontal cortex (DLPFC). Yet
the AIM model only specifies global activation levels in its account of
brain state changes. It is also unclear how global activation of the
forebrain can result in reduced activation levels in the dorsal prefrontal
cortex during REM. Hobson et al. appear to believe that bringing in the

neuromodulatory influence (reduction of aminergic input/enhancement of cholinergic input) can account for selective deactivation of DLPFC. Perhaps the DLPFC is not deactivated during REM but only fails to be activated during REM. Perhaps activation is no different functionally from deactivation or inhibition. Yet inhibitory processes require an active expenditure of resources (e.g., release of inhibitory transmitters with synaptic activation at post-synaptic inhibitory sites on target neurons) while failure to activate requires only a refraining from release of transmitters. Even if we assume that DLPFC is simply not activated, then why is parietal cortex activated when DLPFC is not? They are both complex cortical networks responsible for executive and other high level cognitive functions. What is more: Parietal and DLPFC are densely interconnected via the superior longitudinal fasciculus and other tracts. One would expect an active inhibitory process to be at work on the DLPFC if DLPFC does not "light-up," but parietal operculum does light up during REM.

11.3 Dreams as Virtual Simulation and Predictions of Reality

More recently Hobson has collaborated with Karl Friston (Hobson and Friston, 2012) to produce a new theory of dreams that builds on Hobson's previous work. The new theory formalizes a conception of the dreaming brain as a simulation machine or a virtual reality generator that seeks to optimally model and predict its waking environment and needs REM sleep processes (particularly PGO waves) to do so. The basic idea is that the brain comes genetically equipped with a neuronal system that generates a virtual reality of the waking world during REM sleep because REM sleep processes are essential to optimizing this generative model. Treatments of the mind/brain as a virtual reality machine or a prediction-error device or a "Helmholtz machine" (all roughly the same thing), are rife throughout the cognitive and neurosciences, and it makes a lot of sense to consider dreaming along these lines as well. A dream, after all, is experienced as a fully realized "world" that appears to be generated internally without benefit of current sensory input (as visual input is blocked during REM). Hobson and Friston suggest that sensory data are sampled during wakefulness to build up a complex model of the world that can guide behavior and reduce prediction error and surprises. Then the model is taken off-line during sleep and is subjected to an optimization procedure that prunes redundancy and reduces complexity, thus improving the model's fit to the world.

During waking life, changes in the model's parameters (experienced subjectively as percepts) are driven by the need to explain unpredicted visual input. During dreaming, however, there is no visual or other sensory input so dreaming percepts are driven by the need to explain unpredicted oculomotor input. Dream content therefore is the brain's attempt to find plausible explanations for fictive visual searches triggered by oculomotor input (via rapid eye movements and PGO waves presumably) and by the pruning of synaptic connections that are part of the complexity reduction optimization process. Why is it necessary to go off-line to optimize the simulation machine? The authors in my view never adequately answer this question. The optimization procedure gives us a better model that can better guide behavior. That is fine and good, but it does not explain why optimization has to happen off-line. After all, optimization of the model proceeds during waking life and arguably does so much more efficiently given the sensory feedback available to the waking brain. The authors suggest that using the off-line option was especially acute for the complex brains of mammals (and birds) that exhibit REM sleep. But REM sleep measures are not correlated with brain size or complexity. There are many animals (e.g., marsupials) with a lot of REM sleep and not very complex brains. The authors also suggest that their theory throws some light on the lapse in thermoregulatory reflexes that are characteristic of REM. The reversion during REM to a poikilothermic state has long been one of the many biological mysteries associated with REM. Why does Mother Nature subject the animal to a dangerous lapse in thermoregulation during sleep? The authors argue that among other functions, the simulation machine generates predictions concerning thermal needs and conditions of the organism. But if the machine is taken off-line, "the brain will be impervious to fluctuations in temperature and will not respond to suppress thermal prediction errors, resulting in a suspension of homeothermy." But this is tantamount to saying that thermal regulatory processes cannot proceed because thermal regulatory reflexes are inhibited as part of the REM state. But what we want to know is *why* these reflexes are inhibited in the first place.

Perhaps the authors want to argue that sensory reflexes and input in general are inhibited as part of the REM state *because* the optimization procedure cannot work unless all sensory input is gated. The authors argue that optimization *can* proceed with sensory gating, but they do not establish that it *must* proceed with gating, i.e., that gating is required. The fact that optimization can occur during waking life argues against the idea that gating is absolutely necessary. Note that the benefits of off-line optimization would have to outweigh its risks, including increasing vulnerability to predation, the lapse in thermoregulation, and so forth.

To bolster the argument that off-line optimization is necessary, the authors argue that without periodic off-line repair (pruning), the model will become overly complex and dysfunctional, thus reviving the old idea of Francis Crick that REM dreaming represents a purging or pruning of superfluous associations and complexity in the cognitive system. "In short, taking the brain off-line to prune exuberant associations established during wakefulness may be a necessary price we pay for having a sophisticated cognitive system that can distil complex and subtle associations from sensory samples." But again, there are many species of animals without complex cognitive systems that nonetheless have abundant REM and vice versa – there are species with complex brains with little or no REM (e.g., some sea mammals).

Does viewing the brain as a virtual reality or generative model of the world help us understand dream content? To answer this question the authors urge appropriate caution: "finding order in the real world may not be the same as finding order in the virtual world." A virtual world that is undergoing a process of model-fitting or optimization is likely to generate all kinds of unpredictable content it seems to me. That is why I think the Hobson–Friston theory needs major emendation to work for dream content.

Dreams are not all that unpredictable. Thousands of dream content studies have now clearly established regularities in dream content. Such regularities are broadly consistent with the dream as virtual reality machine theory but the theory needs to take dream content regularities seriously if it hopes to obtain a good fit with the data. To obtain that fit, the authors suggest that more than one modeling process must come into play as part of the optimization procedure. An optimal balance between rehearsing what has already been learned about the world and exploring new hypotheses and possibilities that could be experienced needs to be struck.

Antrobus (Antrobus, 1991) provided a neural network simulation of dreaming. Antrobus assumed that the properties of both dream and wake mentation varied as a function of cortical activation and degree of external stimulation (indexed by sensory thresholds). What created the dream narrative was not so much the brain states NREM or REM, but rather intra-cortical interactions of specialized cortical networks mediating relevant sensorimotor and cognitive functions along with incoming subcortical inputs that needed to be integrated into ongoing cortical processing. This is the kind of theoretical formulation that is consistent with one-generator models of dream generation. With higher forebrain activation levels, one gets the more vivid and bizarre dreams typically associated with REM while lower activation levels produce NREM dreams, etc.

11.4 Solms

The neuropsychoanalyst Mark Solms (Solms 1997) pointed out that REM sleep is neither necessary nor sufficient for dream generation. Therefore, one needed to identify an additional set of brain circuits that participate in dream generation and in the creation of dream phenomenology. Solms used classical neurologic lesion correlation methods to identify the set of brain lesions associated with dream generation, phenomenology, and dream recall. The cholinergic brain stem and basal forebrain mechanisms that generate REM states needed to be supplemented by mesolimbic dopaminergic mechanism. Moreover, specific forebrain structures including higher order association cortices, like the cortical areas surrounding the temporo- parieto-occipital junction (Brodmann area 40), the medial temporo-occipital cortices, as well as the deep white matter structures of the frontal lobes were shown to be significant for the emergence of dreaming.

Solms (1997) submitted a questionnaire on recall of dreams to 332 patients with various types of cerebral lesions (and twenty-nine non-lesioned controls). Reports of global cessation of dreaming were associated with lesions in the region of the inferior parietal lobes on either side or with lesions deep to medial frontal region in the white matter tracts connecting the frontal lobes with both cortical and subcortical sites. These lesions would presumably disconnect anterior frontal cortex from subcortical and limbic sites, preventing generation of dreaming. The dopaminergic tracts that predict reward-related incentives (the appetitive and expectancy circuits) carry the motivational and wish fulfillment aspects of dream content.

Solms' model of dreaming postulates a crucial role for what he calls the appetitive, expectancy, and curiosity circuits associated with ascending meso-limbic-cortical dopaminergic circuits. These dopaminergic circuits project from basal ganglia and limbic sites to medio basal and prefrontal cortex. Independent evidence suggests that meso-cortical catecholaminergic circuits are crucial for predicting reward and are therefore involved in motivational aspects of behavior. Solm's claims that activation of these dopaminergic circuits instigates the dream formation process. Since Solms agrees with Freud that protection of sleep is one of the functions of dreaming, he provides a scheme for propagation and damping of activation levels away from anterior regions to posterior regions. REM-associated activation of anterior limbic sites are hypothesized to simultaneously prevent activation of motor cortex and to facilitate a process Solms calls back-propagation. In back-propagation the activation levels in dopaminergic circuits are kept from prefrontal, supplementary motor and premotor areas and then rerouted posteriorly to sites in the inferior parietal lobes and occipital-temporal visual association areas. The sleeper then can safely experience a visual simulation (hallucination) that satisfies a wish and prevent awakening without becoming fully conscious or motorically active.

While Solm's model is based on well-documented clinical data, the back propagation process is ill-defined and difficult to identify as actually occurring during dreaming. If back-propagation truly occurs and functions to protect sleep, one would expect loss of dreaming to result in waking or at least poor sleep. While Solms claims that some of his patients do indeed report poor sleep it is not clear that this is due to loss of dreaming per se, or to their medical condition. I know of no evidence that suggests patients with frontal leucotomies or with bilateral parietal lesions are rendered permanently awake. Indeed, Jus et al. (1973) demonstrated that REM occurred in leucotomized patients who nevertheless reported very few if any dreams.

Foulkes (1985) argued that dreams are "credible world analogs" or imaginative simulations of waking life that obey fundamental rules of waking cognition but that to a great extent lacked reflective thought. Although he has argued that dreaming plays a role in development of consciousness he has also argued that dreams likely serve no adaptive function. Foulkes recommends that we focus more on the formal cognitive features of dreams rather than on dream content per se as the formal features more likely are functional than are the content themes of dreams. Foulkes proposed that dreaming involved a diffuse activation of mnemonic material and as such could serve no adaptive function. Yet as Foulkes himself points out dream content is not random. The dreamer is typically represented as playing a central role in the dream narrative, which typically involves a summation of selected past experiences personal to the dreamer. The past experiences inform the dream events – the dream is not a mere replay of these past experiences. Instead it is cognitively creative.

Hartmann (1998) has suggested that dreams are the product of spreading excitation between semantic nodes in a semantic network, except that the patterns of activation in dreams are guided by current emotional concerns and make meaning-connections more broadly and more inclusively than does waking cognition. Hartmann suggested that certain dream images function to contextualize intense emotions. This latter capacity allows dreams to facilitate integration of traumatic or overwhelming emotions.

11.5 Emotional Processing Functions of Dreams

Hartmann's position is similar to many contemporary views on functions of dreaming that emphasize potential emotional functions of dreams. All these investigators provide substantial evidence for adaptive emotional problem-solving and processing in dreams. Kuiken and Sikora (1993) argue that impactful dreams reflect activations of components of the classical orienting response and that these emotionally intense, impactful dream have lasting effects on mood states of waking experience.

11.6 Fear Extinction and the Affective Network Dysfunction (AND) Model

Tore Nielsen and Ross Levin (Nielsen and Levin, 2007) formulated a new neuro-cognitive model of nightmares that implicitly carries a basic theory of dreams as well. The AND model suggests that normal REM dreaming involves the stripping away of contextual material from images laden with fear. This stripping process allows the fear image to be more efficiently integrated into long-term memory. REM supported emotional memory consolidation in this view, essentially consists in defanging, so to speak, affecting laden images so that they can be stored into long-term memory. That defanging process involves the stripping of context information from the affect-laden memory fragment and then the fragment is ready for long-term storage. Image contexts are mediated by activation of the hippocampal formation. Fear extinction occurs after contextual information is stripped from the affect-laden images or memory fragments. Nightmares and recurrent dreams occur when the stripping or decontextualization process breaks down and then the affect-laden image fragment remains in short-term memory stores where it gets reactivated periodically whenever semantically related cues activate it.

11.7 Continuity Hypothesis (CH) on Dreams

Schredl (Schredl and Hoffman, 2003) and Domhoff (1996) have been the foremost advocates for the idea that dreams simulate the kinds of things we do and encounter in everyday life. The continuity hypothesis of dreams suggests that the contents of dreams are largely continuous with waking concepts and concerns of the dreamer. Calvin Hall was the first dream researcher to argue that some content of dreams reflected the daily concerns and ideas of the dreamers rather than the hidden libidinal wishes or compensatory emotional strategies that psychodynamic theorists like Freud and Jung advocated. Through creation of standardized dream content scoring inventories (building on the work of Mary Calkins and others), Hall demonstrated that the most frequently appearing content items of dreams were not bizarre images at all but rather mundane social interactions between the dreamer and people he or she interacted with on a daily basis. One did not need to invoke theories concerning elaborate dreamwork to disguise latent libidinal and aggressive wishes buried in the dream.

Instead, simple counts of characters, interactions, objects, actions, and events in the dreams could yield a pretty accurate picture of what the dream was about and it wasn't dramatically different than the daily life of the dreamer. Many dream researchers since Calvin have confirmed that the bread and butter of dreams are the quotidian daily social interactions and concerns most people experience on a daily basis. Domhoff's (2003) impressive content analyses of a longitudinal dream series collected from a middle-aged woman dubbed "Barb Sanders" very convincingly shows that her pattern of aggressive and friendly interactions with key characters in her dreams matched the ups and downs of those same relationships between her and them in waking life.

Thus, the empirical support for some degree of continuity between dream content and waking life is strong. The database supporting the theory has been considerably strengthened by many dream researchers over the years since Hall's pioneering efforts back in the 1950s–1970s. It is therefore clear that any complete theory of dreams must accommodate the data demonstrating substantial continuities between dream content and waking concepts and concerns.

But as every supporter of continuity theory acknowledges, there are also dreams that contain some significant discontinuities between dream content and waking concepts/concerns. For example, most people have had dreams that are like long adventure stories or movies. These "narrative-driven" dreams are less quotidian than everyday dreams. They contain more bizarre elements and imagery and have the dreamer engaged in actions and events that are decidedly not like their ordinary ideas, actions, and concerns. In addition, there is a significant minority of dream reports that have few or no familiar characters, settings, or activities. Can these sorts of dreams be explained with continuity theory approaches? If attempts are made to do so how can one avoid special pleading, circular reasoning, or ad hoc additions to the theory?

Domhoff (2003) draws on Solms data, the recent set of findings gathered from neuroimaging studies, and his own extensive studies on dream content to propose a detailed neurocognitive model of dreaming. Like Hobson et al., Antrobus, and Solms, Domhoff suggests that dreaming depends on brain activation patterns, but the content of dreaming comes from access to the conceptual system of schemata and scripts housed in the cognitive system. The convergence of these data sources indicate large-scale but selective neural networks responsible for dreaming including the brainstem generator, structures in the hypothalamus and thalamus, amygdala, limbic system, anterior cingulate, and cortical sites. Domhoff would later identify the neural networks responsible for dreaming to be essentially large portions of the default mode network. Domhoff suggests both a "continuity principle" and a "repetition principle" in dream content, noting that there is a continuity between waking life and dream life, and there is also a tendency to repeat certain themes in dreams across time. He cites repetitive nightmares, recurrent dreams of childhood and adolescence, and repeated themes found in some dream series elicited from a single individual. Domhoff links this tendency to repeat content to activation of the amygdala's fear-vigilance system. I assume he would largely agree with Nielsen and Levin's AND model of fear extinction functions for dreaming. Dreaming according to Domhoff draws on memory schemata, general knowledge, and episodic memories to produce quasi-veridical simulations of the real world in dreams. Domhoff does not believe that dreaming per se has an adaptive function. He therefore parts company with the next theorist of dream content: the evolutionary theorist Revonsuo.

11.8 Threat Simulation Theory

Revonsuo (2000) proposes that the function of dreaming is to simulate threatening events. Threat simulations are thought to allow for rehearsal of threat perception and thus to enhance threat avoidance. Revonsuo notes that dream content is not random but instead consistently over represents simulations of unpleasant/threatening events. In some cases these simulations are repetitions of previous unpleasant dreams (Domhoff's repetition principle) such as a nightmare of being chased by a wild animal, etc. Repeated simulations of such threatening events in the dreaming mind of an ancestral human event is thought to confer a selective advantage on that individual relative to individuals not experiencing such simulations. The advantage might be a slightly faster response time when confronted with a threat or a slightly improved ability to detect an incipient attack and so forth. Children in particular would benefit from such a threat simulation device and studies of dreams of modern children show that wild threatening animals are overrepresented in their dreams. Nightmares and post-traumatic repetition dreams are thought to be instances of disinhibition of the threat simulation device. While threat simulation can nicely account for some aspects of some dream content, most dreams cannot be assimilated to threat simulation. There are too many dreams that are simply not about threats and/or not even unpleasant. An equally pressing necessity for ancestral humans had to do with interactions with other members of the group: how to find a mate, how to avoid conflict, and how to build coalitions and so forth. This "social simulation theory" of dreaming suggests that dreams also simulate social interactions and if simulating these interactions in dreams enhanced fitness outcomes for the individuals who experienced such dreams, natural selection would have "supported" development of such dreams, as seems to be the case.

11.9 Social Simulation Theory

Social Simulation Theory or SST attempts to capture the fact that many dreams are about social interactions. Many authors have remarked on the probable social functions of dreaming. Anthropologists have long treated the dream as a strategic social act. That is, dreams are used in traditional societies to facilitate negotiations in social alliances and to facilitate change in the social status of the dreamer. Dreams are known to be involuntary experiences and thus they are hard to fake, and if they are hard to fake then they can be considered honest signals concerning the dreamer's capacities and intentions. Freud (1900/1950) and many authors in the psychoanalytical tradition can be read as supporting a kind of SST given that they often interpret dreams in terms of emotional conflict in families of origin or in current families as well as between sexual partners and romantic targets. Revonsuo, Touminin, and Valli (2015) have marshalled some of the data and arguments that support the SST. The SST postulates that dreams virtually simulate socially significant interactions for the dreamer; they simulate human social reality, including the social skills, bonds, interactions, and networks that we engage in during our waking lives. Brereton (2000; see also Franklin and Zyphur, 2005) presented a similar idea in his "Social Mapping

Hypothesis" that suggests that dreaming allows for rehearsal of emotional and perceptual abilities needed for relating the dreamer to emotionally significant others and social groups.

Obviously the social mapping hypothesis and the SST is consistent with the argument I have been presenting in this book concerning the social functions of sleep and dreams. Indeed, I believe the SST is currently the best supported theory of dreams that we have but as Revonsuo et al. point out, the theory has rarely been tested directly. Nevertheless, Revonsuo et al. note (in support of SST) that 95 percent or more of dreams are populated by the dreamer who interacts with two to four other characters, most of whom can be recognized as familiar characters in the dreamer's immediate social network. Friendly interactions (typically verbal conversations) are found in about 40 percent of dreams, while aggressive social interactions occur in about 45 percent of dreams. In addition, mind-reading or inferring the mental states of others, particularly those characters the dreamer interacts with, occurs in over 80 percent of dreams. Finally, people who are most important in the dreamer's waking network regularly appear in that dreamer's dreams. Thus, existing data from dream content studies is certainly consistent with SST and I have tried to show that the existing data on sleep neurobiology is also consistent with SST.

11.10 Conclusions

All of the aforementioned theories of dreaming are supported by a good deal of evidence in the dreaming literature, but all of them cannot be correct as they currently stand. It is likely that elements of each contain building blocks of an ultimate theory of dreaming. That ultimate theory of dreaming must also account for dream variation as summarized in the previous chapter as well as the facts on changing dream content with differing stages in the life cycle. Any theory of dream function must also be consistent with the available neuroscience data on the neuroanatomy of dream recall as well as the neurology of REM and NREM sleep states. Although the neuroscience of sleep and dreams has made tremendous progress in the past few decades it still has not matured to the point where research is theory-guided. Nevertheless, the social hypothesis described in these pages, encompassing the social brain network activated during REM and taken off-line during NREM as well as the social simulation hypothesis that accounts for large amounts of the dream content data, at least provides a heuristic theoretical framework of REM sleep and dreams that can be tested and falsified experimentally in the lab in the years to come. If it is falsified then the field can move beyond the heuristic framework to investigate other potential frameworks, and if it is supported then it will provide the field with theory-guided research questions, instead of blind data-driven research programs for years to come.

Review Questions

- What are the strengths and weaknesses of the continuity hypothesis of dreaming?
- Can any current theory account for the great variety of dream experiences discussed in previous chapters?
- What theory of dreaming is most consistent with neuroscience data concerning dream recall and brain activation patterns during REM?
- Current theories of dreaming all assume that dreaming performs some function for daytime consciousness. What might be the evidence for the claim that dreaming performs some functions for sleep or for nighttime consciousness rather than waking consciousness?

Further Reading

Maquet, P., Ruby, P., Maudoux, A., Albouy, G., Sterpenich, V., Dang-Vu, T., Desseilles, M., Boly, M., Perrin, F., Peigneux, P., & Laureys, S. (2005). Human cognition during REM sleep and the activity profile within frontal and parietal cortices: A reappraisal of functional neuroimaging data. *Progress in Brain Research*, 150, 219–27.

Nir, Y., & Tononi, G. (2010). Dreaming and the brain: From phenomenology to neurophysiology. *Trends in Cognitive Science*, 14(2), 88–100. doi: 10.1016/j.tics.2009.12.001. Epub January 14, 2010.

Schredl, M. & Hofmann, F. (2003). Continuity between waking activities and dream activities. *Consciousness and Cognition*, 12(2), 298–308. 10.1016/S1053–8100(02)00072–7.

Solms, M. (1997). *The Neuropsychology of Dreams*. Mahwah, NJ: Lawrence Erlbaum.

Appendix: Methods

A.1 Methods Used to Study Biological Rhythms

The simplest method used to study biological rhythms in people is to record a suite of variables over a twenty-four-hour period to observe how their values change with time. These variables can include things such as temperature, hunger, rest vs. activity/movement, cognitive processes, hormonal activity, and so on. Using this simple technique has demonstrated that most things cycle on a twenty-four-hour or circadian period; they wax and wane or increase and decrease with regularly occurring twenty-four-hour periods. Internal body temperature, for example, rises in the morning and falls after dark. The hormone cortisol too rises in the morning and falls after dark. The hormone melatonin rises and falls in opposition to the light-dark cycle. Gut hormones rise and fall regularly within the twenty-four-hour period in anticipation of meals. Examples of human physiologic and behavioral variables that cycle in regular periods could be multiplied indefinitely. They are all in some sense regulated by the overarching light-dark cycle. We say that all of these variables are entrained to the light-dark cycle. They work in unison in an orchestrated manner. The temperature and cortisol rhythms rise as the light cycle begins in order, presumably, to prepare us to meet the challenges of the day. If we put someone in a cave where the light-dark cycle is eliminated the rhythmic activity of all of these variables will eventually become desynchronized with one another so that the temperature and cortisol rhythms no longer rise together or at the correct time when light begins to appear in the morning. If the temperature and cortisol rhythms begin to appear or rise during the dark period then sleep will become more difficult as the individual will feel aroused when he should feel ready to sleep.

A common method used to study the functional orchestration of rhythms is the forced desynchrony protocol. In this protocol the sleep-wake cycle is pulled apart from the temperature/arousal cycle such that participants will be asleep or awake at different phases of their normal temperature/arousal cycle. For example, they may be required to sleep for a few minutes at the start of the rise of the temperature cycle and then to wake during the bulk of the dark period and so on.

Another common technique used to identify biological rhythms and rhythm disorders is the sleep diary. If you keep track of your daily sleep-wake schedules for a couple of weeks you will be able to note when there are differences between the daily schedule during the week versus the weekend when many people play catch-up on their sleep. They are sleep-deprived during the week due to social obligations and are able to correct that sleep disturbance over the weekend as demonstrated by the prolonged sleep times on the weekends. We can also record sleep-wake schedules as well as rest-activity rhythms via use of an actigraph watch that is worn on the wrist. It contains an accelerometer that detects any bodily movements and then displays rest-activity patterns over the course of a few days or even weeks. Regularly occurring periods of rest vs. activity can be readily read off the actigraph output graphs depicting these cycles.

A.2 Methods to Study Sleep Mechanisms

Most of our knowledge about the neurobiology of sleep has come from animal studies. You can apply the full armamentarium of the modern "bench laboratory" to study animal's sleep. Studies of animal sleep using genetic and molecular neurobiological techniques have been reviewed when appropriate throughout this book. But if we are primarily interested in human sleep and more particularly interested in dreams, then animal studies have severe limitations. Although animals very likely dream, they cannot communicate these dreams to us. In this chapter therefore we review the neuroscience techniques typically used to study human sleep and dreams. Sleep is produced by the human brain so we begin with a review of key brain systems for sleep.

A.3 Brain Systems Important for Sleep

The cerebral cortex is the outermost layering of the brain and it mediates advanced cognitive functions such as thinking, planning, visuo-spatial reasoning, language, and memory. In most areas the cortex contains six layers of cells with layer IV being the target of projections from the sub-cortical relay center called the thalamus. When a visual stimulus, for example, enters the eye it is converted into neural impulses by the cells in the retina. These cells then send the visual information via the retinol-hypothalamic tract to the hypothalamus, which lies beneath the thalamus.

The visual information is also sent to the thalamus and then to the occipital lobes in the cortex that lie at the back of the brain. After arriving at the central or primary region of the occipital cortex the visual information is sent to the secondary regions of the occipital cortex where the information is analyzed and compared to other information coming from other regions of the cortex.

Similar stories can be told about the other senses. Touch sensation travels to the thalamus and is then sent to the somesthetic sensory strip near the central sulcus in the cortex. After analysis in that primary somatosensory region the touch information is further analyzed in the insula and in the parietal lobes of the cortex. Sound information travels from the ears to the thalamus and thence onto the auditory cortex in the temporal lobes. Speech sounds are analyzed separately in Wernicke's region in the left medial and superior temporal regions. Visual information is analyzed both in the occipital region and in the inferior temporal region. Memory information is also analyzed in the temporal lobes and in structures deep to the temporal lobe such as the amygdala and the hippocampus. The large region of cortex towards the front of the brain is called the frontal lobes. The frontal lobes appear to mediate executive control functions, attentional functions, working memory, prospective forms of cognition, and planning, among other higher order functions. In most people the left prefrontal region contains Broca's region, which is important for speech production.

Beneath the cortex lies a set of structures collectively referred to as the diencephalon. Within the diencephalon one interconnected set of structures is called the limbic system, which appears to be particularly important for emotional responding and emotional memory. Key structures of the limbic system include the amygdala and the hippocampus. Both the amygdala and the hippocampus play important roles in the neurophysiology of REM sleep. Beneath the diencephalon lies the brain stem and the major regulatory structures for sleep. Among these brain stem nuclei are several that manufacture neurotransmitters, or the chemical that allow neurons to communicate with one another.

A.4 Neuromodulators

Neuromodulators are chemicals that facilitate the transfer of information between nerve cells in the central nervous system including the brain. From a methodological point of view we can study the effects of neuromodulators in various regions of the brain to help us identify potential functions (including sleep and dream functions) of those regions of the brain. We can also develop drugs that can either potentiate the actions of certain neuromodulators or inhibit those actions, thereby once again gaining valuable knowledge about the actions and functions of those neuromodulators. For example, if we find that administration of a drug that potentiates the action of the neuromodulator acetylcholine in the pedunculopontine tegmental nucleus of the brainstem/pons (which is in fact the case), is reliably associated with increased activation of REM sleep (again, which is in fact the case), then we can conclude that it is likely that the neuromodulator acetylcholine normally facilitates the activation of REM sleep.

A nerve cell is generally composed of a cell body called a neuron and then an axon or long filament extending from the cell body that sends messages to other neurons. Two neurons can communicate when one axon releases chemicals into the space between the neurons called the synaptic cleft. Once the sender neuron releases those chemicals into the synaptic cleft they drift across the cleft until they reach the receiver neuron. The receiver neuron then uses little pincers on its membrane and literally picks up the chemical messenger molecules from the cleft and attaches them like lock (the transmitter chemical) and key (the membrane "receptors") into its cell membrane. Once captured by a receptor the chemical messengers are then released into the receiver neuron and influence that neuron's ongoing electrical activity.

Some neuromodulators tend to activate brain structures and these are called excitatory neurotransmitters. Other neuromodulators tend to suppress neuronal firing and these are called inhibitory neurotransmitters. Among the excitatory neuromodulators is norepinephrine, serotonin, acetylcholine, glutamate, and dopamine. Norepinephrine is manufactured in the brainstem nucleus called the locus coeruleus. Serotonin is manufactured in another brain stem nucleus called the raphe nuclei. Dopamine is produced in mid-brain nuclei called the substantia nigra and the ventral tegmental region. Acetylcholine is produced in the pedunculopontine tegmental nucleus as well as above the brain stem in several nuclei in the basal forebrain. Glutamate receptors are found throughout the cortex and may be implicated in some aspects of psychosis and some nightmares.

Norepinephrine tends to promote arousal when it is released in the brain. Serotonin tends to regulate mood functions. Dopamine facilitates detection of salience and reward, and acetylcholine supports learning and memory functions. As mentioned, these neuromodulators allow nerve cells to communicate with one another. Once a neurotransmitter is either manufactured in a nerve cell or is taken up into a neuron, its tiny molecules are bundled together into a little packet called a vesicle that is then sent down into the axon awaiting its release. When an electrical charge comes rolling down the axon, it triggers release of the neurotransmitter vesicular bundles into the synaptic cleft. Then these bundles of transmitter molecules diffuse slowly across the synaptic cleft until they are taken up into the receiver neuron. When they are attached to the receiver neuron's receptors they trigger further electrical spikes called post-synaptic action potentials. Each neurotransmitter has its specialized receptor types. So for example, there are neurons that specialize in receiving serotonin transmitter molecules and these are called serotoninergic receptors. There are several such serotoninergic receptors and several dopaminergic (dopamine), noradrenergic (norepinephrine), and cholinergic (acetylcholine) receptor types distributed throughout the brain.

One type of acetylcholine receptor is called the nicotinic receptor, because it is activated both by acetylcholine and by nicotine. Like norepinephrine, nicotine is a stimulating substance promoting arousal. Histaminergic neurons project from the tuberomammillary nucleus to very wide regions of the cortex. When you take antihistamines you get sleepy because these agents block the action of histaminergic receptors on the brain. Selective serotonin reuptake inhibitors like Prozac block the uptake of serotonin when it is diffusing across the synaptic cleft, thus prolonging the action of serotonin in the releasing neuron. L-dopa or levodopa increases the production of dopamine in the substantia nigra and is generally given to patients with Parkinson's disease. Clonidine dampens the firing of cells in the locus coeruleus and thus reduces overall arousal.

The drugs (see Table A.1) that directly produce sleep are mostly the sedatives like the barbiturates (e.g., phenobarbital), and the benzodiazepines (Diazepam (Valium), clonazepam (Klonopin), lorazepam (Ativan), temazepam (Restoril), flunitrazepam (Rohypnol), triazolam (Halcion), alprazolam (Xanax)). Virtually all of these sedative drugs act by increasing the action of the major inhibitory neurotransmitter in the brain: GABA (gamma aminobutyric acid).

The major sleep-promoting nucleus is the GABAergic ventrolateral preoptic nucleus of the hypothalamus. Wakefulness-promoting nuclei include the orexinergic lateral hypothalamic/perifornical area, the histaminergic tuberomammillary nucleus, the cholinergic pedunculopontine tegmental nucleus, the noradrenergic locus coeruleus, the 5-hydroxytryptaminergic raphe nuclei, and the dopaminergic ventral tegmental area. Thus, the drugs that promote wakefulness all tend to be

Table A.1 Drugs that influence sleep

	Drug subgroup	Specific drugs		Mechanism	Major effects	Standard use
		Examples				
Melatonin	Hormone	Supplements		Agonist at melatonin receptor type 1 and 2	Sleepiness	Insomnia, jet lag
Sedatives	Benzodiazepines	Diazepam (Valium), clonazepam (Klonopin), lorazepam (Ativan), temazepam (Restoril), flunitrazepam (Rohypnol), triazolam (Halcion), alprazolam (Xanax)		GABA-A agonist	Muscle relaxation; sleepiness	Anxiety
	Benzodiazepine agonists	Zolpidem (Ambien), eszopiclone (Lunesta), zopiclone, zaleplon (Sonata)		GABA-A agonist	Sleepiness	Insomnia
	Barbiturates	Phenobarbital, pentobarbital, thiopental (sodium pentothal, sodium amytal), secobarbital		Agonist at barbiturate site on the GABA-A receptor	Anesthetized sleepiness	Epilepsy
Stimulants	Amphetamines	Amphetamine (Adderall), methamphetamine (Desoxyn), methylphenidate (Ritalin), MDMA (ecstasy), MDA, MDEA		Increase release of 5-HT, DA, and NE. Releases 5-HT and DA	Euphoric, wakefulness / Euphoric, social bonding	ADHD, narcolepsy / None
	Cocaine			Inhibits 5-HT, NE, and DA reuptake, thus enhancing their effects	Enhances reward-seeking behaviors	None
	Modafinil			Inhibits DA reuptake	Enhances vigilance	Narcolepsy

Table A.1 (cont.)

	Specific drugs		Mechanism	Major effects	Standard use
	Drug subgroup	Examples			
Antidepressives	Selective serotonin reuptake inhibitors (Prozac, Zoloft, Paxil)		Inhibits 5-HT reuptake thus enhancing its effects	Relieves mood disorder; inhibits REM sleep	Depression
	Trycyclics		Inhibits 5-HT reuptake and NE release	Inhibits REM	Depression and anxiety
Antipsychotics	Thorazine, Haldol, Mellaril		Blocks D1 D2 dopamine receptors in limbic system	Inhibits REM and increases SWS	Psychosis
Atypical Antipsychotics	Abilify, Risperdal, Seroquel		Blocks D2 dopamine and 5HT2A receptors in cortex	Inhibit REM and increases SWS	Psychosis
Narcotics	Full opioid agonists	Morphine, heroin (diacetylmorphine), hydrocodone (Vicodin), oxycodone (Percocet, Oxycontin), fentanyl, Demerol, codeine, opium, hydromorphone (Dilaudid), oxymorphone (Opana), methadone	Enhances opioid receptor release	Euphoric sleepiness, pain relief,	Pain

Table A.2 What drug studies have taught us about the neurobiology of sleep and wakefulness

Neurochemical mechanism	Promotes sleep	Promotes wake
H1 histaminergic antagonism	X	
M1 muscarinic antagonism	X	
5HT 2 antagonism	X	
Alpha 1 adrenergic antagonism	X	
D1/D2 antagonism	X	
5HT, NE, and DA reuptake inhibition		X

drugs that enhance the activity (either through direct stimulation of release or via inhibition of the reuptake mechanisms in the synaptic cleft) of the major neuromodulators such as serotonin, norepinephrine, and dopamine.

In sum you can promote sleepiness by decreasing the activity of the major neuromodulators and enhance wakefulness by increasing the activity of the major neuromodulators.

A.5 The EEG and Polysomnography

Aside from pharmacologic and neuroimaging studies of sleep, the primary method used for study of natural sleep processes in humans is the EEG or electroencephalography. When the EEG is combined with measurements of eye movements (electrooculogram or EOG), and muscle movements (electromyogram or EMG) as well as respirations during sleep, we call it polysomnography.

The EEG captures surface electrical activity of the brain, but the mechanisms underlying the brain wave patterns are properties of the billions of neurons that make up the brain. We know that sleep need is reflected in the EEG delta power during sleep, and delta power is a measure of the dominance of slow waves in the EEG.

Slow waves in the EEG are generated when large groups of neurons fire together in a synchronous, rhythmic pattern. The most basic finding uncovered by use of the EEG during sleep is that sleep is associated with mostly slow, high-amplitude synchronized waves, while wakefulness is associated with fast, desynchronized low-amplitude waves.

The synchronized pattern indicates that the brain is (or at least large populations of neurons are) firing single, slow, rhythmic patterns, and the desynchronized pattern reflects different parts of the brain firing out of synchrony in different patterns. Interestingly the desynchronized EEG is also found during REM. So really the synchronized pattern is associated with slow wave stage N3 sleep.

If you perform EEGs on thousands of human subjects you begin to see an average pattern of EEG activity changes over the course of a single night of sleep. That average pattern of EEG changes or brain activity changes over the course of a single night of sleep is called the individual's sleep architecture. We can depict a typical sleep architecture pattern via use of a sleep hypnogram (see Figure 2.1 in Chapter 2).

In the figure you can see the EEG wave forms (panel a) associated with each sleep stage (panel b). Stage N1 (formerly stage 1) is associated with the beginning of the descent into sleep, the EEG changes from the fast, desynchronized wave pattern of alert wakefulness to a slower, more regular wave pattern at a frequency of 8–12 Hz (Hz refers to the number of waves, or cycles, that occur each second). These slow, regular waves in the 8–12 Hz frequency range that characterize a relaxed, drowsy state are called alpha waves. The alpha waves are replaced by a low-amplitude, mixed frequency pattern with a predominance of activity in the 4–8 Hz range. This frequency band is referred to as theta waves. The EOG indicates that slow eye movements are beginning to occur. The sleep study subject has now entered stage 1 non-REM sleep. During the descent into sleep, stage 1 non-REM lasts only a few minutes. Next, the subject goes into stage N2 non-REM sleep (formerly known as stage II). During stage 2, the frequency of the EEG waves continues to slow down even as the amplitude of the waves increases. However, stage 2 non-REM sleep features occasional bursts of higher-frequency oscillations that are called sleep spindles and K-complexes, which are very high amplitude spikes. Sleep spindles are low amplitude 7–14 Hz synchronous waveforms that often precede the so-called K-complex waveform during stage N2 non-rapid eye movement (NREM) light sleep. Stage N2 constitutes the bulk of sleep for most people. Finally, the individual descends into deep sleep consisting of stage N3 (formerly known as stages III and IV). Now the EEG slows even more and shows the high-amplitude, slow waves that are the hallmark of deep sleep, or stage 3 non-REM sleep. Stage 3 sleep is also sometimes referred to as slow wave sleep because the EEG shows a dominance of slow delta waves in the band of 0.5–4.5 Hz. Rolling eye movements occur during stage 3 sleep.

> **Table A.3** Sources for study of sleep and dreams
>
> Large sleep-related datasets are increasingly available for public analysis. For example, the National Sleep Research Resource (NSRR), PhysioNet (www.physionet.com), the Montreal Archive of Sleep Studies (MASS), and even consumer-facing efforts are underway. As "big data" analysis efforts gain momentum, it is increasingly important to understand not only the potential benefits but also the potential pitfalls of PSG phenotyping. In an era when in-laboratory PSG is increasingly restricted, enhancing signal processing and big data analytics could justify resource allocation to inform individual- and population-level insights. The goals of sleep phenotyping span basic and clinical investigations as well as genotype–phenotype associations, especially as academic centers are increasingly banking bio-samples.

After the descent through stages 1, 2, and 3, the individual now quickly cycles back up through 3, 2, and 1, but this time goes into his first period of rapid eye movement or REM sleep (characterized by the dark bar in the Figure 2.1) and thus ends the first cycle of the night's sleep. There will be three to five such cycles during the night with each cycle devoting less time in SWS and more time in REM; the REM cycles gradually increase throughout the night until they reach a crescendo lasting some thirty to forty minutes toward the morning.

A.6 Neuroimaging Methods

With the advent of sophisticated brain imaging devices in the 1980s and 1990s it was not long before these new techniques were used to study the sleeping brain. The most commonly used techniques are functional magnetic resonance imaging (fMRI), positron emission tomography (PET), and single photon emission computed tomography (SPECT). We briefly review each method and the relative advantages and disadvantages as tools to investigate sleep.

In the 1990s fMRI was developed and represents a special form of MRI scanning to measure hemodynamic change in blood. Like any other bodily region the brain requires blood to function, and therefore measuring changes in blood consumption in the brain should reflect changes in brain activity levels. Blood oxygen level exhibits different magnetic properties and therefore emit magnetic signals that can be picked up and measured by a magnetic resonance scanner. Blood-oxygen-level dependent (BOLD) signals reflect transient change in oxyhemoglobin and deoxyhemoglobin levels in the blood. Magnetic properties of oxy-hemoglobin and deoxyhemoglobin are detected by the magnetic reson-ance scanner and neural activity is inferred from local fluctuations in deoxyhemoglobin. BOLD signals are detected by rapid volumetric acquisition of images every one to five seconds (temporal resolution) and mapped onto two to five mm^3 voxels (spatial resolution). Scientists are working on creating the capacity for ever finer temporal and spatial resolutions during image acquisition. Currently all areas (cortical and subcortical) of the brain can be imaged with fMRI.

There are special problems associated with the use of fMRI for the study of sleep or dreams. Even though headphones can be used to block out most of the noise emitted by the scanner, that noise can still prevent most people from falling asleep while in the machine. It is difficult also to record EEG signals from the brain scalp while the individual is in the machine. Finally, fMRI is an expensive procedure currently running at about $800 per hour. Nevertheless fMRI is the preferred method for study of the contribution of differing brain regions to sleep and dreams.

PET scanning (positron emission scanning) is another form of brain imaging that is sometimes used to study brain contributions to sleep. The advantage of PET vs. fMRI is that PET can yield information concerning neurochemical activity during sleep while fMRI does not. PET is an invasive procedure that involves injecting a radioactive isotope into the bloodstream of a patient followed by brain imaging via computation reconstruction methods. The injected radioactive substance with brief half-life circulates through the body (imaging can be for brain or body), the radioactive traces concentrate in biologically active tissue, the tracer beta decays over time emitting positrons (electron antiparticle), which collide in turn with nearby electrons producing gamma particles that travel in opposite directions. The circular detecting device in a PET scanner surrounding the individual's head or body gathers these gamma photons in a scintillator. Normalized data and computational measures are applied to information regarding time and location of gamma photo-emission couplets. The result transforms data streams into three-dimensional brain activation patterns as a function of time. A major drawback to this brain imaging technique is that use of radioactive isotopes is expensive, time-consuming, and must be coordinated within hours of testing a subject in PET scan. Exposing an individual to varying levels of radioactive substance and injection procedures comes with significant health and safety risks. PET is nevertheless a uniquely valu-able procedure for study of sleep in the human brain because it is the only technique that can give us in vivo information concerning neuro-transmitter activity during sleep states. Radionuclides can be prepared as ligands to very specific biochemical substrates, such as dopamine receptors or enzymes, serotonin transporters, etc. And thus we can gain some information about neurochemical events during sleep states.

SPECT, like PET, is a nuclear imaging technique dependent on use of radionuclides and photon emission. SPECT furnishes three-dimensional information of tissue activity. A gamma camera captures photon emission patterns and maps the activity onto cross-sectional slices through patient tissue. Radionuclides can be neurochemically specific to target substrates and the radiopharmaceuticals are injected in a patient's bloodstream. The gamma camera records images approximately every fifteen seconds with spatial resolution around one centimeter. The health risks to patients and cost to perform the procedure are the major drawbacks to this technique.

Aside from a neuroimaging scanner, the standard EEG assessment of sleep can be modified with so-called quantitative EEG techniques. Quantitative EEG's temporal resolution is quite good, on the order of milliseconds. While the standard EEG for sleep assessment contains at most a couple of dozen recent advancements in source localization techniques with high-density electrode arrays (e.g., 64–, 128–, and 256– electrodes) has allowed for the capture of a great deal more information from the cortex and this information can be reconstructed into detailed images of brain activity patterns. Scalp-recorded EEG is a relatively noninvasive method to record micro-voltage potentials at various locations on the cortical surface. Signal processing transformations estimate current sources inside the brain. Spatial and temporal accuracy is approximated at five millimeter and five milliseconds, respectively. Benefits of high density EEG source localization imaging for sleep research is its relatively low cost, portability of equipment for use in varied environments, higher temporal resolution, tolerability of movement, and lack of aggravating noises or tightly enclosed testing space. Its major drawback for sleep is that it does not capture subcortical brain activity.

A.7 Psychophysics

Typically psychophysical paradigms examine the potential relationship between a given stimulus (visual, auditory, etc.) and subjective perceptional response. But these techniques can sometimes be used to investigate a sleeping subject's or recently awakened subject's response. A commonly used visual psychophysics approach is semantic priming.

Table A.4 Functional neuroimaging methods to study the sleeping brain

Method	Spatial resolution	Temporal resolution	What is measured	Strengths for sleep study	Weaknesses for sleep study	Comments
fMRI	cm	seconds	BOLD signal Blood flow	Individual can sometimes sleep in scanner; experiments can be performed while in scanner	Scanner pounds out noise; tight enclosed space	Widely available tool for research
[18F]FDG-PET	cm	10–20 minutes	Glucose metabolism	Can obtain index of energetic needs of sleeping brain	Poor temporal resolution; subject cannot sleep in scanner	
[15O]H2O-PET	cm	minute	Blood flow	Can sometimes sleep in scanner	Poor temporal resolution	
SPECT	cm	minutes	Blood flow and metabolism	Can be used for receptor imaging	Cannot sleep in scanner	

Information processing in semantic networks is quickened when lexical decisions are made following exposure to semantically related concepts compared to those unrelated. For instance, asking a participant to respond to whether a given word is a word or not would yield faster response times to the word "doctor" when preceded briefly by the word "nurse" compared to "purse" or "nursery." Because of the phenomenon of "sleep inertia" your brain remains in the sleep state, perhaps the REM state for about ten minutes after you wake up. Therefore we can probe the REM state if we present stimuli or have you perform tasks during that ten-minute period post-awakening.

Semantic priming techniques have revealed that we are faster in accessing disparate associations after a bout of REM sleep than we are in accessing strong associations. Something about REM enhances our abilities to access more distant semantic associations to a given stimulus. For example, after REM sleep, we are better at making associations between animals not typically associated such as dog–elephant than we are in making more typical associations such as dog–cat. This enhanced ability to cognitively reach for the more distant association is fundamental to thinking outside the box and arriving at novel insights. Indeed, it seems clear now that after a good night's dream-rich sleep, we have improved ability to solve anagram problems, or to suddenly "see" the solution to a difficult problem that eluded us before we engaged in the sleep. The available data suggest that the kind of sleep we need to enhance our creative abilities is dream-rich REM sleep. For example, subjects who had engaged in REM sleep during a daytime nap did better on a remote associates task than those who had engaged in NREM during the nap or those subjects who did not sleep at all during the nap period.

A.8 Methods of Studying Dream Content

All methods for study of dream content depend on the collection of samples of dreams. Dream reports can be collected in the sleep lab by awakening the volunteer whenever he or she enters into the REM state. When lab-collected dreams are compared to spontaneously recalled dreams (e.g., in the home environment) only one difference consistently emerges: Home dreams exhibit slightly greater amounts of aggression than dreams collected in the lab. This may indicate that subjects in the lab are censoring aspects of their dream content or that spontaneously recalled dreams are embellished to spice up the story. The true amount of aggression in the typical dream probably lies somewhere between the amounts reported in the lab versus those spontaneously recalled.

Outside of the lab the most typical way in which dream researchers collect dream samples is to ask groups of subjects to recall their most recent dream and to write it down. Alternatively subjects can be given a notebook, tape recorder or dream diary to keep at their bedside so that they can record a weeks' worth (or longer) of dreams. Occasionally persons may approach dream researchers with a gift: years of journals or dream diaries. These dream journals that contain decades of dreams on a single subject are exceedingly valuable sources for the study of dreams as they can help answer the question as to how dream content changes across the life cycle and in relation to the subject's life events.

Obviously in order for dream scientists to compare results of their analyses of dream content, they need standardized methods of scoring dream content. The "Hall/Van de Castle system" for scoring dream content (Domhoff, 1996; Hall and Van de Castle, 1966) is one such standardized system. The system has built-in techniques for controlling length effects via use of automated scoring of basic categories into percents and ratios. In addition, it is the most comprehensive system yet available encompassing many of the most common dream events, features, and elements. The quantitative scoring system consists of up to sixteen empirical scales and a number of derived scales. The "characters" scale allows for classification of characters known to the dreamer (e.g., family members, friends, etc.) or unknown strangers, and these characters are classified as to gender, age, etc. Animals and imaginary figures are scored as well. Three major types of social interaction are scored: aggression, friendliness, and sexual with other types possible as well. The character that initiated the interaction is identified as well as the target or recipient of the interaction. Subtypes of the interaction are scored as well. For example, aggressive interactions are scored as physical, verbal, etc. Five different types of emotion are scored. The activities scales yield information on dreamer goals or strivings and whether success or misfortune is experienced. The "settings" scale refers to the location (familiar, unfamiliar, indoors, outdoors, etc.) of dream events. The "objects" scale is used to describe any tangible objects in the dream.

In a real service to the dream research community, Domhoff and Schneider have constructed a website (www.dreamresearch.net) that provides complete information on how to best make use of the Hall/Van de Castle system as well as an extensive archive of dreams. A spreadsheet program, DreamSat, allows for automatic tabulation of dream content scores and automatic computation of derived scales and percents. This spreadsheet program greatly increases the reliability of results obtained with use of the system. The program also produces Cohen's h statistic,

Table A.5 Common sleep and dream measures

Test	Summary Variables
Polysomnogram	Total sleep time (TST); total amounts (in minutes and in percent of total sleep time) of stages 1, 2, 3, 4 of NREM; total amount of NREM; spindling activity in S2; total amount of SWS delta activity (stages 3 and 4 summed); total amount of REM; latency in minutes to first REM; REM density; length of the REM-NREM cycle (defined as the elapsed time from the end of each REM episode to the end of the next REM episode); # apneic indices; # hypopneas; # arousals; # awakenings, duration of awakenings, sleep efficiency
Sleep Diary (3 weeks)	Subjective daily rankings of sleep quality; bedtime, sleep onset time, # awakenings, wake-up time, # naps, duration of each nap, sleep location, frequency and content of dreams. (SDI: sleep disturbance index = the average frequency of night wakings per week + the average rating on daily sleep quality)

which is an effect size for comparing differences in content relative to norms or other types of difference (e.g., REM-NREM differences).

While the Hall/Van de Castle system has been criticized as employing too narrow a range of categories (the emotions category for example is biased toward negative emotions), the system is nevertheless reliable and standardized. It should therefore be used as often as possible so that results are comparable across studies and labs. Wingate and Kramer (Winget and Kramer, 1979) describe a number of other scoring systems along with studies on their reliability for scoring content not easily captured by the Hall/Van de Castle system.

A.9 Awakenings Procedures

In order to obtain dreams from EEG-verified sleep states you have to awaken subjects in a sleep lab. Typically each participant will be awakened twice from REM sleep and twice from NREM sleep (stage N2). The order of awakenings will be counterbalanced such that half of the participants will be awakened from REM first, and the other half from NREM first, with all subsequent awakenings alternated between REM and NREM. REM awakenings will occur twenty minutes into each REM period. NREM awakenings will occur twenty minutes into continuous stage 2 sleep. All awakenings will be separated by a minimum of twenty minutes.

To awaken a participant his or her name will be called once per second until he or she responds. The interviewer (sleep tech) will then query:

Tell me everything that was going on through your mind just before I called. Think back and try to remember what was going on in your mind in the time prior to being awakened, and report this as completely as you can. For example, where did you think you were? Who else was there? What were you doing? What was happening around you? What were you seeing, thinking, and feeling? Can you tell what other characters were thinking? If you weren't asleep, state this fact and describe any thoughts, images or feeling that were passing through your mind.

Subjects dictate their mentation reports into an microcassette recorder, which automatically multiplexes a time-and-date stamp onto each recording, allowing subsequent retrieval of the time of each report.

A.10 Transcription of Mentation Reports

All reports are transcribed verbatim, including extraverbal sounds such as "um," "uh," and coughs. To correct for differing word lengths a Word Information Count (WIC) measure is taken. WIC is an estimate of the amount of information about the sleep experience in each report – a count of the words that describe the content. WIC excludes redundancies in the report, commentary, and connections made to the mentation after the participant has awakened. If these WIC scales demonstrate a positive skew (as they have in some other studies, thus violating the standard assumptions of ANOVA), all of the WIC scores will be log transformed ($\log_{10}(\text{WIC}+1)$) to remove their positive skew.

Each dream report will be given a header with the date and time of the report. All subsequent content analyses should be done *with two judges blind to the source of each report* in participant sets of four (two REM and two NREM), to help judges distinguish participant's expressive style from true information. Inter-rater coding reliabilities will be calculated for all major content outcomes.

A.11 Scoring of Characters, Social Interactions, and Emotions

To use the so-called Hall/Van de Castle content scoring system to score see www.dreamresearch.net, which provides a spreadsheet program called "DreamSat," which allows for tabulation of dream content scores and automatic computation of derived scales and percents when using the Hall/Van de Castle scoring system. This spreadsheet program greatly increases the reliability of results obtained with use of the system. The Hall/Van de Castle system for scoring dream content is a standardized and reliable content scoring system that consists of up to sixteen empirical scales and a number of derived scales useful for an analysis of social interactions in dream content. Three primary types of emotional interaction are scored: aggressive, friendly, and sexual with the ability to score subtypes as well (e.g., physical vs. verbal aggression). Along with identification of the physical settings within which these interactions take place, the character that initiated the social interaction is identified as well as the target or recipient of the interaction. The "characters" scale allows for classification of characters known to the dreamer (e.g., family members, friends, etc.) as well as those unknown to the dreamer. Characters (known or unknown) can also be classified as to gender, age, and relation to the dreamer. In addition to scoring all of the basic categories you can also calculate (using the DreamSat software) the following Hall/Van de Castle outcome measures (Table A.6):

Table A.6 Hall/Van de Castle content ratios

- Known and unknown characters by gender
- Number and variety of emotions
- Aggression/Friendliness percent = Dreamer involved aggression/(dreamer-involved aggression + dreamer-involved friendliness)
- Befriender percent = The percentage of all dreamer-involved friendly interactions in which the dreamer befriends some other character. Dreamer as befriender/(dreamer as befriender + dreamer as befriended)
- Aggressor percent = The percentage of all dreamer-involved aggressions in which the dreamer is the aggressor. Dreamer as aggressor/(Dreamer as aggressor + Dreamer as victim)
- Physical aggression percent = The percentage of all aggressions appearing in reports whether witnessed or dreamer involved that are physical in nature. Physical aggressions/all aggressions
- Aggression (A/C) index = Frequencies of aggressions per character (all aggressions/all characters)
- Friendliness (F/C) index = Frequencies of friendly interactions per character (all friendliness/all characters)
- Sexuality (S/C) index = Frequencies of all sexual encounters per character (sexual encounters/all characters)

A.12 Sleep Logs/Diaries

In order to interpret the sleep and waking context in which dreams occur, researchers often request that participants in their studies keep a sleep log/sleep diary. Subjects fill out the sleep diary every evening before going to bed (indicating the time they are going to bed) and every morning upon awakening. Sleep logs record the times subjects go to bed, estimates of sleep latency and wake time after sleep onset, times of morning awakening, and subjective measures of sleep quality. Typically participants fill out daily sleep log information for one week prior to the overnight sleep studies, during the week of the overnight studies and one week after the sleep studies (total of three weeks). Among the information collected is subjective daily rankings of sleep quality: bedtime, sleep onset time, number of awakenings, wake-up time, number of naps, duration of each nap, sleep location, frequency, and content of dreams. A good example of a sleep diary is the *Pittsburgh Sleep Diary*, which reports reasonably stable and high validity/reliability rankings.

A.13 Some Big Data Resources on Sleep and Dreams

The National Sleep Research Resource, (NSRR). "The NSRR is a web-based data portal that aggregates, harmonizes, and organizes sleep and clinical data from thousands of individuals studied as part of cohort studies or clinical trials and provides the user a suite of tools to facilitate data exploration and data visualization. Each de-identified study record minimally includes the summary results of an overnight sleep study; annotation files with scored events; the raw physiological signals from the sleep record; and available clinical and physiological data. NSRR is designed to be interoperable with other public data resources such as the Biologic Specimen and Data Repository Information Coordinating Center Demographics (BioLINCC) data and analyzed with methods provided by the Research Resource for Complex Physiological Signals." **Physionet**, the "Resource for Complex Physiological Signals." See also Dean, D. A., Goldberger, A. L., Mueller, R., et al. "Scaling up scientific discovery in sleep medicine: The National Sleep Research Resource." Sleep. 2016; 39 (5): 1151–1164. Journal of Sleep Research. 2014; 23(6): 628–635.

    The Montreal Archive of Sleep Studies, (MASS). From its website: "MASS is an open-access and collaborative database of laboratory-based polysomnography (PSG) recordings. Its goal is to provide a standard and easily accessible source of data for benchmarking the various systems developed to help the automation of sleep analysis. It also provides a readily available source of data for fast validation of experimental results and for exploratory analyses. Finally, it is a shared resource that can be used to foster large-scale collaborations in sleep studies." "Montreal Archive of Sleep Studies: An open-access resource for instrument benchmarking and exploratory research" is a paper describing MASS by O'Reilly, C., Gosselin, N., Carrier, J., and Nielsen, T.

Dreambank remains the best available depository of dream narratives. Created by psychologists Adam Schneider and G. William Domhoff of the University of California, Santa Cruz, it contains over 20,000 "dream reports" collected from a number of sources and studies. Dreambank has a search tool and analytic tools based on the classic and standardized Hall/Van de Castle scoring system for dreams.

Kelly Bulkeley's sleep and dreams database rivals dreambank.net in the number and variety of dream narratives it contains. You can explore these narratives using the database's built-in tools for word searching and survey analysis.

It would be nice if we had an archive with polysomnographic data like the NSSR and related dream narratives from the same subjects but I do not know of any such archive as of yet. The MASS may post some data along these lines in the future given that teams' expertise in both sleep and dream studies.

In any case, these dream banks contain at most 20,000 dreams. Those numbers will soon be considered small once databases amassed from smartphone apps start to get cleaned up and archived.

Til Roenneberg's Chronotype Questionnaire. Discover your chronotype and whether and why you are a morning or evening person. Roenneberg's group aims to understand the underlying complexity of the biological clock and individual differences in the biological clock, as shown in everyday waking and sleep behavior. Once your questionnaire has been submitted, an automatic evaluation of your chronotype (your personal profile) will be sent to you via email. You will see how your results compare to the ones of more than 50,000 other individuals that have so far filled out the questionnaire.

International Association for the Study of Dreams (ASD). This is the professional society for dream scholars/scientists. It provides a huge range of resources for people interested in dreams and published the APA journal *Dreaming*. Follow ASD on Twitter.

References

Achermann, P., Finelli, L. A., & Borbély, A. (2001). Unihemispheric enhancement of delta power in human frontal sleep EEG by prolonged wakefulness. *Brain Research*, 913(2), 220–223.

Affani, J. M., Cervino, C. O., & Marcos, H. J. A. (2001). Absence of penile erections during paradoxical sleep: Peculiar penile events during wakefulness and slow wave sleep in the armadillo. *Journal of Sleep Research*, 10, 219–228.

Ainsworth, M. S., Blehar, M. C., Waters, E., & Wall, S. (1978). *Patterns of Attachment: A Psychological Study of the Strange Situation*. Hillsdale, NJ: Erlbaum.

Alloy, L. B., Ng, T. H., Titone, M. K., & Boland, E. M. (2017). Circadian rhythm dysregulation in bipolar spectrum disorders. *Current Psychiatry Reports*, 19(4), 21. doi: 10.1007/s11920-017-0772-z. Review. PMID:28321642.

Anderson, J. R. (1998). Sleep, sleeping sites, and sleep-related activities: Awakening to their significance. *American Journal of Primatology*, 46(1), 63–75.

Anderson, C., & Horne, J. A. (2003). Prefrontal cortex: Links between low frequency delta EEG in sleep and neuropsychological performance in healthy, older people. *Psychophysiology*, 40(3), 349–357. PMID:12946109.

Antony, J., Gobel, E. W., O'Hare, J. K., Reber, P. J., & Paller, K. A. (2012). Cued memory reactivation during sleep influences skill learning. *Nature Neuroscience*, 15, 1114–1116.

Antrobus, J. S. (1991). Dreaming: Cognitive processes during cortical activation and high afferent thresholds. *Psychological Review*, 98, 96–121.

Argiolas, A., & Gessa, G. L. (1991). Central functions of oxytocin. *Neuroscience and Biobehavioral Reviews*, 15(2), 217–231.

Arnulf, I., Zeitzer, J. M., File, J., Farber, N., & Mignot, E. (2005). Kleine-Levin syndrome: A systematic review of 186 cases in the literature. *Brain*, 128 (Pt 12), 2763–2776. E-pub October 17, 2005. Review. PMID:16230322.

Aviv, A., & Susser, E. (2013). Leukocyte telomere length and the father's age enigma: Implications for population health and for life course. *International Journal of Epidemiology*. doi:10.1093/ije/dys236.

Barnouw, V. (1963). *Culture and Personality*. Homewood, IL: Dorsey Press.

Beattie, L., Kyle, S. D., Espie, C. A., & Biello, S. M. (2015). Social interactions, emotion and sleep: A systematic review and research agenda. *Sleep Medicine Reviews*, 24, 83–100. doi: 10.1016/j. smrv.2014.12.005.

Beebe, D. W. (2016). WEIRD considerations when studying adolescent sleep need. *Sleep*, 39(8), 1491–1492.

Beijers, R., Jansen, J., Riksen-Walraven, M., & de Weerth, C. (2011). Attachment and infant night waking: A longitudinal study from birth through the first year of life. *Journal of the American Academy of Child and Adolescent Psychiatry*, 32(9), 635–643.

Belsky, J., Steinberg, L., & Draper, P. (1991). Childhood experience, interpersonal development, and reproductive strategy: An evolutionary theory of socialization. *Child Development*, 62, 647–670.

Benington, J. H., & Frank, M. G. (2003). Cellular and molecular connections between sleep and synaptic plasticity. *Progress in Neurobiology*, 69(2), 71–101. Review. PMID:12684067.

Benington, J. H., & Heller, H. C. (1994). Does the function of REM sleep concern non-REM sleep or waking? *Progress in Neurobiology*, 44, 433–449.

(1995). Restoration of brain energy metabolism as the function of sleep. *Progress in Neurobiology*, 45, 347–360.

Benoit, D., Zeanah, C. H., Boucher, C., & Minde, K. K. (1992). Sleep disorders in early childhood: Association with insecure maternal attachment. *Journal of the American Academy of Child and Adolescent Psychiatry*, 31(1), 86–93.

Blanco-Centurion, C., Xu, M., Murillo-Rodriguez, E., Gerashchenko, D., Shiromani, A. M., Salin-Pascual, R. J., et al. (2006). Adenosine and sleep homeostasis in the basal forebrain. *Journal of Neuroscience*, 26(31), 8092–8100.

Bliwise, D. L. (2000). Normal aging. In M. H. Kryger, T. Roth, & W. C. Dement (eds.), *Principles and Practice of Sleep Medicine* (pp. 26–42). Philadelphia: Saunders.

Blurton Jones, N. G., & da Costa, E. (1987). A suggested adaptive value of toddler night waking: Delaying the birth of the next sibling. *Ethology and Sociobiology*, 8, 135–142.

Booker, C. (2006). *The Seven Basic Plots: Why We Tell Stories*. New York: Bloomsbury Academic Press.

Bourguignon, E. (1972). Dreams and altered states of consciousness in anthropological research. In F. L. K. Hsu (ed.), *Psychological Anthropology* (pp. 403–434). Cambridge, MA: Schenkman Publications.

Borbely, A. A. (1980). Sleep: Circadian rhythm versus recovery process. In M. Koukkou, D. Lehmann, & J. Angst (eds.), *Functional States of the Brain: Their Determinants* (pp. 151–161). Amsterdam: Elsevier.
    (1982). A two process model of sleep regulation. *Human Neurobiology*, 1, 195–204.
Borbely, A. A., Tobler, I., & Hanagasioglu, M. (1984). Effect of sleep deprivation on sleep and EEG power spectra in the rat. *Behavioral Brain Research*, 14, 171–182.
Bowlby, J. (1969). *Attachment and Loss* (Vol. 1). New York: Basic Books.
Braun, A. R., Balkin, T. J., Wesensten, N. J., Carson, R. E., Varga, M., Baldwin, P., Selbie, S., Belenky, G., & Herscovitch, P. (1997). Regional cerebral blood flow throughout the sleep-wake cycle. *Brain*, 120, 1173–1197.
Braun, A. R., Balkin, T. J., Wesensten, N. J., Gwadry, F., Carson, R. E., Varga, M., Baldwin, P., Belenky, G., & Herscovitch, P. (1998). Dissociated pattern of activity in visual cortices and their projections during human rapid eye-movement sleep. *Science*, 279, 91–95.
Brereton, D. (2000). Dreaming, adaptation, and consciousness: The social mapping hypothesis. *Ethos*, 28(3), 379–409. 10.1525/eth.2000.28.3.379.
Brubaker, L. L. (1998). Note on the relevance of dreams for evolutionary psychology. *Psychology Reports*, 82(3), 1006.
Bulkeley, K. (2014). Digital dream analysis: A revised method. *Conscious and Cognition*, 29, 159–170. doi: 10.1016/j.concog.2014.08.015. Epub October 3, 2014. PMID: 25286125.
Burnham, M. M., Goodlin-Jones, B. L., Gaylor, E. E., & Anders, T. F. (2002). Nighttime sleep-wake patterns and self-soothing from birth to one year of age: A longitudinal intervention study. *Journal of Child Psychology and Psychiatry*, 43(6), 713–725.
Burns, J. (2007). *The Descent of Madness: Evolutionary Origins of Psychosis and the Social Brain*. New York: Routledge.
Buxton, J. L., Suderman, M., Pappas, J. J., Borghol, N., McArdle, W., Blakemore, A. I., Hertzman, C., Power, C., Szyf, M., & Pembrey, M. (2014). Human leukocyte telomere length is associated with DNA methylation levels in multiple subtelomeric and imprinted loci. *Scientific Reports*, 4, 4954. doi: 10.1038/srep04954.
Buysse, D. (2011). Insomnia: Recent developments and future directions. In M. Kryger, T. Roth, & W. C. Dement (eds.), *Principles and Practice of Sleep Medicine* (5th edn). Philadelphia: W. B. Saunders Co.
Buzsaki, G. (1996). The hippocampo-neocortical dialogue. *Cerebral Cortex*, 6(2), 81–92.
Cajochen, C., Foy, R., & Dijk, D. J. (1999). Frontal predominance of a relative increase in sleep delta and theta EEG activity after sleep loss in humans. *Sleep Research Online*, 2(3), 65–69. PMID: 11382884.

Capellini, I., Barton, R. A., Preston, B., McNamara, P., & Nunn, C. L. (2008). Phylogenetic analysis of the ecology and evolution of mammalian sleep. *Evolution*, 62(7), 1764–1776. PMID: 18384657.

Capellini, I., McNamara, P., Preston, B. T., Nunn, C. L., & Barton, R. A. (2009). Does sleep play a role in memory consolidation? A comparative test. *PLoS ONE*, 4(2), e4609. PMID: 19240803.

Capellini, I., Nunn, C. L., McNamara, P., Preston, B. T., & Barton, R. A. (2008). Energetic constraints, not predation, influence the evolution of sleep patterning in mammals. *Functional Ecology*, 22(5), 847–853.

Carskadon, M. A., Acebo, C., & Jenni, O. (2004). Regulation of adolescent sleep: Implications for behavior. *Annals of the New York Academy of Sciences*, 1021, 276–291.

Carskadon, M., & Dement, W. C. (2000). Normal human sleep: An overview. In M. H. Kryger, T. Roth, & W. C. Dement (eds.), *Principles and Practice of Sleep Medicine* (3rd edn, pp. 15–25). Philadelphia: Saunders.

Cartwright, R. D. (1999). Dreaming in sleep disordered patients. In S. Chokroverty (ed.), *Sleep Disorders Medicine: Basic Science, Technical Considerations, and Clinical Aspects* (pp. 127–134). Boston: Butterworth- Heinemann.

Cartwright, R. (2010). *The Twenty-Four Hour Mind*. Cambridge: Cambridge University Press.

Chauvet, J., Deschamps, E. B., & Hillaire, C. (1995). *Chauvet Cave: The Discovery of the World's Oldest Paintings*. London: Thames and Hudson.

Chemelli, R. M., Willie, J. T., Sinton, C. M., Elmquist, J. Scammell, T., Lee, C., Richardson, J. A., Williams, S. C., Xiong,Y., Kisanuki, Y., Fitch, T. E., Nakazato, M., Hammer, R. E., Saper,C. B., & Yanagisawa, M. (1990). Narcolepsy in orexin knockout mice: Molecular genetics of sleep regulation. *Cell*, 98(4), 437–451.

Chen, Q., Yang, H., Zhou, N., Sun, L., Bao, H., Tan, L., Chen, H., Ling, X., Zhang, G., Huang, L., Li, L., Ma, M., Yang, H., Wang, X., Zou, P., Peng, K., Liu, T., Cui, Z., Ao, L., Roenneberg, T., Zhou, Z., & Cao, J. (2016). Inverse u-shaped association between sleep duration and semen quality: Longitudinal observational study (MARHCS) in Chongqing, China. *SLEEP*, 39(1), 79–86.

Cheyne, J. A. (2002). Situational factors affecting sleep paralysis and associated hallucinations: Position and timing effects. *Journal of Sleep Research*, 11(2), 169–77. PMID: 12028482.

Cheyne, J. A., & Girard, T. A. (2007). Paranoid delusions and threatening hallucinations: A prospective study of sleep paralysis experiences. *Conscious and Cognition*, 16(4), 959–749. Epub March 6, 2007. PMID: 17337212.

Chisholm, J. S. (ed.). (1999). *Death, Hope and Sex: Steps to an Evolutionary Ecology of Mind and Morality*. Cambridge: Cambridge University Press.

Cipolli, C., & Poli, D. (1992). Story structure in verbal reports of mental sleep experience after awakening in REM sleep. *Sleep*, 15, 133–142.

Clayton-Smith, J., & Laan, L. (2003). Angelman syndrome: A review of the clinical and genetic aspects. *Journal of Medical Genetics*, 40(2), 87–95.

Clawson, B. C., Durkin, J., & Aton, S. J. (2016). Form and function of sleep spindles across the lifespan. *Neural Plasticity*. 2016:6936381. doi: 10.1155/2016/6936381. Epub April 14, 2016.

Colace, C. (2010). *Children's Dreams: From Freud's Observations to Modern Dream Research* (1st edn). London: Karnac Books Ltd.

Corsi-Cabrera, M., Miro, E., del-Rio-Portilla, Y., Perez-Garci, E., Villanueva, Y., & Guevara, M. A. (2003). Rapid eye movement sleep dreaming is characterized by uncoupled EEG activity between frontal and perceptual cortical regions. *Brain and Cognition*, 51(3), 337–345.

Crick, F., & Mitchison, G. (1983). The function of dream sleep. *Nature*, 304, 111–114.

(1986). REM sleep and neural nets. *Journal of Mind and Behavior*, 7, 229–250.

Czeisler. C. (2006). Impact of extended-duration shifts on medical errors, adverse events, and attentional failures. *PLOS Medicine*, 3, 12.

Czeisler, C. A., & Gooley, J. J. (2007). Sleep and circadian rhythms in humans. *Cold Spring Harbor Symposia on Quantitative Biology*, 72, 579–597.

Czisch, M., Wehrle, R., Kaufmann, C., Wetter, T. C., Holsboer, F., Pollmacher, T., & Auer, D. P. (2004). Functional MRI during sleep: BOLD signal decreases and their electrophysiological correlates. *European Journal of Neuroscience*, 20(2), 566–574.

Czisch, M., Wetter, T. C., Kaufmann, C., Pollmacher, T., Holsboer, F., & Auer, D. P. (2002). Altered processing of acoustic stimuli during sleep: Reduced auditory activation and visual deactivation detected by a combined fMRI/EEG study. *Neuroimage*, 16(1), 251–258.

Dale, A., Lafrenière, A., & De Koninck, J. (2017). Dream content of Canadian males from adolescence to old age: An exploration of ontogenetic patterns.; *Consciousness and Cognition*, 49, 145–156. doi: 10.1016/j.concog.2017.01.008. Epub February 15, 2017. PMID:28212501.

Dale, A., Lortie-Lussier, M., & De Koninck, J. (2015). Ontogenetic patterns in the dreams of women across the lifespan. *Consciousness and Cognition*, 37, 214–224.

Dang-Vu, T. T., Desseilles, M., Petit, D., Mazza, S., Montplaisir, J., & Maquet, P. (2007). Neuroimaging in sleep medicine. *Sleep Medicine*, 8, 349–372.

Dang-Vu, T. T, Desseilles, M., Laureys, S., Degueldre, C., Perrin, F., Phillips, C., Maquet, P., & Peigneux, P. (2005). Cerebral correlates of delta waves during non-REM sleep revisited. *Neuroimage*, 28(1), 14–21. Epub June 23, 2005.

Dang-Vu, T. T., Schabus, M., Desseilles, M., Sterpenich, V., Bonjean, M., & Maquet, P. (2010) Functional neuroimaging insights into the physiology of human sleep. *Sleep*, 33(12), 1589–603. Review. PMID:21120121.

D'Andrade, R. G. (1961). Anthropological studies of dreams. In F. L. K. Hsu (ed.), *Psychological Anthropology: Approaches to Culture and Personality* (pp. 296–332). Homewood, IL: Dorsey Press.

Daoyun, J., and Wilson, M. A. (2007). Coordinated memory replay in the visual cortex and hippocampus during sleep. *Nature Neuroscience*, 10(1), 100–107.

De Gennaro, L., Vecchio, F., Ferrara, M., Curcio, G., Rossini, P. M., & Babiloni, C. (2004). Changes in fronto-posterior functional coupling at sleep onset in humans. *Journal of Sleep Research*, 13(3), 209–217.

Dement, W. C. (1965). Recent studies on the biological role of rapid eye movement sleep. *American Journal of Psychiatry*, 122, 404–408.

Dement, W. C., & Vaughn, C. (2000). *The Promise of Sleep*. New York: Dell Publishing.

Devereux, G. (1951). *Reality and Dream: Psychotherapy of a Plains Indian*. New York: International Universities Press.

Dew, M. A., Hoch, C. C., Buysse, D. J., Monk, T. H., Begley, A. E., Houck, P. R., et al. (2003). Healthy older adults' sleep predicts all-cause mortality at 4 to 19 years of follow-up. *Psychosomatic Medicine*, 65(1), 63–73.

Dewald, J. F., Meijer, A. M., Oort, F. J., Kerkhof, G. A., & Bögels, S. M. (2010). The influence of sleep quality, sleep duration and sleepiness on school performance in children and adolescents: A meta-analytic review. *Sleep Medicine Review*, 14(3), 179–89. doi: 10.1016/j. smrv.2009.10.004. Epub January 21, 2010.

Dixon, B. R. (1908). Notes on the Achomawi and Atsugewi Indians of Northern California. *American Anthropologist*, 10, 208–220.

Domhoff, G. W. (1996). *Finding Meaning in Dreams: A Quantitative Approach*. New York: Plenum.

(2003). *The Scientific Study of Dreams: Neural Networks, Cognitive Development, and Content Analysis*. Washington, DC: American Psychological Association.

(2011). The neural substrate for dreaming: is it a subsystem of the default network? *Consciousness and Cognition*, 20(4), 1163–1174. doi: 10.1016/j.concog.2011.03.001. Epub March 29, 2011.

Domhoff, G. W., & Kamiya, J. (1964). Problems in dream content study with objective indicators: A comparison of home and laboratory dream reports. *Archives of General Psychiatry*, 11, 519–524.

Dresler, M., Wehrle, R., Spoormaker, V. I., Koch, S. P., Holsboer, F., Steiger, A., Obrig, H., Sämann, P. G., & Czisch, M. (2012). Neural correlates of dream lucidity obtained from contrasting lucid versus non-lucid REM sleep: A combined EEG/fMRI case study. *Sleep*, 35(7), 1017–1020. doi: 10.5665/sleep.1974. PMID: 22754049.

Dumoulin Bridi, M. C., Aton, S. J., Seibt, J., Renouard, L., Coleman, T., & Frank, M. G. (2015). Rapid eye movement sleep promotes cortical plasticity in the developing brain. *Science Advances*, 1(6), e1500105. doi: 10.1126/sciadv.1500105. eCollection July 2015.

Dunbar, R. (1998). The social brain hypothesis. *Evolutionary Anthropology*, 6, 178–190.

Dunbar, R. I. (2012). The social brain meets neuroimaging. *Trends in Cognitive Science*, 16(2), 101–102. doi: 10.1016/j.tics.2011.11.013. Epub December 15, 2011. PMID:22177800.

Durrence, H. H., & Lichstein, K. L. (2006). The sleep of African Americans: A comparative review. *Behavioral Sleep Medicine*, 4(1), 29–44. Review. PMID:16390283.

Eggan, D. (1949). The significance of dreams for anthropological research. *American Anthropology*, 51(2), 177–198.

(1961). Dream analysis. In B. Kaplan (ed.), *Studying Personality Cross-Culturally* (pp. 551–577). New York: Harper and Row.

Eisenberg, D. T. A. (2011). An evolutionary review of human telomere biology: The thrifty telomere hypothesis and notes on potential adaptive paternal effects. *American Journal of Human Biology*, 23, 149–167.

Eisenberg, D. & Kuzawa, C. (2013) Commentary: The evolutionary biology of the paternal age effect on telomere length. *International Journal of Epidemiology*, 42(2), 462-465. doi:10.1093/ije/dyt027.

Eisenberg, D. T., Hayes, M. G., & Kuzawa, C. W. (2012). Delayed paternal age of reproduction in humans is associated with longer telomeres across two generations of descendants. *Proceedings of the National Academy of Sciences of the United States of America*, 109, 10251–1056.

Ekirch, A. (2005). *At Day's Close: Night in Times Past*. New York: W. W. Norton.

Everson, C. A., & Szabo, A. Repeated exposure to severely limited sleep results in distinctive and persistent physiological imbalances in rats. *PLoS ONE*, 6(8), e22987.

Fantini, M. L., Corona, A., Clerici, S., & Ferini-Strambi, L. (2005).
Aggressive dream content without daytime aggressiveness in REM
sleep behavior disorder. *Neurology*, 65(7), 1010–1015.
PMID:16217051.

Finelli, L.A., Borbely, A.A. & Achermann, P. (2001) Functional topography
of the human non-REM sleep electroencephalogram. *European
Journal of Neuroscience*, 13, 2282–2290.

Fogel, S. M., Nader, R., Cote, K. A., & Smith, C. T. (2007). Sleep spindles
and learning potential. *Behavioral Neuroscience*, 121(1), 1–10.
PMID:17324046.

Fosse, M. J., Fosse, R., Hobson, J. A., & Stickgold, R. (2003). Dreaming and
episodic memory: A functional dissociation? *Journal of Cognitive
Neuroscience*, 15, 1–9.

Foulkes, D. (1962). Dream reports from different stages of sleep. *Journal of
Abnormal and Social Psychology*, 65, 14–25.
   (1978). *A Grammar of Dreams*. New York: Basic Books.
   (1982). *Children's Dreams: Longitudinal Studies*. New York: John Wiley.
   (1985). *Dreaming: A Cognitive-Psychological Analysis*. Hillsdale, NJ:
   Lawrence Erlbaum.

Foulkes, D., & Schmidt, M. (1983). Temporal sequence and unit composition
in dream reports from different stages of sleep. *Sleep*, 6(3), 265–280.

Frank, M. G. (1999). Phylogeny and evolution of rapid eye movement
(REM) sleep. In B. N. Mallick & S. Inoue (eds.), *Rapid Eye Movement
Sleep* (pp. 15–38). New Delhi: Narosa.

Frank, M. G., & Benington, J. H. The role of sleep in memory consolidation and
brain plasticity: Dream or reality? *The Neuroscientist*, 12(6), 477–488.

Frank, M. G., & Heller, H. C. Development of REM and slow wave sleep in
the rat. *American Journal of Physiology*, 272, R1792–R1799.

Frank, M. G., Issa, N. P., & Stryker, M. P. Sleep enhances plasticity in the
developing visual cortex. *Neuron*, 30, 275–287.

Frank, R. H. (1988). *Passions within Reason: The Strategic Role of Emotions*.
New York: Norton.

Franken, P., Chollet, D., & Tafti, M. (2001). The homeostatic regulation of
sleep need is under general control. *Journal of Neuroscience*, 21,
2610–2621.

Franklin, M. S. & Zyphur, M. J. (2005). The role of dreams in the evolution
of the human mind. *Evolutionary Psychology*, 3, 59–78.

Freud, S. (1900). *Die Traumdeutung*. Vienna: Franz Deuticke, Leipzig &
Vienna.
   (1950). *The Interpretation of Dreams*. New York: Random House.

French, T., & Fromme, E. (1964). *Dream Interpretation: A New Approach*.
New York: Basic Books.

Fruth, B., & Hohmann, G. (1993). Ecological and behavioral aspects of nest building in wild bonobos. *Ethology*, 94, 113–126.

Fruth, B., & McGrew, W. C. (1998). Resting and nesting in primates: Behavioral ecology of inactivity. *American Journal of Primatology*, 46(1), 3–5.

Garfield, A. S., Cowley, M., Smith, F. M., Moorwood, K., et al. 2011. Distinct physiological and behavioral functions for parental alleles of imprinted Grb10. *Nature*, 469, 534–538.

Gemignani, A., Piarulli, A., Menicucci, D., Laurino, M., Rota, G., Mastorci, F., Gushin, V., Shevchenko, O., Garbella, E., Pingitore, A., Sebastiani, L., Bergamasco, M., L'Abbate, A., Allegrini, P., & Bedini, R. (2014). How stressful are 105 days of isolation? Sleep EEG patterns and tonic cortisol in healthy volunteers simulating manned flight to Mars. *International Journal of Psychophysiology*, 93(2), 211–219. doi: 10.1016/j.ijpsycho.2014.04.008. Epub May 2, 2014.

Giuditta, A., Ambrosini, M. V., Montagnese, P., Mandile, P., Cotugno, M., Grassi, Z. G., et al. (1995). The sequential hypothesis of the function of sleep. *Behavioural Brain Research*, 69, 157–166.

Godbout, R., Bergeron, C., Stip, E., & Mottron, L. (1998). A laboratory study of sleep and dreaming in a case of Asperger's syndrome. *Dreaming*, 8(2), 75–88.

Goodenough, D. R. (1991). Dream recall: History and current status of the field. In S. J. Ellman & J. S. Antrobus (eds.), *The Mind in Sleep: Psychology and Psychophysiology* (2nd edn, pp. 143–171). New York: John Wiley.

Grunebaum, G., & Callois, R. (1966). *The Dream and Human Societies*. Berkeley: University of California Press.

Guevara, M. A., Lorenzo, I., Arce, C., Ramos, J., & Corsi-Cabrera, M. (1995). Inter- and intrahemispheric EEG correlation during sleep and wakefulness. *Sleep*, 18(4), 257–265.

Hafner, M., Stepanek, M., Taylor, J., Troxel, W. M., & van Stolk, C. (2017). Why sleep matters—The economic costs of insufficient sleep: A cross-country comparative analysis. *RAND Health Quarterly*, 6(4), 11. eCollection January 2017. PMID: 28983434.

Haig, D. (2002). *Genomic Imprinting and Kinship*. New Brunswick, NJ: Rutgers University Press.

  (1993). Genetic conflicts in human pregnancy. *Quarterly Review of Biology*, 68(4), 495–532.

  (2000). Genomic imprinting, sex-biased dispersal, and social behavior. *Annals of the New York Academy of Sciences*, 907, 149–163.

  (2014). Troubled sleep: Night waking, breastfeeding and parent-offspring conflict. *Evolution, Medicine, and Public Health*, 2014(1), 32–9. doi: 10.1093/emph/eou005. Epub March 7, 2014. PMID: 24610432.

Haig, D., & Westoby, M. (1988). Inclusive fitness, seed resources and maternal care. In L. L. Doust (ed.), *Plant Reproductive Ecology* (pp. 60–79). New York: Oxford University Press.

Halász, P., Bódizs, R., Parrino, L., & Terzano, M. (2014). Two features of sleep slow waves: Homeostatic and reactive aspects – from long term to instant sleep homeostasis. *Sleep Medicine*, 15(10), 1184–1195. doi: 10.1016/j.sleep.2014.06.006. Epub July 8, 2014. Review. PMID:25192672.

Hall, C. (1963). Strangers in dreams: An empirical confirmation of the Oedipus complex. *Journal of Personality*, 31, 336–345.

Hall, C., & Van de Castle, R. (1966). *The Content Analysis of Dreams*. New York: Appleton-Century-Crofts.

Harrison, Y., Horne, J. A., & Rothwell, A.. (2000). Prefrontal neuropsychological effects of sleep deprivation in young adults – a model for healthy aging? *Sleep*, 23(8), 1067–1073. PMID: 11145321.

Hartmann, E. (1984). *The Nightmare*. New York: Basic Books.

(1996). Outline for a theory on the nature and function of dreaming. *Dreaming*, 6, 147–169.

(1998). *Dreams and Nightmares: The New Theory on the Origin and Meaning of Dreams*. New York: Plenum.

Hartmann, E., Russ, D., van der Kolk, B., Falke, R., & Oldfield, M. (1981). A preliminary study of the personality of the nightmare sufferer: Relationship to schizophrenia and creativity? *American Journal of Psychiatry*, 138, 784–797.

Hartse, K. M. (1994). Sleep in insects and nonmammalian vertebrates. In M. H. Kryger, T. Roth, & W. C. Dement (eds.), *Principles and Practice of Sleep Medicine* (2nd edn, pp. 95–104). Philadelphia: Saunders.

Hennevin, E., Huetz, C., & Edeline, J. M. (2007). Neural representations during sleep: From sensory processing to memory traces. *Neurobiology of Learning and Memory*, 87(3), 416–440; https://doi.org/10.1016/j.nlm.2006.10.006.

Herlin, B., Leu-Semenescu, S., Chaumereuil, C., & Arnulf, I. (2015); Evidence that non-dreamers do dream: A REM sleep behaviour disorder model. *Journal of Sleep Research*, August 25. doi: 10.1111/jsr.12323.

Hertz, G., Cataletto, M., Feinsilver, S. H., & Angulo, M. (1993). Sleep and breathing patterns in patients with Prader Willi syndrome (PWS): Effects of age and gender. *Sleep*, 16(4), 366–371.

Hobson, J. A. (1988). *The Dreaming Mind*. New York: Basic Books.

Hobson, J. A., Pace-Schott, E. F., & Stickgold, R. (2000). Dreaming and the brain: Toward a cognitive neuroscience of conscious states. *Behavioral Brain Sciences*, 23, 793–842.

Hobson, J. A., & Friston, K. J. (2012). Waking and dreaming consciousness: Neurobiological and functional considerations. *Progress in Neurobiology*, 98(1), 82–98. doi: 10.1016/j.pneurobio.2012.05.003; PMCID: PMC3389346.

Hobson, J. A., & McCarley, R. (1977). The brain as a dream state generator: An activation-synthesis hypothesis of the dream process. *American Journal of Psychiatry*, 134, 1335–1348.

Hobson, J. A., & Pace-Schott, E. F. (2002). The cognitive neuroscience of sleep: Neuronal systems, consciousness and learning. *Nature Reviews, Neuroscience*, 3, 679–693.

Hobson, J. A., Pace-Schott, E. F, & Stickgold, R. (2000a). Consciousness: Its vicissitudes in waking and sleep. In M. Gazzaniga (ed.), *The New Cognitive Neurosciences* (2nd edn, pp. 1341–1354). Cambridge, MA: MIT Press.

Hobson, J. A., Stickgold, R., & Pace-Schott, E. F. (1998). The neuropsychology of REM sleep dreaming. *Neuroreport*, 9(3), R1–R14.

Hofle, N., Paus, T., Reutens, D., Fiset, P., Gotman, J., Evans, A. C. & Jones, B. E. (1997). Regional cerebral blood flow changes as a function of delta and spindle activity during slow wave sleep in humans. *The Journal of Neuroscience*, 17, 4800–4808.

Hofer, M. A., & Shair, H. (1982). Control of sleep-wake states in the infant rat by features of the mother-infant relationship. *Developmental Psychobiology*, 15(3), 229–243.

Hofle, N., Paus, T., Reutens, D., Fiset, P., Gotman, J., Evans, A. C., et al. (1997). Regional cerebral blood flow changes as a function of delta and spindle activity during slow wave sleep in humans. *Journal of Neuroscience*, 17, 4800–4808.

Hollan, D. (2003). The cultural and intersubjective context of dream remembrance and reporting: Dreams, aging, and the anthropological encounter in Toraja, Indonesia. In R. I. Lohmann (ed.), *Dream Travelers: Sleep Experiences and Culture in the Western Pacific* (pp. 169–187). New York: Palgrave Macmillan.

Hong, C. C. H., Gillin, J. C., Dow, B. M., Wu, J. & Buchsbaum, M. S. (1995) Localized and lateralized cerebral glucose metabolism associated with eye movments during REM sleep and wakefulness: A positron emission tomography (PET) study. *Sleep*, 18, 570–80.

Horne, J. A. (1993). Human sleep, sleep loss and behaviour: Implications for the prefrontal cortex and psychiatric disorder. *British Journal of Psychiatry*, 162, 413–419. Review. No abstract available. PMID: 8453439.

   (2000). REM sleep—by default? *Neuroscience and Biobehavioral Reviews*, 24, 777–797.

Hrdy, S. B. (1999). *Mother Nature*. New York: Pantheon.

Huber, R., Ghilardi, M. F., Massimini, M., & Tononi, G. (2004). Local sleep and learning. *Nature*, 430(6995), 78–81. Epub June 6, 2004. PMID:15184907.

Hultkrantz, A. (1970). Attitudes to animals in Shoshoni Indian Religion. *Studies in Comparative Religion*, 4, 70–79.

    (1987). *Native Religions of North America: The Power of Visions and Fertility*. New York: Harper and Row.

Hunt, H. T. *The Multiplicity of Dreams: Memory, Imagination and Consciousness*. New Haven, CT: Yale University Press.

Irwin, L. (1994). *The Dream Seekers: Native American Visionary Traditions of the Great Plains*. Norman: University of Oklahoma Press.

Isles, A. R., Davies, W., & Wilkinson, L. S. 2006. Genomic imprinting and the social brain. *Philosophical Transactions of the Royal Society of London B: Biological Sciences*, 361, 2229–2237.

Jackowska, M., Hamer, M., Carvalho, L. A., Erusalimsky, J. D., Butcher, L., et al. (2012). Short sleep duration is associated with shorter telomere length in healthy men: Findings from the Whitehall II Cohort Study. *PLoS ONE*, 7(10), e47292. doi:10.1371/journal.pone.0047292.

Janecka, M., Rijsdijk, F., Rai, D. Modabbernia. A. & Reichenberg, A. (2017). Advantageous developmental outcomes of advancing paternal age. *Translational Psychiatry*, 7, e1156; doi:10.1038/tp.2017.125; published online June 20, 2017.

Jedrej, M. C., & Shaw, R. (eds.). (1992). *Dreaming, Religion, and Society in Africa*. Leiden: E. J. Brill.

Jouvet, M. (1999). *The Paradox of Sleep: The Story of Dreaming*. Cambridge, MA: MIT Press.

Jouvet, D., Vimont, P., Delorme, F., & Jouvet, M. (1964). Study of selective deprivation of the paradoxal sleep phase in the cat. *Comptes Rendus des Seances de la Societe de Biology et de ses Filiales*, 158, 756–759.

Kahn, D., Stickgold, R., Pace-Schott, E. F., & Hobson, J. A. (2000). Dreaming and waking consciousness: A character recognition study. *Journal of Sleep Research*, 9(4), 317–325.

Karmanova, I. G. (1982). *Evolution of Sleep: Stages of the Formation of the Wakefulness-Sleep Cycle in Vertebrates*. Basel: Karger.

Kaufmann, C., Wehrle, R., Wetter, T. C., Holsboer, F., Auer, D. P., Pollmacher, T., & Czisch, M. (2006). Brain activation and hypothalamic functional connectivity during human non-rapid eye movement sleep: An EEG/fMRI study. *Brain*, 129(3), 655–667.

Keller, P. S. (2011). Sleep and attachment. In M. El-Sheikh (ed.). *Sleep and Development* (pp. 49–77). New York: Oxford University Press.

Kennedy, D. P., & Adolphs, R. (2012). The social brain in psychiatric and neurological disorders. *Trends in Cognitive Science*, 16(11), 559–572. doi: 10.1016/j.tics.2012.09.006. Epub October 6, 2012. Review. PMID: 23047070.

Kern, S., Auer, A., Gutsche, M., Otto, A., Preuß, K., & Schredl, M. (2014). Relationship between political, musical and *sports* activities in waking life and the frequency of these dream types in *politics* and psychology students. *International Journal of Dream Research*, 7(1), 80–84.

Keverne, E. B., & Curley, J. P. (2008). Epigenetics, brain evolution and behavior. *Front Neuroendocrinol*, 29, 398–412.

Keverne, E. B., Martel, F. L., & Nevison, C. M. (1996). Primate brain evolution: Genetic and functional considerations. *Proceedings of the Royal Society of London B: Biological Sciences*, 263, 689–696.

Kilborne, B. J. (1981). Moroccan dream interpretation and culturally constituted defense mechanisms. *Ethos*, 9(4), 294–312.

Kilduff, T. S., Krilowicz, B., Milsom, W. K., Trachsel, L., & Wang, L. C. (1993). Sleep and mammalian hibernation: Homologous adaptations and homologous processes? *Sleep*, 16(4), 372–386.

Kirkwood, T. B. L., & Holliday, R. (1979). The evolution of ageing and longevity. *Proceedings of the Royal Society of London B: Biological Sciences*, 205, 531–546.

Kochanek, K. D., Murphy, S. L., Xu, J., & Arias, E. (2014). Mortality in the United States, (178), 1–8. NCHS Data Brief. PMID: 25549183.

Kracke, W. (1979). Dreaming in Kagwahiv: Dream beliefs and their psychic uses in Amazonian culture. *Psychoanalytical Study of Society*, 8, 119–171.

Krakow, B., & Zadra, A. (2010). Imagery rehearsal therapy: Principles and practice. *Sleep Medicine Clinics*, 4(2), 289–298.

Kramer, M. (1993). The selective mood regulatory function of dreaming: An update and revision. In A. Moffit, M. Kramer, & R. Hoffman (eds.), *The Functions of Dreaming*. Albany: State University of New York Press.

Kripke, D. F., Langer, R. D., Elliott, J. A., Klauber, M. R., & Rex, K. M. Mortality related to actigraphic long and short sleep. *Sleep Medicine*, 12,(1), 28–33.

Krueger, J. M., Obal, F., & Fang, J. (1999). Why we sleep: A theoretical view of sleep function. *Sleep Medicine Reviews*, 3(2), 119–129.

Kuiken, D. L., & Sikora, S. (1993). The impact of dreams on waking thoughts and feelings. In A. Moffitt, M. Kramer, & R. Hoffman (eds.), *The Functions of Dreaming*. Albany: State University of New York Press.

Kuiken, D. L., Nielsen, T. A., Thomas, S., & McTaggart, D. (1983). Comparisons of the story structure of archetypal dreams, mundane dreams, and myths. *Sleep Research*, 12, 196.

Kushida, C. A., Bergmann, B. M., & Rechtschaffen, A. (1989). Sleep deprivation in the rat: Paradoxical sleep deprivation. *Sleep*, 12, 22–30.

LaBerge, S. P., Kahan, T. L., & Levitan, L. (1995). Cognition in dreaming and waking. *Sleep Research*, 24A, 239.

Lai, Y.-Y., & Siegel, J. (1999). Muscle atonia in REM sleep. In S. Inoue (ed.), *Rapid Eye Movement Sleep* (pp. 69–90). New York: Dekker.

Lakoff, G. (2001). How metaphor structures dreams. The theory of conceptual metaphor applied to dream analysis. In K. Bulkeley (ed.), *Dreams: A Reader on Religious, Cultural and Psychological Dimensions of Dreaming* (pp. 265–284). New York: Palgrave.

Laughlin, C. D. (2011). *Communing with the Gods: Consciousness, Culture, and the Dreaming Brain*. Brisbane: Daily Grail.

Ledoux, J. (ed.). (1996). *The Emotional Brain*. New York: Simon and Schuster.

Li, W., Ma, L., Yang, G., & Gan, W. B. (2017). REM sleep selectively prunes and maintains new synapses in development and learning. *Nature Neuroscience*, 20(3), 427–437. doi: 10.1038/nn.4479. Epub January 16, 2017. PMID: 28092659.

Lieberman, M. (2014) *Social: Why Our Brains Are Wired to Connect*. New York: Broadway Books Inc.

Lincoln, J. S. (1935). *The Dream in Primitive Cultures*. Oxford: Cresset Press.

Lohmann, R. (2003) *Dream Travelers: Sleep Experiences and Culture in the Western Pacific*. New York: Palgrave Macmillan.

Lyamin, O. I., Manger, P. R., Ridgeway, S. H., Mukhametov, L. M., & Siegel, J. M. (2008). Cetacean sleep: An unusual form of mammalian sleep. *Neuroscience and Biobehavioral Reviews*, 32, 1451–1484.

Lyamin O. I. et al. (2016). Monoamine release during unihemispheric sleep and unihemispheric waking in the fur seal. *Sleep*, 39(3), 625–636.

Lugaresi, E., Medori, R., Montagna, P., Baruzzi, A., Cortelli, P., Lugaresi, A., et al. (1986). Fatal familial insomnia and dysautonomia with selective degeneration of thalamic nuclei. *New England Journal of Medicine*, 315, 997–1003.

Madsen, P. C., Holm, S., Vorstup, S., Friberg, L., Lassen, N. A. & Wildschiodtz, L. F. (1991) Human regional cerebral blood flow during rapid eye movement sleep. *Journal of Cerebral Blood Flow and Metabolism*, 11, 502–507.

Mahowald, M. W., & Cramer Bornemann, M. A. (2011). Non-REM arousal parasomnias. In M. Kryger, T. Roth, & W. C. Dement (eds.), *Principles and Practice of Sleep Medicine* (5th edn). Philadelphia: W. B. Saunders Co.

Mahowald, M. W., & Schenck, C. H. (2011). REM sleep parasomnias. In M. Kryger, T. Roth, & W. C. Dement (eds.), *Principles and Practice of Sleep Medicine* (5th edn). Philadelphia: W. B. Saunders Co.

Manford, M., & Andermann, F. (1998) Complex visual hallucinations: Clinical and neurobiological insights. *Brain*, 121, 1819–1840.

Margoliash, D. (2005). Song learning and sleep. *Nature Neuroscience*, 8, 546 – 548 doi:10.1038/nn0505-546.

Maquet, P. (2000). Functional neuroimaging of normal human sleep by positron emission tomography. *Journal of Sleep Research*, 9, 207–231.

Maquet, P., & Franck, G. (1997). REM sleep and amygdala. *Molecular Psychiatry*, 2(3), 195–196.

Maquet, P., Smith, C., & Stickgold, R. (eds.) (2003). *Sleep and Brain Plasticity*. Oxford: Oxford University Press.

Maquet, P., Degueldre, C., Delfiore, G., Aerts, J., Peters, J.M., Luxen, A., & Franck, G.(1997). Functional neuroanatomy of human slow wave sleep. *The Journal of Neuroscience*, 17, 2807–2812.

Maquet, P., Peters, J. M., Aerts, J., Delfiore, G., Degueldre, C., Luxen, A., & Franck, G. (1996). Functional neuroanatomy of human rapid-eye-movement sleep and dreaming. *Nature*, 383, 163–66.

Maquet, P., Ruby, P., Maudoux, A., Albouy, G., Sterpenich, V., Dang-Vu, T., Desseilles, M., Boly, M., Perrin, F., Peigneux, P., & Laureys, S. (2005). Human cognition during REM sleep and the activity profile within frontal and parietal cortices: A reappraisal of functional neuroimaging data. *Progress in Brain Research*, 150, 219–227.

Maquet, P., Ruby, P., Schwartz, S., Laureys, S., Albouy, G., Dang-Vu, T., Desseilles, M., Boly, M., & Peigneux, P. (2004). Regional organisation of brain activity during paradoxical sleep (PS). *Archives Italiennes de Biologie*, 142(4), 413–419.

Marks, G. A., Shaffrey, J. P., Oksenberg, A., Speciale, S. G., & Roffwarg, H. (1995). A functional role for REM sleep in brain maturation. *Behavioural Brain Research*, 69, 1–11.

Mars, R. B., Neubert, F. X., Noonan, M. P., Sallet, J., Toni, I., & Rushworth, M. F. (2012). On the relationship between the "default mode network" and the "social brain." *Frontiers in Human Neuroscience*, 6, 189. doi: 10.3389/fnhum.2012.00189. eCollection 2012.

Matheson, E., & Hainer, B. L. (2017). Insomnia: Pharmacologic therapy. *American Family Physician*, 96(1), 29–35. Review. PMID: 28671376.

McKenna, J. J., & Mosko, S. S. (1994). Sleep and arousal, synchrony and independence, among mothers and infants sleeping apart and together (same bed): An experiment in evolutionary medicine. *Acta Paediatrica*, 397, 94–102.

McKenna, J. J., Mosko, S., Dungy, C., & McAninch, J. (1990). Sleep and arousal patterns of co-sleeping human mother/infant pairs: A preliminary physiological study with implications for the study of sudden infant death syndrome (SIDS). *American Journal of Physical Anthropology*, 83, 331–347.

McKenna, J. J., Thoman, E. B., Anders, T. F., Sadeh, A., Schechtman, V. L., & Glotzbach, S. F. (1993). Infant- parent co-sleeping in an evolutionary perspective: Implications for understanding infant sleep development and the Sudden Infant Death Syndrome. *Sleep*, 16, 263–282.

McNamara K. (1997). *Shapes of Time: The Evolution of Growth and Development*. Baltimore: Johns Hopkins University Press.

McNamara, P. (2008). *Nightmares: The Science and Solution of those Frightening Visions during Sleep*. Westport, CT: Praeger Perspectives.

(2004). *An Evolutionary Psychology of Sleep and Dreams*. Westport, CT: Praeger/Greenwood Press.

(2000). Counterfactual thought in dreams. *Dreaming*, 10(4), 237–246.

McNamara, P., Anderson, J., Clark, C., Zborowski, M., & Duffy, C. A. (2001). Impact of attachment styles on dream recall and dream content: A test of the attachment hypothesis of REM sleep. *Journal of Sleep Research*, 10, 117–127.

McNamara, P., Ayala, R., & Minsky, A. (2014). REM sleep, dreams, and attachment themes across a single night of sleep: A pilot study. *Dreaming*, 24(4), 290.

McNamara, P., Belsky, J., & Fearon, P. (2003). Infant sleep disorders and attachment: Sleep problems in infants with insecure-resistant versus insecure-avoidant attachments to mother. *Sleep and Hypnosis*, 5(1), 7–16.

McNamara, P., Dowdall, J., & Auerbach, S. (2002). REM sleep, early experience, and the development of reproductive strategies. *Human Nature*, 13, 405–435.

McNamara, P., Johnson, P., McLaren, D., Harris, E., Beauharnais, C., & Auerbach, S. (2010). REM and NREM sleep mentation. *International Review of Neurobiology*, 92, 69–86.

McNamara, P., McLaren, D., Kowalczyk, S., & Pace-Schott, E. (2007). "Theory of Mind" in REM and NREM dreams. In D. Barrett & P. McNamara (eds.), *The New Science of Dreaming: Volume I: Biological Aspects* (pp. 201–220). Westport, CT: Praeger Perspectives.

McNamara, P., McLaren, D., Smith, D., Brown, A., & Stickgold, R. (2005). A "Jekyll and Hyde" within: Aggressive versus friendly social interactions in REM and NREM dreams. *Psychological Science*, 16(2), 130–136. PMID: 15686579.

McNamara, P., Minsky, A., Pae, V., Harris, E., Pace-Schott, E., & Aurbach, S. (2015). Aggression in nightmares and unpleasant dreams and in people reporting recurrent nightmares. *Dreaming*, 25(3), 190–205.

McNamara, P., Pace-Schott, E. F., Johnson, P., Harris, E., & Auerbach, S. (2011). Sleep architecture and sleep-related mentation in securely and insecurely attached young people. *Attachment and Human Development*, 13(2), 141–154.

McNamara, P., Pae, V., Teed, B., Tripodis, Y., & Sebastian, A. (2016) Longitudinal studies of gender differences in cognitional process in dream content. *Journal of Dream Research*, 9(1). doi: hhtp://dx.doi.org/10.11.588/ijord.2016.

Merritt, J. M., Stickgold, R., Pace-Schott, E. F., Williams, J., & Hobson, J. A. (1994). Emotion profiles in the dreams of men and women. *Consciousness and Cognition*, 3, 46–60.

Mikulincer, M., Shaver, P. R., & Avihou-Kanza, N. (2011). Individual differences in adult attachment are systematically related to dream narratives. *Attachment & Human development*, 13(2), 105–123. doi:10.1080/14616734.2011.553918.

Mikulincer, M., Shaver, P. R., Sapir-Lavid, Y., & Avihou-Kanza, N. (2009). What's inside the minds of securely and insecurely attached people? The secure-base script and its associations with attachment-style dimensions. *Journal of Personality and Social Psychology*, 97(4), 615. doi:10.1037/a0015649.

Mirmiran, M. (1995). The function of fetal/neonatal rapid eye movement sleep. *Behavioural Brain Research*, 69(1–2), 13–22.

Mirmiran, M., Scholtens, J., van de Poll, N. E., Uylings, H. B., van der Gugten, J., & Boer, G. J. (1983). Effects of experimental suppression of active (REM) sleep during early development upon adult brain and behavior in the rat. *Brain Research*, 283, 277–286.

Montangero, J., & Cavallero, C. (2015). What renders dreams more or less narrative? A microstructural study of REM and stage 2 dreams reported upon morning awakening. *International Journal of Dream Research*, 8(2), 105–119.

Morrell, J., & Steele, H. (2003). The role of attachment security, temperament, maternal perception, and care-giving behavior in persistent infant sleeping problems. *Infant Mental Health*, 24(5), 447–468.

Muzur, A., Pace-Schott, E. F., & Hobson, J. A. (2002) The prefrontal cortex in sleep. *Trends in Cognitive Sciences*, 16, 475–481.

Nathanielsz, P. W. (1996). *Life Before Birth: The Challenges of Fetal Development*. New York: W. H. Freeman.

National Sleep Foundation. https://sleepfoundation.org/media-center/press-release/lack-sleep-affecting-americans-finds-the-national-sleep-foundation (downloaded November 16, 2017).

Nielsen, T. A. (2000). A review of mentation in REM and NREM sleep: "Covert" REM sleep as a possible reconciliation of two opposing models. *Behavioral and Brain Sciences*, 23(6), 851–866; discussion 904–1121.

Nielsen, T. A., Deslauriers, D., & Baylor, G. W. (1991). Emotions in dream and waking event reports. *Dreaming*, 1, 287–300.

Nielsen, T. A., Kuiken, D., Hoffman, R., & Moffitt, A. (2001). REM and NREM sleep mentation differences: A question of story structure? *Sleep and Hypnosis*, 3(1), 9–17.

Nielsen, T. A., Kuiken, D., Alain, G., Stenstrom, P., & Powell, R. A. (2004). Immediate and delayed incorporations of events into dreams: Further replication and implications for dream function. *Journal of Sleep Research*, 13(4), 327–336.

Nielsen, T. A., & Levin, R. (2007). Nightmares: A new neurocognitive model. *Sleep Medicine Reviews*, 11, 295–310.

Nir, Y., & Tononi, G. (2010). Dreaming and the brain: From phenomenology to neurophysiology. *Trends in Cognitive Science*, 14(2), 88–100. doi: 10.1016/j.tics.2009.12.001. Epub January 14, 2010.

Nofzinger, E. A., Buysse, D. J., Miewald, J. M., Meltzer, C. C., Price, J. C., Sembrat, R. C., Ombao, H., Reynolds, C. F., Monk, T. H., Hall, M., Kupfer, D. J., & Moore, R. Y. (2002) Human regional cerebral glucose metabolism during non-rapid eye movement sleep in relation to waking. *Brain*, 125, 1105–1115.

Nunn, C. L., McNamara, P., Capellini, I., Preston, B. T., & Barton, R. A. (2010). Primate sleep in phylogenetic perspective. In P. McNamara, R. A. Barton, & C. L. Nunn (eds.), *Evolution of Sleep: Phylogenetic and Functional Perspectives* (pp. 123–144). New York: Cambridge University Press.

Nunn, C. L., Samson, D. R., & Krystal, A. D. (2016). Shining evolutionary light on human sleep and sleep disorders. *Evolution, Medicine, and Public Health*, (1), 227–243. doi: 10.1093/emph/eow018. Print 2016. Review. PMID: 27470330.

Oberst, U., Charles, C., & Chamarro, A. (2005). Influence of gender and age in aggressive dream content of Spanish children and adolescents. *Dreaming*, (15), 170–177.

Offenkrantz, W., & Rechtschaffen, A. (1963). Clinical studies of sequential dreams: A patient in psychotherapy. *Archives of General Psychiatry*, 8, 497–508.

Ohayon, M. M., Carskadon, M. A., Guilleminault, C., & Vitiello, M. V. Meta-Analysis of quantitative sleep parameters from childhood to old age in healthy individuals: Developing normative sleep values across the human lifespan. *Sleep*, 27(7), 1255–1273.

Ohayon, M. M., Morselli, P. L., & Guilleminault, C. (1997). Prevalence of nightmares and their relationship to psychopathology and daytime functioning in insomnia subjects. *Sleep*, 20, 340–348.

Oksenberg, A., Shaffery, J. P., Marks, G. A., Speciale, S. G., Mihailoff, G., & Roffwarg, H. P. (1996). Rapid eye movement sleep deprivation in kittens amplifies LGN cell-size disparity induced by monocular deprivation. *Brain Research: Developmental Brain Research*, 97, 51–61.

Opp, M. R., & Krueger, J. M. (2015). Sleep and immunity: A growing field with clinical impact. *Brain, Behavior, and Immunity*, 47, 1–3. doi: 10.1016/j.bbi.2015.03.011. Epub April 4, 2015. PMID:25849976.

Oudiette, D., Dealberto, M. J., Uguccioni, G., Golmard, J. L., Merino-Andreu, M., Tafti, M., Garma, L., Schwartz, S., & Arnulf, I. (2012). Dreaming without REM sleep. *Consciousness and Cognition*, 21(3), 1129–1140. doi: 10.1016/j.concog.2012.04.010. Epub May 29. PMID:22647346.

Pace-Schott, E. F., & Picchioni, D. (2017). Neurobiology of dreaming. In M. Kryger, T. Roth, & W. C. Dement (eds.)*Principles and Practice of Sleep Medicine* (6th edn, pp. 529–538). Philadelphia: Elsevier.

Pace-Schott, E. F. (2013). Dreaming as a story-telling instinct. *Frontiers in Psychology*, 4, 159. doi: 10.3389/fpsyg.2013.00159.

Pace-Schott, E. F., & Hobson, J. A. The neurobiology of sleep: Genetics, cellular physiology and subcortical networks. *Nature Reviews Neuroscience*, 3, 591–605.

Pack, A. I. (1995). The prevalence of work-related sleep problems. *Journal of General Internal Medicine*, 10(1), 57. PMID: 7699486.

Parker, J. D., & Blackmore, S. (2002). Comparing the contents of sleep paralysis and dream reports. *Dreaming*, 12(1), 45–59.

Peluso, D. M. (2004). "That which I dream is true": Dream narratives in an Amazonian community. *Dreaming*, 14(2–3), 107–119.

Peña, M. M., Rifas-Shiman, S. L., Gillman, M. W., Redline, S., & Taveras, E. M. (2016). Racial/ethnic and socio-contextual correlates of chronic sleep curtailment in childhood. *Sleep*, 39(9), 1653–1661.

Perogamvrosa, L., & Schwartz, S. (2012). The roles of the reward system in sleep and dreaming. *Neuroscience and Biobehavioral Reviews*, 36, 1934–1951.

Plihal, W., & Born, J. (1997). Effects of early and late nocturnal sleep on declarative and procedural memory. *Journal of Cognitive Neuroscience*, 9, 534–547.

Preston, B. T., Capellini, I., McNamara, P., Barton, R. A., & Nunn, C. L. (2009). Parasite resistance and the adaptive significance of sleep. *BMC Evolutionary Biology*, 9(7). PMID: 19134175.

Proud, L. (2009). *Dark Intrusions*. San Antonio, TX: Anomalist Books.

Rattenborg, N. C., Amlaner, C. J., & Lima, S. L. (2000). Behavioral, neurophysiological and evolutionary perspectives on unihemispheric sleep. *Neuroscience and Biobehavioral Reviews*, 24, 817–842.

Rattenborg, N. C., Martinez-Gonzalez, D., & Lesku, J. A. Avian sleep homeostasis: Convergent evolution of complex brains, cognition and sleep functions in mammals and birds. *Neuroscience and Biobehavioral Reviews*, 33, 253–270.

Rechtschaffen, A., Bergmann, B. M., Everson, C. A., Kushida, C. A., & Gilliland, M. A. Sleep deprivation in the rat. *Sleep*, 12(1), 68–87.

Reite, M., & Short, R. (1978). Nocturnal sleep in separated monkey infants. *Archives of General Psychiatry*, 35, 1247–1253.

Reite, M., Stynes, A. J., Vaughn, L., Pauley, J. D., & Short, R. A. (1976). Sleep in infant monkeys: Normal values and behavioral correlates. *Physiology and Behavior*, 16(3), 245–251.

Resnick, J., Stickgold, R., Rittenhouse, C. D., & Hobson, J. A. (1994) Self-representation and bizarreness in children's dream reports collected in the home setting. *Consciousness and Cognition*, 3, 30–45.

Revonsuo, A. (2000). The reinterpretation of dreams: An evolutionary hypothesis of the function of dreaming. *Behavioral and Brain Sciences*, 23, 877–901; discussion 904–1121.

Revonsuo, A., Tuominen, J. & Valli, K. (2015). The avatars in the machine-dreaming as a simulation of social reality. In T. Metzinger & J. M. Windt (eds), *Open MIND: 32(T)* (pp. 1–28). Frankfurt am Main. doi: 10.15502/9783958570375.

Runyan, M. (2010). Do twins dream twin dreams? A quantitative comparison with singles' dreams (UMI Number: 3389215 ProQuest LLC 789 East Eisenhower Parkway P.O. Box 1346 Ann Arbor, MI 48106–1346).

Sándor, P., Szakadát, S., & Bódizs, R. (2014). Ontogeny of dreaming: A review of empirical studies. *Sleep Medicine Reviews*. 18(5), 435–449. doi: 10.1016/j.smrv.2014.02.001. Epub February 12, 2014. Review. PMID: 24629827.

Sagi, A., van Ijzendoorn, M. H., Aviezer, O., Donnell, F., & Mayseless, O. (1994). Sleeping out of home in a Kibbutz communal arrangement: It makes a difference for infant-mother attachment. *Child Development*, 65(4), 992–1004.

Salzarulo, P., & Ficca, G. (eds.). (2002). *Awakening and Sleep Cycle across Development*. Amsterdam: John Benjamins.

Samson, D. R., Crittenden, A. N., Mabulla, I. A., Mabulla, A. Z., & Nunn, C. L. (2017). Hadza sleep biology: Evidence for flexible sleep-wake patterns in hunter-gatherers. *American Journal of Physical Anthropology*, 162(3), 573–582. doi: 10.1002/ajpa.23160. Epub January 7, 2017. PMID: 28063234.

Samson, D. R., & Nunn, C. L. (2015). Sleep intensity and the evolution of human cognition. *Evolutionary Anthropology*, 24(6), 225–237. doi: 10.1002/evan.21464. PMID: 26662946.

Saper, C. B., Scammell, T. E., & Lu, J. (2005). Hypothalamic regulation of sleep and circadian rhythms. *Nature*, 437(7063), 1257–1263.

Scher, A. (2001). Attachment and sleep: a study of night waking in 12-month-old infants. *Development Psychobiology*, 38(4), 274–85.

Schouten, D.I., Pereira, S. I., Tops, M., & Louzada, F. M. (2017). State of the art on targeted memory reactivation: Sleep your way to enhanced cognition. *Sleep Medicine Reviews*, 32, 123–131. doi: 10.1016/j.smrv.2016.04.002. Epub April 21, 2016. Review. PMID: 27296303.

Schredl, M., & Hofmann, F. (2003). Continuity between waking activities and dream activities. *Consciousness and Cognition*, 12(2), 298–308. 10.1016/S1053–8100(02)00072–7.

Schwartz, S., & Maquet P. (2002). Sleep imaging and the neuro-psychological assessment of dreams. *Trends in Cognitive Science*, 6(1), 23–30. PMID:11849612.

Schweickert, R. (2007). Social networks of characters in dreams. In D. Barrett & P. McNamara (eds.), *The New Science of Dreaming*. Westport, CT: Praeger.

Sejnowski, T. J., & Destexhe, A. (2000). Why do we sleep? *Brain Research*, 886(1–2), 208–223.

Selterman, D. F., Apetroaia, A. I., Riela, S., & Aron, A. (2014). Dreaming of you: Behavior and emotion in dreams of significant others predict subsequent relational behavior. *Social Psychological and Personality Science*, 5(1), 111–118. doi: 10.1177/1948550613486678.

Selterman, D., Apetroaia, A., & Waters, E. (2012). Script-like attachment representations in dreams containing current romantic partners. *Attachment and Human Development*, 14, 501–515. doi:10.1080/14616734.2012.706395.

Selterman D., & Drigotas S. (2009). Attachment styles and emotional content, stress, and conflict in dreams of romantic partners. *Dreaming*, 19, 135–151. doi: 10.1037/a0017087.

Shein-Idelson, M., Ondracek, J., Liaw, H.-P., Reiter, S., & Laurent, G. (2016). Slow waves, sharp-waves, ripples and REM in sleeping dragons. *Science*, 29.

Siclari, F., Khatami, R., Urbaniok, F., Nobili, L., Mahowald, M. W., Schenck, C. H., Cramer Bornemann, M. A., & Bassetti, C. L. (2010). Violence in sleep. *Brain*, 133(12), 3494–3509. doi: 10.1093/brain/awq296.

Siclari, F., Baird, B., Perogmvros, L., Bernardi1, G., LaRocque, J., Riedner, B., Boly, M., Postle B., & Tononi; G. (2017). The neural correlates of dreaming. *Nature Neuroscience*; published online April 10, 2017; doi:10.1038/nn.4545.

Siegel, J. M. (2008). Do all animals sleep? *Trends in Neuroscience*, 31(4), 208–213.

(2005). Clues to the functions of mammalian sleep. *Nature*, 437, 1264–1271.

Simard, V., Chevalier, V., & Bédard, M. M. (2017). Sleep and attachment in early childhood: a series of meta-analyses. *Attachment and Human Development*, 19(3), 298–321. doi: 10.1080/14616734.2017.1293703. Epub February 20, 2017. PMID: 28277095.

Smith, C. (1995). Sleep states and memory processes. *Behavioural Brain Research*, 69(1–2), 137–145.

(1996). Sleep states, memory processes and synaptic plasticity. *Behavioural Brain Research*, 78, 49–56.

Smith, M. R., Antrobus, J. S., Gordon, E., Tucker, M. A., Hirota, Y., Wamsley, E. J., Ross, L., Doan, T., Chaklader, A., & Emery, R. N. (2004). Motivation and affect in REM sleep and the mentation reporting process. *Conscious and Cognition*, 13(3), 501–511.

Solms, M. (1997). *The Neuropsychology of Dreams*. Mahwah, NJ: Lawrence Erlbaum.

(2000). Dreaming and REM sleep are controlled by different brain mechanisms. *Behavioral and Brain Sciences*, 23, 843–850; discussion 904–1121.

Spoormaker, V. I., Schredl, M., & van den Bout, J. (2006). Nightmares: From anxiety symptom to sleep disorder. *Sleep Medicine Reviews*, 10(1), 19–31.

Spoormaker, V. (2008). A cognitive model of recurrent nightmares. *International Journal of Dream Research*, 1(1), 15–22.

Stepansky, R., Holzinger, B., Schmeiser-Rieder, A., Saletu, B., Kunze, M., & Zeitlhofer, J. (1998). Austrian dream behavior: Results of a representative population survey. *Dreaming*, 8, 23–30.

Stickgold, R. (2013). Parsing the role of sleep in memory processing. *Current opinion in neurobiology*, 23(5), 847–853.

(2005). Sleep-dependent memory consolidation. *Nature*, 437, 1272–1278.

Stickgold, R., Scott, L., Fosse, R., & Hobson, J. A. (2001). Brain-mind states: Longitudinal field study of wake-sleep factors influencing mentation report length. *Sleep*, 24(2), 171–179.

Stickgold, R., Scott, L., Rittenhouse, C., & Hobson, J. A. (1998). Sleep induced changes in associative memory. *Journal of Cognitive Neuroscience*, 11, 182–193.

Stickgold, R, & Walker, M. P. (2005). Memory consolidation and reconsolidation: What is the role of sleep? *Trends in Neuroscience*, 28(8), 408–145. Review. PMID: 15979164.

Stickgold, R., & Walker, M. P. (2013). Sleep-dependent memory triage: evolving generalization through selective processing. *Nature Neuroscience*, 16(2), 139–145. doi: 10.1038/nn.3303. Epub January 28, 2013. Review. PMID: 23354387.

Stranges, S., Tigbe, W., Gómez-Olivé, F. X., Thorogood, M., & Kandala, N. B. (2012). Sleep problems: An emerging global epidemic? *Sleep*, 35(8), 1173–1181. doi: 10.5665/sleep.2012. PMID: 22851813.

Strauch, I. (2005) REM dreaming in the transition from late childhood to adolescence: a longitudinal study. *Dreaming*, 15, 155–169.

Strauch, I., & Meier, B. (1996). *In Search of Dreams: Results of Experimental Dream Research*. Albany: State University of New York Press

Steiger, A. (2003). Sleep and endocrinology. *Journal of Internal Medicine*, 254, 13–22.

Stearns, S. (1992). *The evolution of life histories*. New York: Oxford University Press.

Strecker, R. E., Basheer, R., McKenna, J. T, & McCarley, R. W. (2006). Another chapter in the adenosine story. *Sleep*, 29(4), 426–428.

Tafti, M., & Franken, P. (2002). Invited review: Genetic dissection of sleep. *Journal of Applied Physiology*, 92, 1339–1347.

Tedlock, B. (1987). Dreaming and dream research. In B. Tedlock (ed.), *Dreaming: Anthropological and Psychological Interpretations* (pp. 1–30). Cambridge: Cambridge University Press.

(1992). *Dreaming: Anthropological and Psychological Interpretations*. Albuquerque, NM: School of America Research Press.

Terzano, M. G., Mancia, D., Salati, M. R., Costani, G., Decembrino, A., & Parrino, L. (1985). The cyclic alternating pattern as a physiologic component of normal NREM sleep. *Sleep*, 8(2), 137–145.

Tononi, G., & Cirelli, C. (2006). Sleep function and synaptic homeostasis. *Sleep Medicine Reviews*, 10(2006), 49–62.

Trivers, R. L. (1974). Parent offspring conflict. *American Zoologist*, 14, 249–264.

Trosman, H., Rechtschaffen, A., Offenkrantz, W., & Wolpert, E. (1960). Studies in psychophysiology of dreams: Relations among dreams in sequence. *Archives of General Psychiatry*, 3, 602–607.

Troxel, W. M. (2010). It's more than sex: Exploring the dyadic nature of sleep and implications for health. *Psychosomatic Medicine*, 72(6), 578–586. doi: 10.1097/PSY.0b013e3181de7ff8. Epub May 13, 2010. Review. PMID: 20467000.

Troxel, W. M., Trentacosta, C. J., Forbes, E. E., & Campbell, S. B. (2013). Negative emotionality moderates associations among attachment, toddler sleep, and later problem behaviors. *Journal of Family Psychology*, 27(1), 127–136.

Tucci, V. (2016) Genomic imprinting: A new epigenetic perspective of sleep regulation. *PLOS Genetics*, 12(5), e1006004. https://doi.org/10.1371/journal.pgen.1006004.

Ubeda, F., & Gardner, A. (2010). A model for genomic imprinting in the social brain: Juveniles. *Evolution*, 64, 2587–2600.

(2011). A model for genomic imprinting in the social brain: Adults. *Evolution*, 65, 462–475.

Uguccioni, G., Golmard, J.-L., de Fontréaux, A. N., Leu-Semenescu, S., Brion, A., & Arnulf, I. (2013). Fight or flight? Dream content during sleepwalking/sleep terrors vs. rapid eye movement sleep behavior disorder. *Sleep Medicine*, 14(5), 391–398.

Van de Castle, R. (1994). *Our Dreaming Mind*. New York: Ballantine.

(1970). Temporal patterns of dreams. In E. Hartmann (ed.), *Sleep and Dreaming* (pp. 171–181). Boston: Little, Brown.

Van der Helm, E., & Walker, M. P. (2011a). Sleep and emotional memory processing. *Sleep Medicine Clinics*, 6(1), 31–43. PMID:25285060.

van der Helm, E., Yao, J., Dutt, S., Rao, V., Saletin, J. M., & Walker, M. P. (2011b) REM sleep de-potentiates amygdala activity to previous emotional experiences. *Current Biology*, 21(23), 2029–2032.

Vela-Bueno, A., Kales, A., Soldatos, C. R., Dobladez-Blanco, B., Campos-Castello, J., Espino-Hurtado, P., et al. (1984). Sleep in the Prader-Willi syndrome: Clinical and polygraphic findings. *Archives of Neurology*, 41(3), 294–296.

Velasquez-Moctezuma, J., Salazar, E. D., & Retana-Marquez, S. (1996). Effects of short- and long-term sleep deprivation on sexual behavior in male rats. *Physiology and Behavior*, 59, 277–281.

Verdone, P. (1965). Temporal reference of manifest dream content. *Perceptual and Motor Skills*, 20, 1253–1268.

Verrier, R. L., Muller, J. E., & Hobson, J. A. (1996). Sleep, dreams, and sudden death: The case for sleep as an autonomic stress test for the heart. *Cardiovascular Research*, 31(2), 181–211. Review. PMID: 8730394.

Vgontzas, A. N., Kales, A., Seip, J., Mascari, M. J., Bixler, E. O., Myers, D. C., et al. (1996). Relationship of sleep abnormalities to patient genotypes in Prader-Willi syndrome. *American Journal of Medical Genetics*, 67, 478–482.

Vogel, G., & Hagler, M. (1996). Effects of neonatally administered iprindole on adult behaviors of rats. *Pharmacology, Biochemistry, and Behavior*, 55(1), 157–161.

Vogel, G. W. (1999). REM sleep deprivation and behavioral changes. In S. Inoue (ed.), *Rapid Eye Movement sleep* (pp. 355–366). New York: Dekker.

Wagner, U., Gais, S., & Born, J. (2001). Emotional memory formation is enhanced across sleep intervals with high amounts of rapid eye movement sleep. *Learning and Memory*, 8(2), 112–119.

Wagner, U., Gais, S., Haider, H., Verleger, R., & Born, J. (2004). Sleep inspires insight. *Nature*, 427, 352–355.

Walker, M. P. (2005). A refined model of sleep and the time course of memory formation. *Behavioral and Brain Sciences*, 28(1), 51–64; discussion 64–104. Review. PMID:16047457.

Walker, M. P., & Stickgold, R. Sleep-dependent learning and memory consolidation. *Neuron*, 44, 121–133.

Walker, M. P., & Stickgold, R. (2006). Sleep, memory, and plasticity. *Annual Review of Psychology*, 57, 139–166. Review. PMID: 16318592.

Walker, M. P., Brakefield, T., Morgan, A., Hobson, J. A.,& Stickgold, R. (2002). Practice with sleep makes perfect: Sleep-dependent motor skill learning. *Neuron*, 35, 205–211.

Werth, E., Achermann, P., & Borbely, A. A. (1996). Brain topography of the human sleep EEG: Antero-posterior shifts of spectral power. *NeuroReport*, 8, 123–127.

Werth, E., Achermann, P., & Borbely A. A. (1997). Fronto-occipital EEG power gradients in human sleep. *Journal of Sleep Research*, 6, 102–112.

White, H. (1999). *Figural Realism: Studies in Mimesis Effect*. Baltimore: Johns Hopkins University Press.

Wilson, M. A., & McNaughton, B. L. (1994). Reactivation of hippocampal ensemble memories during sleep. *Science*, 265, 676–679.

Windt, J. M. (2015). *Dreaming: A Conceptual Framework for Philosophy of Mind and Empirical Research*. Cambridge, MA: MIT Press.

Winget, C., & Kramer, M. (1979). *Dimensions of the Dream*. Gainesville: University of Florida Press.

Winson, J. (1985). *Brain and Psyche*. New York: Doubleday.

Yetish, G., Kaplan, H., Gurven, M., et al. (2015) Natural sleep and its seasonal variations in three pre-industrial societies. *Current Biology*, 25, 2862–2868.

Index

acetylcholine, 211–212
Activation-Input Source-Neuromodulation (AIM) model, 195–197
active sleep (AS), 46–47
adenosine, 29, 33–34, 103–104
adolescent sleep, 5, 54–55
adults
    dreams of, 146–149
    sleep expression in, 55–57
advanced sleep phase wake disorder (ASPD), 36–38
affective network dysfunction (AND) model, 202
age. *See* lifespan dream content; lifespan sleep expression
aggression
    in dreams, 157–161, 164–165
    in REM sleep behavior disorder, 91–92
AIM model. *See* Activation-Input Source-Neuromodulation model
alpha waves, 61, 174, 216
amnesia, of dreams, 127–128
amygdala, 210
    in memory consolidation, 109–111
    in REM sleep behavior disorder, 91–92
    sleep deprivation effects on, 15–16
    in social brain network, 12–14, 142–143
amyloid proteins, 102
ancestral humans, sleep in, 26
AND model. *See* affective network dysfunction model
Angelman syndrome, 116
anorexia nervosa, 113–116
anti-depressants, 213–214
anti-histamines, 212
anti-psychotics, 213–214
anxiety, 80
apnea. *See* sleep apnea
aquatic mammals, sleep in, 23–24
arousal, confusional, 53–54

arousal thresholds, 19
AS. *See* active sleep
Asclepian rituals, 182–183
ASPD. *See* advanced sleep phase wake disorder
atonia. *See* paralysis
attachment dreams, 149–151
attachment theory
    childhood sleep expression and, 54
    infant sleep expression and, 48–49
    REM dreaming and, 143–144
    of sleep state development, 44–46
attacks, sleep, 83–85
automaticity, of dreams, 128
autonomic nervous system, 67–68, 73
awakenings procedures, 223–224

bad dreams. *See* nightmares
barbiturates, 212–214
behavioral traits, of sleep, 7–9
benzodiazepines, 212–214
big dreams, 186–187
bimodal sleep pattern, 26
binge eating, sleep-related, 87
biological rhythms, 28–29
    circadian rhythm. *See* circadian rhythm
    disorders of, 36–38
    methods of studying, 208–209
    social modulation of, 35–36
    in two process sleep regulation model, 33–35
    ultradian cycle. *See* ultradian cycle
bipolar disorder, 37–38, 80
birds, sleep in, 22, 42
body. *See* physiologic systems
brain
    dream recall and, 174–176
    energy restoration in, 102–104, 106
    hybrid states of, 95–97

brain (cont.)
  NREM connectivity and plasticity effects in, 105
  NREM sleep mechanisms of, 64–65
  REM sleep mechanisms of, 70–71
  sleep regulation by, 11–14
  social. See social brain network
  systems important for sleep, 209–210
brain development
  N3 slow wave sleep role in, 67
  REM promotion of, 41–43, 111–112
  sleep pattern response to, 41
brain stem, 210
Bulkeley, Kelly, sleep and dreams database of, 227

caffeine, 33
CAP. See cyclic alternating pattern
cardiac arrest, 73
Cartwright, Rosalind, 88–95
cataplexy, 83–85
catch-up sleep. See rebound sleep
central sleep apnea, 81
cerebral cortex, 109–111, 209–210. See also prefrontal cortex
CH. See continuity hypothesis
characters, dream, 163–164
children
  dreams and nightmares in, 144–146
  sleep deprivation among, 5
  sleep expression in, 53–54
  slow wave sleep role in, 67
chronotherapy, 38
cingulate cortex, 12–14
circadian rhythm
  adenosine role in, 29, 33–34
  master clock regulating, 29–30, 32
  melatonin release in, 29–30
  sleep organization by, 14–16, 28–30
  social modulation of, 35–36
  in two process sleep regulation model, 33–35
  ultradian cycle in, 30–32
clitoral engorgement, in REM sleep, 74–75
clonidine, 212
cognitions, dreams as, 123–127

cognitive functions, NREM restoration of, 104–105
cognitive processing, in dreams, 133, 146–149
cognitive-restructuring techniques, 90–91
compensatory rebound. See rebound sleep
confabulation, 168–169
confusional arousals, 53–54
continuity hypothesis (CH), 149, 202–204
co-sleeping, 15, 40
creativity, in dreams, 130
criminal acts, during sleep, 88–95
cyclic alternating pattern (CAP), 61–62
cytokines, 100–101

daydreams, 123, 136
death. See also mortality
  dream content and, 152
debt, sleep, 10
default mode network (DMN), 70–71, 142–143
delayed sleep phase wake disorder (DSPD), 36–38
delta power, 10–11, 60–61
delta waves, 60–61, 63–65
depression, 80–82
deprivation. See sleep deprivation
development. See brain development
diary, sleep, 209, 223, 226
diencephalon, 210
diurnal lifestyle, 28–29
DMN. See default mode network
dopamine, 211–215
doppelganger dreams, 187–188
dorsomedial prefrontal cortex, 12–14, 143
dream lag effect, 108–109
Dreambank, 227
DreamON, 176–177
dreams
  amnesia for, 127–128
  attachment, 149–151
  automaticity of, 128
  bad. See nightmares
  big, 186–187
  as brain state-regulated, 11–12
  in children, 144–146

cognitive processing in, 133, 146–149
data resources on, 217, 226–227
in dying people, 152
in elderly, 151–152
emotions in, 127
enactment of. *See* enacted dreams
false awakenings, 188–189
fear extinction by, 89–90, 202
hyper creativity in, 130
hypermnesia within, 127–128
incubated, 182–183
lifespan content of. *See* lifespan dream
    content
loss of, 155–156
lucid, 176–177, 183–185
meeting one's double in, 187–188
in memory consolidation, 108–109
methods for studying, 221–223
    awakenings procedures, 223–224
    scoring of characters, social
        interactions, and emotions, 224–225
    sleep logs/diaries, 209, 223, 226
    transcription of mentation reports, 224
mind-reading in, 130–131
in multiple personality disorder/
    dissociative identity disorder, 181
musical, 190
narrative structure of, 133–135
NREM. *See* NREM dreams
ontology, 131–133
perceptual disengagement during, 129
physical symptom, 180–181
recall of. *See* recall
recurrent, 191
REM. *See* REM dreams
self in, 125–127
self-reflectiveness in, 130, 163
of sensorially limited patients, 191
sexual, 74–75, 181–182
sleep paralysis, 188–190
as sleep-dependent cognitions, 123–127
theories of, 194–195, 206–207
    AIM theory, 195–197
    continuity hypothesis, 149, 202–204
    dreams as virtual simulation and
        predictions of reality, 197–200

emotional processing functions, 202
    AND model, 202
    social simulation theory, 205–206
    Solm's model, 200–202
    threat simulation theory, 204–205
in traditional societies, 177–180
twin, 185–186
variation in, 171–172, 192
visitation, 188
visual sense in, 128
drowsiness, 17, 61
DSPD. *See* delayed sleep phase wake
    disorder
dyssomnias, 78–79
    hypersomnolence, 82
        Kleine-Levin Syndrome, 82–83,
            113–116
        narcolepsy, 83–85
    insomnia. *See* insomnia

eating, during sleep, 87
EEG. *See* electroencephalography
elderly
    dreams in, 151–152
    sleep expression in, 57
electroencephalography (EEG)
    of dream recall neural correlates,
        174–176
    as method for sleep study, 215–217
    of NREM stages, 61–64, 216
    quantitative, 219
    of rebound sleep, 10
    of REM-NREM cycle, 31–32
    sleep measurement using, 7, 9
electrophysiological traits, of sleep, 7–9
emotion
    in dreams, 127
    processing of, 166–167, 202
    REM regulation and balance of, 112–113
    sleep deprivation effects on, 15–16
emotional memories, 108–109
enacted dreams, 195
    dream recall and, 173–174
    NREM-REM content differences in
        studies of, 160–161
    REM atonia and, 73–74, 91–92

energy, sleep restoration of, 102–104, 106
erections, in REM sleep, 74–75
ERK. *See* extracellular signal–regulated
        kinase
evolution, sleep
    attachment theory of, 44–46
    functions, 99
    heterochrony role in, 41
    immune system evolution and, 101–102
    life history theory of, 43–44
    NREM, 18–23, 99, 113–118
    parent-offspring conflict theory of, 43
    REM, 18–23, 41–43, 99, 113–118
excessive daytime sleepiness. *See* dyssomnias
exploding head syndrome, 88
extracellular signal–regulated kinase
        (ERK), 41–42

Falater, Scott, 88–95
false awakenings, 188–189
fatal familial insomnia (FFI), 68–69, 79–80
fear extinction, 89–90, 202
fetal sleep, 46
FFI. *See* fatal familial insomnia
fitness signals, 75
flip-flop switch, 34–35
fMRI. *See* functional magnetic resonance
        imaging
forced desynchrony protocol, 208–209
Freud, Sigmund, 134, 194
friendliness, in dreams, 157–161, 164–165
Friston, Karl, 197–200
frontal lobes, 210
    delta power link to, 60–61
    NREM restoration of, 104–105
    slow wave activity and, 66–67
frontopolar region, 12–14, 143
full polygraphic sleep, 7
functional magnetic resonance imaging
        (fMRI), 217–218, 220
functional traits, of sleep, 7–9
fusiform gyrus, 12–16, 143

gamma aminobutyric acid (GABA), 212
genetic conflict
    human lifespan and, 50–53

infant sleep expression and, 49–50
    NREM-REM interactions and, 113–118
    sleep state development and, 43
genomic imprinting, 113–118
GH. *See* growth hormone
glial cells, 102–104
glutamate, 211
glycogen, 102–104
glymphatic system, 102
Gnas gene, 117
Grb10 gene, 117
growth hormone (GH), 65–66

Hall, Calvin, 194–195, 203
Hall/Van de Castle system, 131–133,
        222–225
    development of, 194–195
    norms on male and female dreams,
        147–148
hallucinations
    dreams as, 125–126
    isolated sleep paralysis with, 92–95
    in narcolepsy, 83–85
heart rate, REM effects on, 73
heterochrony, in evolution of sleep
        development, 41
hibernation, 20, 104
hippocampus, 109–111, 143, 210
Hobson, Allan, 195–200
homeostatic regulation, 10–11, 33–35
homicide, during sleep, 88–95
hypermnesia, within dreams, 127–128
hypermorphosis, in evolution of sleep
        development, 41
hypersomnolence, 82
    Kleine-Levin Syndrome, 82–83, 113–116
    narcolepsy, 83–85
hypnogram, 216
    of NREM-REM cycle, 31–32
hypocretin, 83
hypothalamus, 32

idiopathic hypersomnia, 82
IL1. *See* interleukin I
illness dreams, 180–183
imagery rehearsal therapy (IRT), 90–91

immersive spatiotemporal hallucination (ISTH), 125–126
immune system, NREM maintenance of, 67–68, 100–102
imprinting. *See* genomic imprinting
incubated dreams, 182–183
indeterminate sleep, 46
infant sleep, 15, 43, 48–50
inflammation, sleep loss causing, 100–101
insomnia, 79
    primary, 79–80
        fatal familial insomnia, 68–69, 79–80
    secondary, 80
        major depression, 80–81
        sleep apnea, 81–82
    two-process model of, 34
insula, 12–14, 143
interleukin I (IL1), 100–101
International Association for the Study of Dreams, 227
IRT. *See* imagery rehearsal therapy
isolated sleep paralysis (ISP), 92–96, 189–190
ISTH. *See* immersive spatiotemporal hallucination

jet lag, 37–38
Jung, Carl, 194

K-complexes, 60–63, 216
Kleine-Levin Syndrome (KLS), 82–83, 113–116

latency, sleep, 57–58
law, on criminal acts committed during sleep, 88–95
learning
    NREM role in, 105–108
    REM role in, 106–109
    sleep spindle activity and, 62–63
    slow wave activity and, 66–67
levodopa, 212
life history theory, 43–44
lifespan dream content, 138–140, 153
    in adult males compared with adult females, 146–149

age-related changes in, 151–152
attachment dreams, 149–151
childhood dreams and nightmares, 144–146
death and, 152
social interactions in, 138–144
lifespan sleep expression
    adult woman, 55–57
    child, 53–54
    elderly, 57
    evolutionary background to
        attachment theory, 44–46
        heterochrony, 41
        life history theory, 43–44
        parent-offspring conflict theory, 43
        REM promotion of brain development, 41–43
    fetal, 46
    infant, 48–50
    longevity and, 50–53
    neonatal, 47–48
    normal patterns of, 40–41, 57–58
    teenage, 54–55
light-dark cycle, 28–30
limbic system, 210
log, sleep. *See* sleep diary
longevity, sleep expression and, 50–53
lucid dreams, 176–177, 183–185

magnetic resonance imaging (MRI), 217–218, 220
major depression, 80–81
mammals, sleep in, 22–26
MASS. *See* Montreal Archive of Sleep Studies
master clock, 29–30, 32
melatonin, 213–214
    in circadian cycle, 29–30
    for delayed sleep phase wake disorder, 36–38
memory
    NREM consolidation of, 106–111
    REM consolidation of, 106–111
    sleep spindle activity and, 62–63, 109–111
    slow wave activity and, 66–67
men, dreams of, 146–149

mentation reports, 224
metabolic rate, 102, 106
microsleeps, 17
migration, sleep during, 22
mind-reading, in dreams, 130–131
monotremes, sleep in, 22–23
Montreal Archive of Sleep Studies
     (MASS), 226–227
mortality
   lifespan sleep expression and, 50–53
   sleep architecture as predictor of, 76
mothers
   infant co-sleeping with, 15
   in infant sleep state development, 43
motivational reward, 72
motor paralysis. See paralysis
MPD/DID. See multiple personality
     disorder/dissociative identity
     disorder
MRI. See magnetic resonance imaging
multi-oscillator sleep regulation models,
     34–35
multiple personality disorder/dissociative
     identity disorder (MPD/DID), 181
musical dreams, 190
mutual dreams, 185–186

N1 sleep, 60–61, 216
N2 sleep, 60–63, 216
N3 sleep, 60–61, 63–64, 216. See also slow
     wave sleep
narcolepsy, 83–85
narcotics, 213–214
narrative structure, dream, 133–135
National Sleep Research Resource
     (NSRR), 226
Native American Plains Indians, 178
neonatal sleep, 47–48
neurodevelopment. See brain development
neuroimaging, 217–220
neuromodulators, 210–215
neuronal connectivity, NREM optimization
     of, 105
neurons, 211
   sleep-on, 32
   S-R , W-A, and W-R, 34–35

neurotransmitters. See neuromodulators
nicotine, 212
night terrors, 53–54, 64, 87
nightmares, 88–91, 187, 202
   in children, 144–146
night-wakings, 43, 48–50
non-rapid eye movement (NREM) sleep,
     7–8
   bodily changes during, 67–68
   brain mechanisms in, 64–65
   in children, 53–54, 67
   disorders of
      fatal familial insomnia, 68–69,
         79–80
      parasomnias, 64, 85–88, 95–97
   dreams during. See NREM dreams
   EEG characteristics of, 61–64, 216
   in elderly, 57
   electrophysiologic measures of, 9
   evolution of, 18–23, 99, 113–118
   functions of, 99–100, 114–115, 118–119
      antagonistic REM interactions and,
         113–118
      cognitive performance restoration,
         104–105
      energy restoration, 102–104
      immune system maintenance, 67–68,
         100–102
      memory consolidation, 106–108
      neuronal connectivity optimization,
         105
   growth hormone release during, 65–66
   lifespan trends in, 57–58
   memory and, 66–67
   multi-oscillator sleep regulation models
      of, 34–35
   in neonates, 47–48
   pathway to deep sleep in, 61–64
   in pregnancy, 55–57
   rebound, 10–11, 34
   REM compared with, 76–77, 114–115
   REM cycle with. See ultradian cycle
   social brain network deactivation during,
      13–14
   stages of, 60–64, 216
norepinephrine, 211–215

NREM dreams, 155–159
  REM compared with, 72, 157–161, 169
  REM dream interactions with, 161–162
NREM sleep. *See* non-rapid eye movement
  sleep
NSRR. *See* National Sleep Research
  Resource

obstructive sleep apnea (OSA), 81–82
occipital cortex, 175–176
Ojibwa Algonguin speaking Indians, 179–180
OSA. *See* obstructive sleep apnea
oxytocin, 142–143

pacemaker, circadian, 29–30, 32
paradoxical sleep (PS), 42
paralysis. *See also* sleep paralysis
  during REM, 73–74, 91–92
parasomnias, 78, 85
  criminal acts during, 88–95
  hybrid brain states in, 95–97
  NREM, 64, 85–88, 95–97
  REM, 88–97
parasympathetic nervous system, 67–68
parent-offspring conflict theory, 43, 49–50
parents
  infant co-sleeping with, 15
  reproductive age of, 50–53
Parkinson's disease, 173–174
Pawaganak, 179
perception
  during dreams, 129
  during sleep, 17
PET. *See* positron emission tomography
PGO waves. *See* pontine-geniculo-occipital
  waves
physical activity, during sleep, 17
physical symptom dreams, 180–181
physiologic systems
  NREM effects on, 67–68
  REM effects on, 72
    autonomic nervous system storms, 73
    dream content, 72
    motor paralysis, 73–74, 91–92
    sexual activation, 74–75
    thermoregulation lapses, 73

social nature of sleep and, 14–16
physiologic traits, of sleep, 7–9
Physionet, 226
plasticity
  NREM promotion of, 105
  REM promotion of, 41–43
  sleep spindle activity and, 62–63
polysomnography, 215–217, 223
pontine-geniculo-occipital (PGO) waves, 9, 69
positron emission tomography (PET),
  217–220
posterior cingulate, 175–176
posture, sleep, 17–19
Prader-Willi syndrome (PWS), 116
precognitive dreams, 185–186
precuneus, 12–14, 175–176
predictions, dreams as, 197–200
prefrontal cortex, 210
  in dream recall, 174–176
  in memory consolidation, 109–111
  in REM sleep behavior disorder, 91–92
  sleep deprivation effects on, 15–16
  in social brain network, 12–14, 143
pregnancy, 55–57
primates
  diurnal lifestyle of, 28–29
  sleep in, 25–26
prion disease, 68–69, 79–80
PRL. *See* prolactin
Process C, 33–34
Process S, 33–34
prolactin (PRL), 75
PS. *See* paradoxical sleep
psychophysics, 219–221
puberty, 54–55
PWS. *See* Prader-Willi syndrome

QS. *See* quiet sleep
quantitative EEG, 219
Quiche Maya, dreams of, 178
quiescent state, sleep as, 17
quiet sleep (QS), 46–47

RAM. *See* Reward Activation Model
rapid eye movement (REM) sleep, 7–8
  bihemispheric nature of, 24

rapid eye movement (REM) sleep (cont.)
  biobehavioral characteristics of, 69
  brain mechanisms in, 70–71
  in children, 53–54
  deprivation of, 11, 34, 75, 105–106
  dreams during. *See* REM dreams
  in elderly, 57
  electrophysiologic measures of, 9
  evolution of, 18–23, 41–43, 99, 113–118
  fetal development of, 46
  functions of, 76, 99, 105–106, 114–115,
      118–119
    antagonistic NREM interactions and,
        113–118
    brain development, 41–43, 111–112
    emotion regulation and emotional
        balance, 112–113
    memory consolidation, 106–111
  lifespan trends in, 57–58
  in major depression, 81
  motivational reward and, 72
  multi-oscillator sleep regulation models
      of, 34–35
  in neonates, 47–48
  NREM compared with, 76–77, 114–115
  NREM cycle with. *See* ultradian cycle
  parasomnias of, 88–97
  physiologic phenomena related to, 72
    autonomic nervous system storms, 73
    dream content, 72
    motor paralysis, 73–74, 91–92
    sexual activation, 74–75
    thermoregulation lapses, 73
  in pregnancy, 55–56
  rebound, 11, 34, 105–106
  REM on and REM off cellular networks
      controlling, 69–70
  sexual signaling and, 75
  social brain network reactivation during,
      13
  in teens, 55
RBD. *See* REM behavior disorder
reality prediction, dreams as, 197–200
rebound dreams, 125
rebound sleep, 10–11
  for energy restoration, 104

REM, 11, 34, 105–106
  two process sleep regulation model
      explaining, 33–35
recall, dream, 172–174
  boosting of, 176–177
  by lucid dreamers, 176–177
  neural correlates of, 174–176
recurrent dreams, 191
religious dreams. *See* spiritual dreams
REM behavior disorder (RBD), 73, 91–92,
      96, 173–174
REM dreams, 155–159, 162–163
  characters in, 163–164
  emotional processing in, 166–167
  NREM dream interactions with, 161–162
  NREM dreams compared with, 72,
      157–161, 169
  self-reflectiveness in, 163
  social brain network and, 142–144
  social interactions and aggression in,
      164–165
  story-like complexity of, 167–169
REM sleep. *See* rapid eye movement sleep
REM-NREM cycle. *See* ultradian cycle
reptiles, sleep in, 21–22
respiratory functions, REM effects on, 73
restorative process, sleep as, 9
restorative theory, 102–104, 106
reversible state, sleep as, 9–10
Reward Activation Model (RAM), 72
rhythm disorders, 36–38
Roenneberg, Til, Chronotype
      Questionnaire of, 227

SAD. *See* seasonal affective disorder
schizophrenia, 80
SCN. *See* suprachiasmatic nucleus
scoring, of dreams, 224–225
script, in recurrent nightmares, 90–91
seasonal affective disorder (SAD), 37–38
sedatives, 212–214
selective serotonin reuptake inhibitors,
      212
self, in dreams, 125–127
self-reflectiveness, in dreams, 130, 163
semantic priming, 219–221

senses
  during dreams, 128–129
  dreams of patients with impaired, 191
serotonin, 211–215
sex, sleep, 64, 86
sexual activation, 15, 74–75
sexual dreams, 74–75, 181–182
sexual dysfunction, REM deprivation and,
  42
sexual signaling, REM and, 75
shamans, 178–179
sharp-wave ripple events, 109–111
shell cells, 30
shift work, 37
Sigmund, 177
simulations, dreams as, 197–200, 204–206
single photon emission computed
    tomography (SPECT), 217, 219–220
sleep
  arousal thresholds during, 19
  behavioral habits restoring, 5–6
  biological need for, 3–4
  biological rhythms of. *See* biological
    rhythms
  as brain state-regulated, 11–14
  brain systems important for, 209–210
  criminal acts committed during, 88–95
  data resources on, 217, 226–227
  definition of, 5–9
  evolution of. *See* evolution
  full polygraphic, 7
  functions of, 99
  hibernation and torpor, 20, 104
  homeostatic regulation of, 10–11, 33–35
  lifespan expression of. *See* lifespan sleep
    expression
  methods for studying, 209–210
    EEG, 215–217
    neuroimaging, 217–220
    neuromodulators, 210–215
    polysomnography, 215–217, 223
    psychophysics, 219–221
  mortality and
    lifespan sleep expression effects on,
      50–53
    sleep architecture as predictor of, 76

multi-oscillator models of, 34–35
NREM. *See* non-rapid eye movement
  sleep
perceptual disengagement during, 17
posture during, 17–19
as quiescent state, 17
rebound. *See* rebound sleep
REM. *See* rapid eye movement sleep
as restorative process, 9
as reversible state, 9–10
as social behavior, 14–16, 18–19
species comparisons in, 20–21
  ancestral humans, 26
  aquatic mammals, 23–24
  birds, 22
  monotremes, 22–23
  primates, 25–26
  reptiles, 21–22
  terrestrial mammals, 24–25
triggering of, 32
two process regulation of, 33–35
yawning and, 19–20
sleep apnea, 81–82
sleep architecture, 216
sleep attacks, 83–85
sleep debt, 10
sleep deprivation
  in animals with unihemispheric sleep,
    23–24
  causes of, 4–5
  consequences of, 3–5
  dream rebound after, 125
  emotional effects of, 15–16
  global epidemic of, 4–5
  inflammation associated with, 100–101
  neuronal plasticity and, 41–43
  rat studies of, 100
  sexual impairment and, 75
  sleep rebound after. *See* rebound sleep
sleep diary, 209, 223, 226
sleep disorders
  dyssomnias. *See* dyssomnias
  hybrid brain states in, 95–97
  parasomnias. *See* parasomnias
  rhythm, 36–38
  two-process model of, 34

sleep hygiene, 5–6
sleep latency, 57–58
sleep paralysis
  dreams of, 188–190
  isolated, 92–96, 189–190
  in narcolepsy, 83–85
sleep sex, 64, 86
sleep spindles, 60–63, 109–111, 216
sleep state misperception, 80
sleep talking, 64, 87–88, 96
sleep traits, 7–9
sleep walking, 64, 85–86, 88–96
sleep-dependent cognitions, dreams as,
        123–127
sleepiness, excessive. *See* dyssomnia
sleep-on neurons, 32
sleep-onset REM (SOREM), 83
sleep-related binge eating, 87
slow wave activity (SWA), 64–65, 215–216
  as indicator of Process S, 34
  memory and, 66–67
  types of, 62
slow wave sleep (SWS), 31, 60–61, 63–65,
        216
  in children, 67
  in elderly, 57
  functions of, 100
    cognitive performance restoration,
        104–105
    energy restoration, 102–104
    immune system maintenance, 100–102
    memory consolidation, 106–111
    neuronal connectivity optimization,
        105
  growth hormone release during, 65–66
  lifespan trends in, 57–58
  memory and, 66–67
  in pregnancy, 55–57
Snord116 gene, 117
social behavior, sleep as, 14–16, 18–19
social brain hypothesis, dream content and,
        138–142
social brain network, 11–14
  dream recall and, 174–176
  in NREM sleep, 64–65
  NREM-REM interactions and, 117–118

in REM dreaming, 142–144
  in REM sleep, 70–71
social cues, biological rhythm response to,
        35–36
social interactions
  in REM compared with NREM dreams,
        157–161
  REM dream levels of, 164–165
social simulation theory (SST), 205–206
Solms, Mark, 200–202
somatostatin (SS), 65–66
somnambulism, 64, 85–86, 88–96
somniloquy, 64, 87–88, 96
SOREM. *See* sleep-onset REM
SPECT. *See* single photon emission
        computed tomography
sperm, telomeres in, 51–53
spindles, sleep, 60–63, 109–111, 216
spiritual dreams
  big dreams, 186–187
  doppelganger dreams, 187–188
  in traditional societies, 177–180
  visitation dreams, 188
S-R neurons, 34–35
SS. *See* somatostatin
SST. *See* social simulation theory
stimulants, 213–214
  for narcolepsy, 85
story structure, dream, 133–135, 167–169
strangers, dream, 163–164
superior temporal sulcus, 12–14, 143
suprachiasmatic nucleus (SCN), 29–30, 32
SWA. *See* slow wave activity
SWS. *See* slow wave sleep
sympathetic nervous system, 67–68, 73
synapses, 105, 211

talking, sleep, 64, 87–88, 96
targeted memory reactivation (TMR), 111
teenagers. *See* adolescent sleep
telomeres, 50–53
temporal–parietal junction, 12–14, 143,
        174–176
terrestrial mammals, sleep in, 24–25
thalamic alerting neurons, 79–80
thalamus, 209–210

theory of mind (ToM) capacity, 141–142
thermoregulation, 73
theta waves, 61, 110, 174, 216
threat simulation theory, 161, 204–205
TMR. *See* targeted memory reactivation
ToM capacity. *See* theory of mind capacity
torpor, 20, 104
traditional societies, dreams in, 177–180
traits, sleep, 7–9
twin dreams, 185–186
two process sleep regulation model, 33–35

ultradian cycle, 30–32
    social modulation of, 35–36
    triggering of, 32
unihemispheric sleep, 22–24

Van de Castle, Robert, 194–195. *See also*
        Hall/Van de Castle system
vasopressin, 142–143
ventrolateral preoptic nucleus (VLPO),
        34–35, 212

ventromedial prefrontal cortex, 12–14, 143,
        174–176
virtual simulation, dreams as, 197–200
visitation dreams, 188
visual sense, in dreams, 128
VLPO. *See* ventrolateral preoptic nucleus

W-A neurons, 34–35
wake after sleep onset (WASO),
        57–58
waking, NREM and REM hybrid brain
        states with, 95–97
walking, sleep, 64, 85–86, 88–96
WASO. *See* wake after sleep onset
white blood cells, 101–102
wish fulfillment, 194–195
women. *See also* mothers
    dreams in, 146–149
    sleep expression in, 55–57
W-R neurons, 34–35

yawning, 19–20